# DATE DUE

| | | | |
|---|---|---|---|
| | | | |
| | | | |
| | | | |
| | | | |
| | | | |
| | | | |
| | | | |
| | | | |
| | | | |
| | | | |
| | | | |
| | | | |
| | | | |
| | | | |
| | | | |
| | | | |
| | | | |
| | | | |

DEMCO 38-296

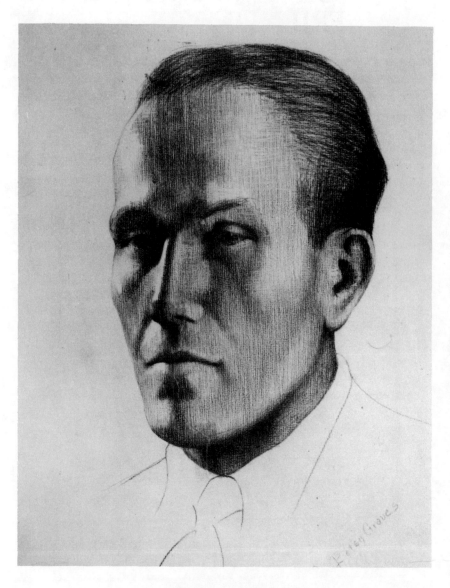

Eduard C. Lindeman
Drawing by Betsy Graves

# FRIENDLY REBEL

## A Personal and Social History
## of Eduard C. Lindeman

Elizabeth Lindeman Leonard
Research Associate, School of Social Work,
University of Illinois at Urbana-Champaign

Introduction by Clarke A. Chambers
Professor Emeritus, University of Minnesota, Twin Cities

ADAMANT PRESS
Adamant, Vermont, USA
1991

Copyright © 1991, by Elizabeth Lindeman Leonard

First Edition


**Library of Congress Cataloging-in-Publication Data**

Leonard, Elizabeth Lindeman, 1918-
  Friendly rebel: a personal and social history of Eduard C.
Lindeman/by Elizabeth Lindeman Leonard: introduction by Clark
A. Chambers.
    p. cm.
  Includes bibliographical references and index.
  ISBN 0-912362-11-1 (alk. paper)
  1. Lindeman, Eduard, 2. Social workers—United States—
Biography. 3. Social reformers—United States—Biography. 4. Social
work education—United States—History—20th century. I. Title.
HV40.32.L56L46 1991
361.92—dc20
[B]
                                                        91-31364
                                                             CIP


    Book and jacket design and production by Pine Hill Press,
P.O. Box 340, Highway 81 South, Freeman, South Dakota 57029
USA.

    Drawings of E. C. Lindeman by Betsy Graves.

    Published by Adamant Press, Box 7, Adamant, Vermont 05640
USA.

ii

# Contents

# Contents

# Preface

Writing this book was a long and arduous journey into the past, sometimes painful, but always exciting. I discovered a father from a poverty-stricken background, whose early life was filled with hard manual labor, illness, and death. A young man, who—with little or no formal education—broke with family tradition and enrolled in a special program for sub-freshmen at the age of twenty-one. Slowly he transformed himself from laborer to scholar, overcoming poverty, discrimination, and illiteracy. I also discovered a very private life along with a very public life.

It has taken nearly a decade to gather materials from primary sources, including interviews with more than sixty individuals who knew Lindeman either as colleague, student, associate, friend, or intimate. Scores of scrapbooks were perused, as well as correspondence both to and from him, and works by or about him, published and unpublished.

Many individuals and institutions contributed to the completion of this project. For financial support to conduct field investigations, the author is indebted to the Jerome Foundation in St. Paul, Minnesota. Special gratitude and thanks are due the then Executive Director of the foundation, Mr. Heckman, a pioneer and leader in Minnesota philanthropy. Mr. Heckman, an admirer of Lindeman, believed that Lindeman needed to be reclaimed by the social work profession. Foundation support was based on the belief that Lindeman's work is of lasting importance, has relevance for today, and that pertinent records about Lindeman should be collected and preserved. Those collected materials are now located in the Social Welfare History Archives at the University of Minnesota. Al Heckman's ongoing encouragement and support of my efforts was a major factor in the preparation, analysis, and completion of the book.

Librarians at Columbia University's Oral History and Rare Book Manuscript archives were enormously helpful to me, as were those at the Roosevelt Library at Hyde Park, and the Library of Congress. Archivist David Klaasen was especially helpful in accessing the Lindeman materials at the University of Minnesota. Also the librarian at the St. Clair Public Library in St. Clair, Michigan, provided valuable assistance in locating information related to pioneer life in St. Clair. I am indebted also to Mary Bride Nicholson of Dartington Hall who made it possible for me to work in the Records Room at Dartington Hall, Totnes, England.

In the mid-1960's, long before I had thought of writing a book about my father, Dorothy Straight Elmhirst sent me a box of letters written to her by Lindeman during the years 1922 to 1930. I was deeply touched by the letters. In retrospect, I realize that her unexpected gift may have been a factor in my decision to write this book.

Special thanks go to Dr. Clark A. Chambers, Professor Emeritus, University of Minnesota. Not only has he written a thoughtful Introduction, but in 1980 he surprised me with seventeen missing notebooks which Lindeman had used while teaching and lecturing in India in 1949. A University of Minnesota student had rescued them many years after Lindeman's hasty departure and given them to Dr. Chambers for safekeeping. Throughout the writing of this book, his valuable suggestions clarified my thinking and kept me on track.

Letters written to Marion Beers by Lindeman between the years 1937 and 1940, supplemented by multiple interviews, provided a dimension to Lindeman that had not previously been revealed. Dorothy Shaw was also kind enough to send me letters from Lindeman to her husband, Charles Shaw, and to discuss with me the Shaw friendship with the Lindeman family, which began in Greensboro and lasted a lifetime. She also provided me with new insights into the relationship between Hazel and Eduard, and a glimpse of a side of my mother I had not known before.

The University of North Carolina at Greensboro provided the author with correspondence pertaining to Lindeman's confrontation with the Ku Klux Klan and his subsequent resignation from the college in 1922. Lewis and Clark College in Portland, Oregon contributed correspondence pertaining to Lindeman's encounter with McCarthyism in Portland in 1952.

I am indebted also to the many friends, colleagues, students, and associates of Lindeman's who permitted me to tape their oral histories and generously shared their recollections, memories, and experiences. They provided valuable information about Lindeman's early life, the North Carolina Klan incident, Bohemian life in Greenwich Village, memories of life at Greystone, and Lindeman as colleague at Columbia University. I am especially grateful to Roger Baldwin, with whom I spent many hours in Puerto Rico, and to Marion Beers who shared memories of her intimate relationship with Lindeman. Bradley Buell provided me with insight into the special contribution of Lindeman's book *Social Discovery* to the field of social research, and Dr. Frederick H. Burkhardt, pragmatist friend of Lindeman's, made important observations after reading the Otto/Lindeman chapter.

For a personal account of Lindeman's WPA program Community Organization for Leisure, I am indebted to Sally Ringe Goldmark in Seattle, Dorothy Cline in Albuquerque, Byron Mock in Salt Lake City, Howard White, Elizabeth Wickenden and Arthur Goldschmidt, UCLA Professor Donald Howard, and Hilda Smith. For impressions of Lindeman by former colleagues at Columbia, I am grateful to Clara Kaizer, Lucille Austin, Philip Klein, Fern Lowry, Gertrude Wilson, Nathan Cohen and Leonard Mayo. Maurice Connery, formerly Dean, UCLA School of Social Welfare and a former student of Lindeman's, provided me with invaluable insight into Lindeman's personality and some of his difficulties in trying to relate to WW II veterans who returned as students.

Numerous colleagues and friends took the time to comment on various aspects of the book. In each and every case their suggestions contributed to the improvement of the final product. The author is especially grateful for suggestions from the following people: Lela B. Costin, Professor Emerita, University of Illinois at Urbana; Professor Joseph B. Harris, Parkland College, Champaign, Illinois, mentor and then teacher of a special Creative Writing Seminar; Phyllis Cooper, close friend, wise critic and member of the Writing Seminar; Patricia Stevens, member of the Writing Seminar; Harding and Dorothy Lemay of New York City; John Ohliger, adult educator, of Springfield, Illinois; and my sisters Ruth O'Neil of Ft. Pierce, Florida, and Barbara Sanford of Dallas, Texas.

Special thanks go to Dr. Edmund V. Mech, Professor, University of Illinois, who, over the years, has served as a sounding board for my ideas and provided me with support and encouragement. In all likelihood this book would never have been completed had it not been for Dr. Mech's conviction that Lindeman was an important figure whose recognition by the social work profession was long overdue.

Innumerable scholars have joined me in the process of discovering Lindeman. Credit must be given to each and every one of them for furnishing different contexts, different impressions and angles from which to view the Lindeman legacy. The letters, the impressions, the records together comprise a collective consciousness of Eduard C. Lindeman. Although this book has been an attempt to capture this collective consciousness, in the end, it represents the author's solitary struggle to define Lindeman, his experience, and his relevance for our time.

—Elizabeth Lindeman Leonard
University of Illinois at Urbana-Champaign
March 1991

# Introduction

Some years ago in preparation for composing a brief summary of the life and career of Eduard C. Lindeman for a biographical dictionary, I studied his major publications, surveyed some of the bound notebooks in which he had recorded passages selected from his readings together with his responses, and consulted the usual range of obituaries and eulogies on the occasion of his death. I had also the advantage of having before me Gisela Konopka's critical biographical study of Lindeman and his influence upon social work philosophy, and the appreciative essay by his son-in-law, Robert Gessner. As a scholar whose subject of research had come to focus on the history of social welfare policies and practice and the history of the profession of social work as it evolved in the twentieth century, I had naturally attended to the role Lindeman had played in defining the fields of community organization, and group work, and in providing a core concern with social theory in graduate programs of social work education from his base in the influential New York School of Social Work. My interest in Lindeman was subsequently enlivened and deepened by conversations and correspondence with his daughter, Betty Lindeman Leonard, who set out some years ago on a voyage of discovery into her father's life, the end product of which we now have in this splendid biography. Thanks to her and to other concerned scholars, we began to gather primary historical records bearing on his career at the University of Minnesota's Social Welfare History Archives.

I was, then, no stranger to Lindeman when I was asked, on the eve of my retirement, to provide an introductory essay to this book that would attempt to assess the significance of his contributions to so many crucial issues of society and education over the course of his career beginning in the early 1920s and extending to his death in 1953. For that assignment I determined to go back and study again the main corpus of his published works—books,

ix

articles, essays, and scattered occasional pieces. From that concentrated exercise I came to a fresh appreciation of the range of his intellect, the prescient understanding he had of issues largely neglected by others, and the philosophic vision that informed all his scholarly inquiries.

Others have observed that his was not an original mind, and in general I am inclined to concur with that judgment; yet his talents manifested themselves most dramatically in opening up new fields in inquiry, policy, and practice just as they were being formed—community organization in 1921, adult education in 1925, philanthropy in 1936, leisure and recreation in 1939. In each instance he delved into developments in which many others were currently active; he drew from the experience of associates and friends and, more notably, from his own personal engagement. Proud of being a social philosopher or social theorist, he rejoiced in the freedom independent scholarship and membership in the academy of higher learning provided; but his work (perhaps with the major exception of his monograph *Social Discovery*, 1924, which labored to address diverse methods of social science research) rarely smacked of the ivory tower. He was always deeply engaged in the vital issues that marked his time and place; he was personally involved in concerns of civil rights and civil liberties, the rights of minorities, political and governmental processes, social justice in industry, the unionization of labor, the function of schooling, unemployment, war and peace. He was, in the French sense of the word, a scholar/citizen *engagé*. His writing, his teaching, his outreach to larger communities through the spoken word on the lecture circuit were all laced with personal experience and common sense. As he himself was the first to credit, his social vision was rooted in the transcendental principles of Ralph Waldo Emerson, and in his devotion to practice, to experimentation, to empiricism in the pragmatic system of philosophy set forth by John Dewey.

Reviewing his scholarship and teaching, I was struck anew by the dialectic he sustained between theory and application. His philosophical ruminations were grounded in felt realities. In an era marked by increasing specialization in all arenas of life, in higher education and in social work, Lindeman remained a general practitioner. This conscious determination not to specialize was, at once, a major source of the influence he enjoyed during his lifetime and probably provides, as well, one explanation for the relative neglect into which his work plunged soon after his death, for academic guilds over the past three or four decades came to recognize and reward chiefly those who carved out very specialized spheres of technical expertise whatever the discipline. Generalists, in recent years, tended to suffer a loss of authority and respect. Especially was this evident in the discipline of philosophy, which scorned what Lindeman and his friend Max Otto defined as social philosophy while turning to the intense examination of highly technical issues of logic. That being the case, what could one make of a scholar/teacher like Lindeman whose contributions spanned a wide range of themes and methods, none of which did he spin out in elaborate detail much beyond an initial statement? After Lindeman's 1926 statement on adult education, for example, there later came occasional reflections, informal essays, and reports but no subsequent major extensions or revisions from him on the subject. So it was also with the opening he made to the study of philanthropy in the mid-1930s: the task had been so arduous and frustrating owing to the resistance of the foundations to the opening of their records, that he never pursued the heroic initiative he had launched, and it had to be left to other scholars a generation later to pick up what Lindeman had begun.

From Professor Konopka's book, published in 1958, little was heard of his work again until Stephen Brookfield and David W. Stewart rediscovered in the late 1980s the formative influence he had exerted on the developing field of adult education. Other related studies are now underway. Betty Leonard's biography is bound to stimulate renewed attention that is long overdue. It may be premature, until this new set of studies has been accomplished, to attempt even a brief reassessment of Lindeman's influence; but this is the assignment I have cheerfully accepted.

Arising from his experiences as a young man involved in extension work in rural communities and with the YMCA, and informed as well by his observations of federated welfare work coordinated by community chests during the teens and early 1920s, Lindeman sought to make sense of new dynamics in American society in a book he titled *The Community: An Introduction to the Study of Community Leadership and Organization,* published by the Association Press of the YMCA in 1921. The style was that of a primer; at the conclusion of each chapter came lists of "student's problems," exercises that students could complete as they studied the basics of community organization. Stated, simply and directly, were principles Lindeman would emphasize throughout his career in different settings: Man's destiny "to live in cooperation with his fellow-men" (p. 1); the authentic and powerful impulse of a "people who live in a small, compact, local group to assure their own responsibilities and to guide their own destinies" (p. 58); the need to reconcile democratic will as expressed in local communities with the technical skills that specialized experts could provide; the elaboration of strategies to enable national agencies, including government, to advance institutions of democracy built "upward from the smaller unit" (p. 161); and the search for ways to inspire and empower "resident leaders" in the achievement of the general welfare (p. 161).

Lindeman was quick to note that grassroots communities were themselves composed of diverse self-interest groups, each with its own agendas and goals, and that competition and conflict among these groups was both natural and salutary. Conflict was not to be repressed but welcomed and expressed, for in the contest of competing interests, ideas, and needs could be clarified. "All life," he declared, "is a compromise" (p. 135). Through open and frank discussion, consensus could be achieved, and in the process, as he was often to emphasize later, the true consent of the citizenry could be achieved. Consent, in his view, emerged not from passive assent but through active participation; only thus could balanced programs for progress achieve community-wide support.

For examples to illustrate these principles he turned to models provided by farm associations (the Farm Bureau, for example), consumers' cooperatives, the settlement house movement, scouting, the YM and YWCA, the Red Cross, and community chests and councils, which were engaged at that time in forging tactics for the rationalization, coordination, and federation of agencies engaged in the delivery of social services. In varied ways, such efforts loosed dynamic spiritual forces to affirm the value of individuals and the efficacy of love over hatred. Lindeman's selection of words would later stray away from religious metaphors, but in 1921 his indebtedness to the Social Gospel was manifest in the assertion that the Kingdom of God was an ideal to be realized on earth, in his belief in a "God who is Love, Truth, and Purpose," and in a perception of Christianity primarily as "a philosophy of life, and secondarily a system of belief" (p. 197). From the gospel was derived the pragmatic principle — "By their fruits ye shall know them."

*The Community* was something more than a handbook for community organization, although its intent was in part to instruct persons pioneering that field of practice. Written with disarming directness, the volume set forth a number of basic strategies for organizing that came to constitute the common sense of the matter for those who followed. A diverse lot of persons teaching and practicing the art of community organizing would restate Lindeman's principles over the next generation, not always with his idealistic assumptions, of course, and not always citing his pioneer work: the crucial importance of encouraging indigenous (Lindeman had written "resident") leadership, the creative uses to which the conflict of interest groups could be put, the fundamental requirement of broad citizen participation.

*Social Discovery: An Approach to the Study of Functional Groups,*, published in 1924 by the New Republic and boasting an introduction by Lindeman's friend and mentor, Herbert Croly, had another order of importance entirely. It was apparently the springboard for Lindeman's appointment to the faculty of the New York School of Social Work, and it did open up consideration of the importance of research into the structure and functions of groups and, in a way, informed the development of group work as a method of social work practice opposed to the prevailing model of social casework, whose design had been imprinted in Mary Richmond's authoritative text, *Social Diagnosis* (1917). Lindeman's volume had been inspired by Croly and had been originally intended as a work to be jointly written with Mary Parker Follett, whose *Creative Experience* composed her separate statement. The collaboration, for complex personal reasons beyond the purpose of this introduction, had faltered and the two had agreed to go their own ways, both acknowledging their indebtedness to the other. *Social Discovery* and *Creative Experience* shared many perceptions and suppositions; each, in my judgment, exhibited a turgidity of exposition that makes the reading of them a demanding task, particularly now that the enthusiasms of that moment in the mid-1920s have faded.

Social science in that era was infused with a heady self-confidence that by applying scientific principles of research all problems of society could be managed and resolved. Prominent sociologists were imbued with that conceit; Lindeman cited such exemplars as Graham Wallas, J. A. Hobson, Walter Lippmann, and Mary Parker Follett among those who had influenced his own prescriptions. It was a guiding faith of *The New Republic* under Croly's editorship. Lindeman set out to provide a method of research into group behavior that would focus on collective behavior and move with increasing certainty toward enhancing the predictive reliability of social science. The key, in Lindeman's judgment, was to recognize that in contemporary society, the group constituted the basic functional unit. "The individual . . . who has no vital adherence to and expression through a group is an individual who plays a diminishing role," he asserted. "The task of social scientists is to discover the nature of these groupings and their functional attributes" (pp. 111-112). All groups in society must be seen, then, in functional terms, as providing the means through which individuals could achieve their ends.

Lindeman's style of presentation in this volume reflects a mode of expression to which social scientists in their methodological modes were generally addicted. A careful reader may, however, discern some principles of research that still make sense: that a disciplined participant observer has access to levels of understanding that a distanced observer may miss; that understanding must take into account what a group *thinks* it is doing, whatever the objective reality may be; that a skilled observer must attend to "emotions, prejudices, habits, customs, mores, sentiments" (p. 193); that groups are integrated, given cohesion, and resist collectivism by the free give and take of discussion. There were lessons here for persons engaged in that generation in forging methods of group work in the profession of social work, and Lindeman himself would assist that pioneer work in the classroom and in the conduct of workshops; but one has to struggle through clouded prose to see clearly what that influence must have been. Beneath it all, for Lindeman and other pragmatists, was the intuition that men could, by taking thought, control human destiny. As Croly, in his complimentary introduction, observes—the book describes society as "the product fundamentally of human contrivance and volition" (p. xvi). In retrospect it would seem as much a matter of faith as of method.

*The Meaning of Adult Education*, that appeared but two years later in 1926, was altogether a happier and, as the passage of decades confirms, a more influential work. Indeed, two scholars in the field, Stephen Brookfield and David W. Stewart, have recently hailed it as a classic in its field, if not original in its formulations, a synthesis of fresh and elegant authority. Perhaps it was the case that Lindeman spoke most eloquently when he started from his own experience, not when he strayed into abstractions. In this instance, as Leonard's biography relates the story, Lindeman was introduced to formal education late in his youth and found it to be difficult and largely rigid and stultifying. Directing rural extension work and performing teaching roles in church and through the YMCA in his twenties, Lindeman learned first-hand the excitement of shared intellectual discovery in informal settings. His discovery, in 1920, of Danish cooperative folk education provoked in him a still deeper passion in his search for alternative strategies of learning. No wonder that in the preface to his book he declares his hope to "free education from stifling ritual, formalism and institutionalism," to take education out of "college halls and into the lives of the people who do the work of the world" (pp. xiv-xv).

His attack on traditional schooling is brisk and blunt. So are his affirmations: "*education is life* — not a mere preparation for an unknown kind of future living" (p. 6). Learning is a continuous process to be centered around "*non-vocational* ideals" in order "to put meaning into the whole of life" and to promote the "fruitful use of leisure" (pp. 7-8). The principles set forth in 1926 were so quickly absorbed by adult educators that to many it must have seemed that there had never been a time they were not operative; yet even today his initial statement seems fresh and powerful. A curriculum, he argued, should take the "route of *situations*, not subjects," and should be constructed around "the students' needs and interests" (p. 8). Adult education draws on the "*learner's experience*"; it must unite thinking and doing; it must be experiential for "experience is the adult learners' textbook" (pp. 9-10). Adult education finds its ultimate expression in both self-improvement and the betterment of society; its goal was "to change the social order so that vital personalities will be creating a new environment in which their aspirations may be properly expressed" (p. 14). From John Dewey he drew the prescription that all life is evolving, that intelligence at its best is experimental and to be judged by its ability "to solve problems" (p. 25). It was the teacher's (read discussion leader's) responsibility to keep conversation going, to sum up arguments, and above all else to facilitate wide participation in discussion in small groups in order to achieve "as much decentralization, diversity and local autonomy as is consistent with order" (p. 141). From Dewey again, and from the Sage of Concord, Lindeman calls for adult education to keep the "creative spark" alive; "creativeness is less dependent upon its ends than its means, the creative process, not the created object, is of supreme importance."

I resort to the use of direct quotations and close paraphrase of Lindeman's words, including his frequent resort to the use of italics for purposes of emphasis, for in this book, above all others, there is a clarity and power of expression that must have arisen from deeply-held convictions of the good life founded upon democratic processes. Social intelligence, the command of knowledge, the empowerment of the individual in relationship to others, freedom of discussion, the testing of ideas in action—these constituted the processes by which one could reaffirm a "belief in the possibilities of creating a new world," as he declared in a pamphlet, *Workers' Education and the Public Libraries*, printed in 1926 by the Workers Education Bureau. Some years later, 1944, in the midst of war, he chaired a committee of the New York Adult Education council whose report echoed his earlier sentiments: adult education must be "accessible," "cheerful and friendly," and experimental; it must "help solve everyday problems, add variety to life, and prepare for the assumption of greater civic responsibility" (p. 6). These and related themes recur later, but as was the case with other themes, once he had outlined a position in an initial statement, he then went on to explore other concerns.

Soon after addressing the meaning of adult education, Lindeman turned to another topic, the cultural role of philanthropic foundations and trusts in contemporary American society. In the one case he could draw on the formulations of associates and, more significantly, from his own experience; he could draft his chapters deep from his heart and off the top of his head, quickly and easily, with directness and natural flow, characteristics that also explain the authority he commanded and the enthusiasm he stirred with the spoken word from the lecture platform. In preparing to examine foundations, he had no guide, he was on his own. And everywhere, to his surprise and dismay, philanthropic trusts proved unwilling to share with him the data his study required. Had it occurred to him at the outset of his research "that it would require eight years of persistent inquiry at a wholly disproportionate cost to disclose even the basic quantitative facts desired," he complained, "I am sure that the study would have been promptly abandoned" (p. vii).

There is something heroic in the persistence he demonstrated in whittling away at this monstrous undefined problem. Launched at a time of roaring prosperity in 1928, his study—*Wealth and Culture: A Study of One Hundred Foundations and Community Trusts and Their Operations During the Decade 1921-1930*—found publication in the depth of the Great Depression, 1936. His personal frustrations in conducting research were probably sharpened by the social frustrations that accompanied hard times. His perceptions of how surplus wealth had been created reflected the mounting opposition to unregulated, speculative capitalism that burgeoned in the years following the Panic of 1929. Foundations had arisen, he declares, when the "vast surplus of wealth accumulated by industrialists, financiers, and speculators was not needed for reinvestment" (p. 5). There was a limit to how much of those surpluses could be squandered on "conspicuous consumption" (Lindeman had read and digested Thorstein Veblen); speculation using surplus funds had collapsed in 1929. The private foundation allowed "those who had accumulated large fortunes . . . to determine how the wealth was to be redistributed and what social effects it was intended to bring about" (p. 5). Lindeman denied the existence of a conspiracy on the part of capital, but "vested wealth" provided the means to set social priorities and thus determine "cultural values" (p. 11).

In an effort to understand how this authority was exercised, he presented an analysis of 402 trustees drawn from such foundations as provided data. From these data he drew a profile of control—a majority of trustees in the 1920s had spent their formative years and formal education before the turn of the century; two-thirds had been educated in private eastern colleges and universities, a disproportionately large number were graduates of but four ivy league institutions; corporation officials, bankers, university administrators, lawyers, doctors, and financiers dominated the boards; 85 percent were from elite denominations, Episcopalian, Presbyterian, Jewish, Methodist, and Baptist; men outnumbered women 391 to 11 (the latter, with one exception, were represented only in family foundations). In such hands was concentrated the authority to impose cultural norms with no warrant other than "pecuniary success" (p. 46). Projects for health, welfare, recreation, and religion underwritten by the foundations became pilot programs that enjoyed authority quite beyond their numbers. The trustees and the foundations they governed remained unaccountable to society, while those "who have an anticipation of receiving grants are the more servile" (p. 19).

Lindeman's pioneer study was the first of its kind, none other followed for some years. In this instance as in others his insights proved prescient. In 1921 he had outlined processes of community organization that seemed as relevant in the 1960s and today as they did seventy years ago; in *Social Discovery* (1924) he set forth the importance of studying basic groups in American society, affirmed the validity of participant observation, and suggested principles of group work that others were subsequently to elaborate. *The Meaning of Adult Education* (1926) still speaks essential common-sense truths. The questions he raised in 1936 about the overweening power of elite groups exercised through philanthropic foundations, operating out of sight, raised questions not yet fully addressed. The wonder is how quickly his influence faded with his death in 1953, and only now is being rediscovered.

*Leisure — A National Issue: Planning for the Leisure of a Democratic People*, published in 1939 under the joint sponsorship of the Association Press and the American Association for the Study of Group Work, reflected Lindeman's experience as Consulting Director of Recreation of the Works Progress Administration, 1935-1939. It was essentially an extended essay on by-now familiar themes. Constructive use of leisure time was essential to counter the stultifying consequences of performing routinized and repetitive tasks demanded by modern industrial and bureaucratic agencies. Leisure was not mere idleness, but rather involved active participation in learning (now Lindeman was back to the lessons of adult education). Learning in leisure hours was not to be for "narrowly vocational" or "pecuniary" goals but aimed at promoting balanced personal growth, engagement in "aesthetic experiences," and the enhancement of one's power as a citizen in a democracy (pp. 23, 20). Planning for leisure might require a degree of national funding and coordination (that's what the WPA had provided), but planning for the creative use of leisure must arise from "conference, consultation, and consent" at every level of life from the local community up (p. 13). The wide distribution and sharing of the authority and responsibility to plan constituted the best means to resist the coercion, regimentation, uniformity, and subservience that flowed from centralized planning imposed by central organs of government. Clearly, more than leisure and learning were at stake in Lindeman's mind in 1939; like other thoughtful citizens he was searching ways to strengthen democracy at the grass roots against the threat of totalitarianism posed by fascist, nazi, and communist regimes. The nation's government had to address nation-wide issues, only the federal government had the resources to accomplish national ends; but democracy rested ultimately on an informed citizenry actively involved in their own communities, settings in which the consent of the governed was worked out in argument and discussion that led to compromise and cooperation. Not in the avoidance of conflict, but in its resolution lay the road to dynamic democracy. "The true purpose of government," he concluded, "is to promote the growth of freedom and thereby produce that form of inner security upon which a social order may reach stability with a minimum of force and coercion" (p. 59). It is important in this context to recall that for many years Lindeman counted Roger Baldwin, director of the American Civil Liberties Union, among his closest friends, and that dedication to free speech, press, worship, and assembly took first priority in making the democratic process secure. All his life Lindeman shaped his political philosophy on the bedrock foundation of first Amendment rights; in the last years of his life, as Betty Leonard's biography tells the story, he was engaged in fighting the repressive forces centered around Senator Joseph McCarthy.

However diverse the subjects Lindeman pondered and explored—community, learning, leisure, social planning—certain themes persisted throughout his career. He was an unblushing pragmatist devoted to empiricism, experimentation, and the testing of truth in practice. He celebrated diversity over uniformity. Social philosophy consisted not of logic-chopping but of shaping strategies for action and for life.

John Dewey was a chief mentor. Lindeman turned for inspiration and insight also to Ralph Waldo Emerson and declared, in an essay published in the *American Scholar* (Winter 1946-47), that their two systems were fully compatible. Emerson, like Dewey, believed in an evolving world containing no ultimate or final solutions; change was the rule of life. The optimism he found in Emerson matched his own—it was tentative, not dogmatic, and faithful to "an unfinished but promising world" (p. 64). From Emerson he drew confirmation of what he had learned from the pragmatic way; Emerson saw that "we become what we do. *The end pre-exists in the means*" (p. 62). Inappropriate or bad means corrupted even the best of ends.

The capacity of democracy to survive and thrive came down finally to the acting out of all these principles and processes in daily life. Democracy found meaning and strength in the small group. In one of his last formal statements (a short essay published in the Winter 1951 issue of the *University of Kansas City Review*) he summed up that faith: "Self-government is learned in the daily round of life, in family circles, play groups, staff meetings, conferences, neighborhood and community meetings" (p. 130).

In 1991 it may be difficult for many of us to embrace all these enthusiasms as our own. But we are asked not to imitate or to emulate but to create our own strategies of life. In studying the life and career of Eduard C. Lindeman we can find much that remains relevant and vital in our own day.

—Clarke A. Chambers
Professor of History, Adjunct Professor of Social Work, and Director of the Social Welfare History Archives, Emeritus, University of Minnesota, Twin Cities Campus. January 1991

## Prologue

# On the Mountain

*It was clear the search had just begun
and the journey would be long.*

On a beautiful fall day in 1973 while hiking with a group
of friends in the Central Oregon Cascades, I was introduced to
Paul Unger from Cleveland, Ohio.[1] Paul and I trailed behind the
others and struck up a conversation. When I asked him how a
businessman became involved in international social work,* he replied
that fresh out of Harvard University, in the middle of the Depression, a man named Eduard Lindeman had given him his first job
in a WPA program called "Community Organization for Leisure."
Paul worked for Lindeman, the director, for four years. "That man,"
he told me, "had the biggest influence of anyone on my entire life!"

I was so startled I didn't speak. Vivid memories flooded my
mind. I saw once again my father's whimsical smile, his half-closed
eyes; I smelled the pungent, maple-scented tobacco from his pipe;
I touched the rough tweed of his jacket and I felt his comforting
hand in mine. I heard him say again, as he did whenever he returned from a trip, "Well, now, what do you have to say for yourself?"
Or, "Do you think you'll ever amount to anything?" Although
he said it impishly, somehow I thought he wasn't kidding. I
remembered also that when playing tennis (his favorite pastime),
walking, or dancing, Lindeman moved purposefully and energe-
tically. But in spite of being a graceful dancer and tennis player,

---

*The International Program to which Unger referred was called C.I.P.,
The Council of International Programs for Youth Leaders and Social Workers,
Inc., located in Cleveland, Ohio.

he frequently embarrassed himself and others by his clumsiness, and he had a way of listing to one side when walking or driving a car. Someone attributed the listing to long hours of walking steel girders when he was a shipbuilder during his youth. Unger would tell me later he thought it was from walking in the furrows of farm fields, or perhaps from leaning to one side as he held onto a plow.

After a long silence, I announced, "I am Lindeman's daughter." Stunned by this amazing coincidence, Unger thought I would be surprised to know of the many other people whose lives Lindeman had touched: Sally Ringe Goldmark,[2] who was Lindeman's administrative assistant and lived in Seattle; Byron Mock,[3] his secretary, from Salt Lake City; and Dorothy Cline,[4] Albuquerque. There are many others, he said, who still look upon Lindeman as he does. Then, somewhat hesitantly, he added, "And don't forget, you must talk to Marion Beers."[5]

Paul's voice trailed off into the ravine below, and I was deep again in my own memories.

A scene flashed into my mind. I was driving my father to Boston where he was to deliver a speech. We talked about how I was to whisk him away from the crowd as he descended the podium, but, as often happened, the audience was electrified by the tall figure, his voice charged with emotion, his thoughts inseparable from his words, quietly persuasive. When he finished people huddled around him so that he couldn't get away. Although he had an escape plan, I doubt that he really wanted to escape. I knew even then how important adulation was to him. Clearly, he was enjoying, and maybe he needed, the recognition. It probably made up for some of the deprivation of his youth and may have also helped to satisfy a deep yearning for acceptance.

In his lifetime Lindeman had earned the respect of students, colleagues, audiences, and readers; was an established figure in adult education and social philosophy; and was considered an elder statesman of the social work profession. He was called the "Father of Adult Education" by adult educators, and his book *The Meaning of Adult Education*[6] was referred to as possibly the greatest book of the century in the field. Malcolm Knowles,[7] the current Father of Adult Education, had told me that the practice of adult education today is built upon Lindeman's philosophical base.

And it was Gertrude Wilson,[8] renowned professor of group work, who told me that Lindeman conceptualized group work theory. "You see, he was a philosopher, and had that rare combination of theory and a wonderful spirit. His theories had life to them . . . and there just aren't enough people reading Lindeman today. He's the one. He was the leader!"

Certainly Lindeman had been a strong advocate of group work and community organization. He could often be heard remonstrating, "I can't see why groups and group experience do not stand at the very center of social work's concern." Wilson also reminded me that Lindeman's 1949 definition of social work remains as valid today as it was then: "It is a profession which emanates from a humanitarian faith . . . founded upon the assumption that science can help human beings to lead a better life by applying scientific principles to individual, neighborhood, and community processes and situations."[9]

However, Lindeman refused to be contained within the boundaries of any one discipline. His career, stretching from 1911 to 1953, defied categorization. Not only could he relate education, social sciences and social problems to the problems of the day; he could also combine concepts from social sciences with both natural sciences and philosophy. He was a pioneer on many interlocking fronts—a pioneer social scientist with an allegiance to both science and to society and its processes, and also a pioneer in adult education and social philosophy.

In some respects, Lindeman was an Emersonian individualist, a nineteenth century romanticist, and a Jeffersonian agrarian as well. There were times when his strong belief in "individualism" on the one hand, and an equally strong belief in "collectivism" on the other, created a conflict for him. Fearing the power of large organizations, he sought individual and group expression. "How can you achieve a sense of community in a society in which science, technology, and industry are the chief sources of dynamics?" and "How shall science be employed to serve and enhance rather than endanger the quality of life?" were two key questions he asked his audiences and readers. That challenge remains as relevant today as it was then. The philosophical questions he posed were amazingly prophetic and predated others by some fifty years.[10]

Lindeman paid a price, though, for involvement in the social and political issues of the day. Because he was easily outraged by conditions of poverty, discrimination and social injustice, he joined hundreds of organizations that he thought promised hope for change. He was soon labeled a radical, and thus he became a target for reactionaries from 1922 until his death in 1953.

But that was the public man. The more I thought about the private man, the more I realized how little I knew about his personal life. He was away from home a lot and talked very little about himself. At his home in Greystone in High Bridge, New Jersey, he was the country gentleman, but he led another life in New York City, where he taught. Symbolically, the Hudson River came to separate his two lives. He may have believed he could keep the two apart, but there were those who felt he sacrificed the companionship of his family for his professional life.

In the following poem I wrote at about age 14, I challenged his wisdom and infallibility in all matters:

### To My Father

How do you know, Mr. Lindeman, how do you know
That what you say is right?
Don't you think that other
People might see things in a different light?

You have things all worked out
In beautifuly drawn charts,
And then proceed to make wholes
Out of what are seemingly parts.

You know too much, Mr. Lindeman,
About too many things
But it's too much for one man
To know what the future brings.

How do you know, Mr. Lindeman,
How do you know,
That what you say is true?
Don't you sometimes find
That what you say conflicts with what you do?

Although Unger and I talked of other things during our hike, again and again our conversation turned to Lindeman, and my thoughts to Lindeman the man. I realized there were a host of questions that needed answers and there were people who could provide them—friends, students, colleagues, associates—whose lives Lindeman had transformed. There were also his precious black notebooks that he always took with him wherever he went. They contained his random thoughts, quotes from his favorite authors, jokes, and newspaper clippings on current economic, social, and political problems—his efforts to trace political and social change. Addicted to writing course and lecture outlines on trains and airplanes, complete with doodles, the scrapbooks were full of these as well. Letters? Scrapbooks?[11] Unpublished manuscripts and other writings?[12]

An idea was taking shape. It was time to find out more about this man who had influenced so many. Through his experiences, scrapbooks, letters, writings, and memories of those who had been influenced by him, I would try to reconstruct a life that had such power to touch and change the lives of others. It would not be easy. "Lindeman was a man who painted on a seven-league canvas with brushes of camel's hair," an old friend from Dallas eulogized at Lindeman's memorial service.[13] And, on the same occasion, a former chairman of the American Civil Liberties Union suggested that "a careless visitor from Mars might think this is not a man but a syndicate."[14]

There was a need to explore Lindeman's background and the way his early experience may have contributed to his fundamental ideas and beliefs. There was the basic element, so American in concept, of a young man, son of immigrants, who somehow rose above poverty, discrimination, and obscurity to become a giant in several fields; a unique individual; a scholar who contributed to the knowledge base of many fields.

I was prepared to discover a complicated man, a troubled man, a study in contradictions. I knew he loved his family and his home, but he was seldom home. He was a man who epitomized youthful energy and vitality, and yet he was seriously ill and in pain much of his lifetime. I had been told that he could send students soaring, mesmerizing them with the forceful presentation of his ideas, but also that he was perhaps a superb showman and spell-binder, called by some a gadfly, even a ladies' man. Speeches that seemed so magnificent could result in terrible articles because of constant repetition, convoluted sentence structure, and sentences within sentences.

As I descended the mountain late that afternoon, I knew I would start another venture to investigate Lindeman the private and the public man, to discover the father I had never really known.

It was clear that the search had only just begun and the journey would be long.

# Chapter 1

# Early Beginnings

*The time will come when you will speak knowingly*
*about important topics.*

Frederecka von Piper Lindemann

Lindeman had rarely, if ever, discussed his childhood or his parents and their background with members of his family. Most of what the family knew was what we had gleaned from two publications after his death, *The Democratic Man* by his son-in-law, Robert Gessner, in 1956, and *Eduard C. Lindeman and Social Work Philosophy*, Gisela Konopka's 1958 doctoral dissertation.

The two books offered little biographical information and, not surprisingly, contained identical stories about his origin. This data must have been what Lindeman told Gessner, who, in turn, served as a primary source of information for Dr. Konopka. Gessner somewhat romantically described Lindeman's mother, Frederecka Johanna von Piper, as a "young Danish noblewoman, born in the unhappy province of Schleswig Holstein in a time of great political upheaval." Frederecka fell in love with "a poor, but stolid, godfearing shepherd, Frederick Lindemann, who had escaped from a German war camp. Together they sailed to the new world." Gessner concluded that Frederecka's "high-caste parents thereupon disowned her" and that she "relinquished social position and wealth to bear ten children in a strange land, and to die in poverty."[1]

Konopka quoted from autobiographical notes that she had found in one of Lindeman's early scrapbooks in the Columbia University Archives:

I grew up in this country as the son of immigrant parents who had migrated from Denmark after the Prussian-Danish war. . . . We lived in a neighborhood where Scandinavians were held in low esteem,

1

in fact, the lowest in the community. Thus I was born, and spent my early childhood and youth, in an environment in which there was segregation and demeaning of personality.[2]

This was most of what I knew about Lindeman's heritage and early life, and I did not know this until after his death in 1953. However, earlier I had met two of his sisters, Rose and Minnie, and knew he was very fond of them. While he was still alive my sister Ruth showed me a letter he had written to her in 1932 from Frankfurt, Germany. In it he showed a curious interest in the origin of the name Lindeman.

> This morning, I was called out of a conference session to meet a man whose name was Hugo Lindeman; he teaches at the University of Cologne. . . . He said he wanted to find out if we might be related; and he thinks there is some likelihood. He told me the name originated in the Middle Ages and means the man who lived by the Linde. The Linde in early days was a man who meted out justice in the community. Since many could live near him, there are many people by that name, scattered all over Europe. When I told him my father came from (Sleswig) [sic] when it was still Danish, he said he thought that must have been the same family.[3]

It was important for Lindeman to be of Danish origin, and he had traveled to Denmark in 1920, and again in 1922 and 1926, ostensibly in search for the roots of progressive Danish social legislation. In a letter to his close friend Charles Shaw, however, he confided that he viewed these trips as "pilgrimages," attempts to pick up "lost ancestral threads," a "quest" that he said arose from his "dislocated youth."[4] But we knew of no indication anywhere that he had ever made an attempt to locate either relatives or ancestral sites on any of these visits.

Yet clearly Denmark was special for him, the one country, outside of his own, where he seemed to fit into the pattern of life without any difficulty. Dorothy Shaw, wife of Charles Shaw, had sent me a packet of letters Lindeman had written to Shaw from 1922 to 1950. In a 1926 letter, Lindeman described his deep regret in leaving Denmark, writing, "My Copenhagen friends presented me with a beechwood cane as a token, they said, of my understanding of the Danish people."[5]

2

During his visits he had also become intimately acquainted with the Danish folk high schools (*folkehojskoler*) or people's colleges, conceived by Danish educator, Nikolai Grundtvig[6] and shaped by others, notably Christen Kold.[7] Lindeman's impressions of the *folkehojskoler* led to his lifelong interest in adult education and the worker's education movement, and perhaps they also explain his complete captivation by Denmark.

He often extolled Denmark's virtues in his articles and lectures. The story goes that once as he read a paper in which he praised Denmark at a meeting of academics, he felt a tug at his coattails. It was Felix Frankfurter, the presiding officer, who in a loud whisper reportedly said, "Good Lord, Lindeman, isn't there anything rotten in Denmark?" Lindeman frequently asked his lecture audiences, "If Denmark can do it, why can't we? Why can't we have a society which furnished basic security from the hazards of unemployment, accident and old age?"[8]

Konopka speculated that because Lindeman had grown up as a member of a minority ethnic group, and was "torn by allegiance to several cultures," he may have had a strong need to be accepted.[9] It seemed that he may have found that acceptance in Denmark. He was proud of his heritage, of a country whose bold social, economic, and educational experiments he so admired.

In 1974 I spent several days at the University of Puerto Rico interviewing Roger Baldwin, founder of the American Civil Liberties Union. Because Baldwin and Lindeman had lived together in Greenwich Village from 1928 to 1935, I hoped he would shed more light on Lindeman's childhood and his heritage. But I was dead wrong. Although recalling vividly their Greenwich Village days together, their fall vacations in the wilds of British Columbia, and life at Greystone with Lindeman's happy, tennis-playing family, Baldwin knew nothing about Lindeman's ancestry because he spoke so little about himself personally.

Baldwin reported that Lindeman knew many women young and old, who were devoted to him and who in fact also "adored him, admired him, indeed, some of them loved him." At one point they had both been interested in the same woman. Roger believed Lindeman won her affections because he was very sociable. "More than I, he enjoyed sitting around and chatting in bars and restaurants, and he loved to play tennis, go to ball games, to the theater, and he loved to dance."

3

Up to this point I knew that Lindeman had had many friends and admirers, both men and women, and that he had had a serious affair with a "Mrs. C." But Baldwin suggested that there were in fact many more women, although he was quite sure that Lindeman "did not allow himself to get involved with his students."

Baldwin confirmed what I had already begun to suspect: since little biographical information existed, I might have to rely on stories Lindeman told and wrote about himself to friends, colleagues, and students. One thing was certain: what little he had chosen to relate about his childhood was consistent.

According to these stories, Lindeman was orphaned at a young age. His father died when he was ten, and his mother, he revealed, died when he was nine. He had been so upset he refused to attend her funeral, and when his older sisters tried to force him, he ran away and hid in a barn nearby.[10]

Lindeman seldom spoke about his older brothers except to say that five had died accidentally, including in a fire and by drowning.[11] A mysterious entry in an early scrapbook mentioned a plank "which one brother allowed to drop on another brother, and killed him." Still, there is no way to be sure that he was referring to one of his own brothers. In a letter written in 1925 to a very dear friend, Dorothy Straight, Lindeman said, "I am obliged to speak to you when crises appear. Word has just come of the death of my last brother. I mean the last of us. Curiously enough, his death was also due to an accident."[12] It was characteristic of Lindeman to dramatize, but it did seem strange that five brothers could have died by accident and that no one had ever questioned that fact.

Friends and colleagues recalled how much Lindeman loved his mother, but some thought he had feared his father. One told of how as a small boy Lindeman had been curious about a picture that hung on the wall over his parents' bed. When he thought they were asleep, he crept softly into their bedroom and climbed onto a chair to get a better look at the picture by candlelight. His parents woke up when the chair slipped from under him and his curiosity resulted in a sound spanking by his father. Oddly, a brief entry in an early scrapbook stated, "Incident of punishment by father, confusion as to ethical implications; resulting attitude one of fear toward father and reinforcement of affection toward mother."[13] Could Lindeman have been referring to the incident in his parents' bedroom?

A different and contradictory viewpoint of his father is expressed in an unpublished book manuscript entitled *Egoism* that he wrote at age 40:

It is possible that filial duty was more developed in me than in other men. For my part, the innate feeling of my duty to my father was the most profound of all my sentiments. I had the good fortune, it is true, to have a father whose high intelligence and severe probity commanded the respect of all, but I knew very well that I should not have been able to free myself from this hereditary filial veneration even if I had been the son of an unworthy father.[14]

I headed for St. Clair, Michigan, to locate his birthplace, the old homestead. In the general area north of what is now Pine Street, Lindeman's father had built a log cabin in the wilderness over one hundred years ago. There, on May 9, 1885, Lindeman was born, the last of ten children. By then his mother, Frederecka, was forty-seven and his father, Frederick, was forty-nine.

To continue my quest for information on Lindeman's heritage and early life, I wandered around the neighborhood, noting that the lots had been subdivided many times. It no longer looked like the poverty-stricken neighborhood Lindeman had described. Now, it seemed a pleasant enough working-class community. Unable to find the homestead, I asked for directions from a woman who turned out to be a Mrs. Kenneth Mayhew, the mother-in-law of a Marjorie DuChêne who had come to live with the Lindeman family after Frederecka's death and later was adopted by them. I recall that Gessner had suggested that Lindeman may have resented Marjorie because she replaced him as the youngest child and also because she was taken care of by his favorite older sister, Minnie. Mrs. Mayhew reported that Marjorie had been taken into the home because she was the illegitimate child of Lindeman's sister Rose.

According to Mrs. Mayhew, Lindeman, or "Uncle Ed," had always been close to his sister Minnie. Minnie took in laundry as Frederecka had, not only to help support Marjorie but also to help Lindeman pay his way through college. Later on, when he could afford it, he sent Minnie $25 a month for the special orthopedic shoes she needed because of an injury to her foot. "Everyone loved Aunt Minnie," said Mrs. Mayhew, recalling that Lindeman visited Minnie at the old homestead every year until her death in 1949,

5

when he returned for the last time to attend her funeral. On this occasion Lindeman wrote to a friend:

> Death once more touched the Lindeman family. Minnie was 78 and had been an invalid most of her life. Now there are but two of us left of that large pioneer family of ten. The saddest part of it all was the funeral. . . . I had forgotten how medieval it really is. She was such a warm, human person. The one touching element in the whole affair was the flag at half mast on the little town hall. Ours was the most poverty-stricken family in the community, and the people were paying tribute to character alone. My heart warmed and my faith in people was restored.[15]

It would be impossible to say how much influence Minnie might have had on Lindeman's life, but it is possible that some of his concern for people could be attributed to her.

Mrs. Mayhew and I wandered around the neighborhood, and I tried to visualize what life must have been like for Lindeman growing up in St. Clair at the turn of the century. An article in *The Gleaner*, "Save the Grand Old Trees," that he had written in 1912 mentioned his favorite tree:

> In the yard of my old home, there stands a crooked chestnut tree. It is far from beautiful in shape; but to me it has a charm so intense that I renew its acquaintance as often as my work permits. Down its crooked trunk I slid from my window when they tried to keep me in bed with the mumps. Under its shade I started my first pinstore and with its fruit I've won many battles. . . . To go back to the old home and find the chestnut tree missing would be like finding a forever empty chair at a dinner table.

Mrs. Mayhew and I looked for the old chestnut tree, but there was no trace of it. As for the house, it had been remodeled many times and was now the office of an ambulance business. Only the basement of the original structure remained.

According to the St. Clair librarian, by the time Frederick Lindemann had hewn the last timber for his homestead in 1864, the town had 2,550 settlers and was booming. Early St. Clair was described as a pioneer community where "immigrants pitched their tents and began the task of taming the wilderness . . . first came the French, then the Yankees." By 1842 a little group of pioneer

6

farmers from New England were living in a cleared stretch above the town, known as Yankee Street. Then between 1845 and 1848 a wave of Germans, Scandinavians, and Hollanders arrived. It is said that many of the Germans came because the villages along the St. Clair River reminded them of the towns along the Rhine.[16]

The St. Clair River, with its exquisitely blue water, extends seventy miles from Lake Huron to Lake Erie and was the lifeline of the towns along its banks. Hardy sailors from St. Clair regularly left town to ship out on the Great Lakes or on a tug, or to raft logs downstream.

In spite of the fact that by 1870 there were seven saw mills, twelve salt mines, and a large brickyard, work in St. Clair was sporadic and seasonal, and wages were low. Lindeman's father was frequently out of work and his mother, with the help of Rose and Minnie, had to take in laundry to supplement the family income. No doubt some of the laundry belonged to wealthy out-of-towners who came to St. Clair for the summer and owned the fashionable homes that bordered the river.

Not surprisingly, each child was expected to contribute to the meager family income. When Lindeman was old enough, he helped his mother pick up and deliver laundry. His older brothers contributed by working in the nearby brickyards and salt mines and as store clerks. Lindeman described a variety of jobs he held as a child. "As a boy I drove a delivery wagon for a grocery store, and in the summer I transported huge quantities of food to camps along the beautiful river near our town. I first became accustomed to hard manual labor in the brickyards near our home at a very early age."[17] When older, he worked on farms, in the salt mines, in shipyards in nearby Port Huron, and in factories in Detroit. Factory work and a riveting job on the tunnel between Detroit and Windsor, Ontario, marked the beginning, he said, of his concern about the social and economic injustices accompanying the industrial revolution. He was especially concerned about its impact on the working classes.

In 1870 when the Lindemanns' fourth child was born, there were good schools in the community, and yet none of the Lindemann children attended them. Even if the family had not been poor, illiterate, and discriminated against as immigrants, it is unlikely they would have taken advantage of the good schools. Why was it that a few months in a Lutheran church school was all the Lindemann

7

children had in the way of formal education? Although Lindeman hinted that his mother may have valued education, he suggests that his father's disinterest in education for himself and his family was passed on to other family members with the possible exception of Eduard and Minnie. This under-valuing of education caused much grief for Lindeman. Understandably, it resulted in a breach with remaining family members. Minnie may have helped her brother with his education from her heart and not because she valued education.

Because Lindeman was the youngest, he may have been the favorite of his mother and perhaps of Rose and Minnie as well. His letters to Dorothy Straight suggest that his mother could spare little time from her busy schedule to minister to his needs, hence the time she did spend with him must have been very special.

Although Frederecka spoke only German and the only book in the house was the Lutheran Bible, she might have had more education than her husband and passed some of this on to her youngest child. In some way she may have been responsible for Lindeman's momentous decision at age twenty-one to veer from family tradition and seek a college education.

In the book he wrote about his college experience Lindeman described the important role his mother played in his life. What emerges from this early book, and later in letters to Straight, is the profound sense of loss he felt at her death. He never ceased mourning her. "I recall one Christmas," he wrote Dorothy in 1923, "a long time ago, when my mother presented me with woolen mittens and stockings which she made by lamplight. [She must have seen how great my joy was] because I still remember her [saying]: *'Deine Augen scheinen wie's Himmelslicht.'* (Your eyes shine like the heavens.) And this became her favorite expression." He told Dorothy that if he ever wrote his autobiography, "I shall say something about my mother." Enclosed with the letter was a sentimental poem by Du Bose Hayward, which included the following lines:


> Having no books, you said a shining word into my open palms and closed tight.
> Then there were the nights—do you remember still? forgetting playthings we could never buy,

We journeyed out beyond the farthest hill adventuring along the evening sky; and you would teach the meaning of the stars.[18]

On another occasion he wrote about the "secret knowledge" his mother seemed to possess, and that when she could find time to share his childish aspirations and fancies, she would confide in him, "The time will come when you will read books and speak knowingly about important topics."[19]

In addition to the theme of loneliness that emerges from his childhood, there is the ever-recurring theme of death. In the outline for his autobiography he alluded to his early years as "Youth, Death, and Many Beginnings." In his copy of a biography of Lincoln he marked the sentences describing the death of Lincoln's mother.

The overwhelming sense of loss at the death of his mother, and the deaths of eight family members during his early youth, contributed to feelings of bereavement and even abandonment that resurfaced throughout his life.

# Chapter 2

## Discovery at the St. Clair County Courthouse

*Life may have seemed like an endless series of losses.*
*Did his only hope for the future lie in reshaping his past*
*and creating a new personal mythology?*

Author

After leaving Lindeman's old neighborhood, I stopped at the St. Clair County Courthouse to verify the vital statistics of the Lindemann family. There I found information in federal, state and local census records, and in birth and death records, that surprisingly did not corroborate the data I had.

I read and reread the very old records dating back to 1864 when Lindeman's oldest brother, William, was born. They were handwritten and did require a magnifying glass to read, but they were legible and meticulously recorded.

Reluctantly, I had to accept the fact that I had made a number of startling discoveries. The first of these was the fact that his parents did *not* come from Schleswig-Holstein, or even from anywhere near Denmark, because record after record clearly established that their homeland was Württenberg, Bavaria, in southern Germany. Therefore, it was unlikely that Lindeman's mother was the daughter of a Danish noble family, which then makes it highly unlikely that her parents ever disowned her when she married Frederick. There was no evidence that Frederick had ever been a shepherd or a prisoner of war. Furthermore, the records said nothing of Lindeman's older brothers dying in accidents. Yet another surprise was learning that Lindeman had not been orphaned at ten, but rather in 1901 when he was sixteen his father had died of cancer, and at seventeen his mother died of "stomach trouble."

Spurred on by these unexpected discoveries, I next checked Frederick's occupations prior to and after emigrating to the United

States. Because Lindeman insisted that, like his father, he too was a "simple man" who moved in "simple ways" and that like the peasant his father was, "I'd like my feet placed solidly in some piece of soil,"[1] I searched the records to see if his father had ever owned or worked any land, or even farmed after emigrating. On the contrary, there was clear evidence that before emigrating Frederick was a "common laborer" and that after settling in St. Clair he worked in nearby sawmills and brickyards and was, at times, only seasonally employed. This information corresponded to the information I found in the St. Clair library concerning opportunities for employment for immigrants during the latter part of the nineteenth century.

Despite the image Lindeman chose to create of a "peasant heritage," he was not generally perceived as a simple man. On the contrary, a Columbia University colleague, Lucille Austin, described him to me as an "aristocrat. He could, and did, often give the impression of being suave and sophisticated; but always he was a complex man."[2]

I came away from the courthouse certain that my grandparents had emigrated to the United States in 1863 during the Danish-Prussian War and that quite possibly Frederick had fled the old country to avoid being conscripted. However, these courthouse findings posed numerous contradictions. Moreover, an air of mystery had begun to surround Lindeman's identity and that of his family. Why would he have made up these stories about himself and falsified past events concerning his parents and their background, his childhood and youth?

Next I noticed that Lindeman's birth certificate cites his name as *Edward Lindemann*, with no middle name and the last name spelled with the Teutonic two *n*'s. His parents and their ten children all had the identical Teutonic spelling. Was the act of changing his name a deliberate and well-thought-out decision, or a spontaneous one? It has been said that, apart from the name given at birth, there is very little a person can change at will. Could it be that by changing his name slightly, Lindeman was, like the immigrants before him, striking out on his own? Why did the name *Eduard* appeal to him more than *Edward*? Why and when did he decide to add a middle name of *Christian*? And when did he drop the second *n* in his last name?

11

I was convinced that altering a name was an important act, no matter how or why it occurred. In *The Biographer Himself,* Kaplan states, "By changing a name an unfinished person may hope to enter into more dynamic—but not necessarily more intimate—transactions. Assuming a name that is not your given name suggests that the change is more than nominal—it is organic—and revolutionary. Making a name deserves to be regarded with awe."[3]

It was more than the mere changing of his name, though, that aroused my curiosity, and concern. It was the other facts I had uncovered in the courthouse records that upset certain cherished notions and beliefs held by our family over the years. Why would Lindeman want to change his parents' place of origin? In spite of the fact that he persisted, even insisted, over the years in calling himself Danish, he was not Danish. I knew that his parents passed on to him a strong dislike of the Prussians. He was never to forget the motto that he saw over the First People's College in Denmark on his first visit in 1920: *"Hvad udad tabes, det ma indad vindes"* (What the Prussians have taken away from us by force, we shall regain by education from within; or, what outwardly is lost must inwardly be gained). He had no doubt also been influenced by the glowing accounts of writers returning from Denmark extolling the virtues of a country that had put an end to poverty and illiteracy. Some of these reports may have been exaggerated, but even to the critical, Denmark's social, economic, and educational experiment was impressive.

As we learned in chapter 1, Lindeman made prolonged observations of Denmark's folk high schools, which provided much of the impetus for his remarkable publication, *The Meaning of Adult Education.* He claimed that Denmark seemed like a "cultural oasis in the desert of nationalism." He saw farmers studying for the purpose of "making life more interesting," and he saw evidence that education "not only changed citizens from illiterate to literate, but rebuilt the total structure of life's values."[4]

Another explanation for his wanting to change his origin from Germany to Denmark might lie in his desire to distance himself from his family. The family was poor, illiterate, and foreign-born in a time when immigrants and their children were looked down upon; a family where sickness and death lurked; that knew only hard work; that was, above all, German, which in those days could only mean Prussian. And what must have been the hardest for

12

Lindeman was that they were a family that did not value education. Growing up in this atmosphere and in a community with so much animosity toward Germans, he must have experienced a painful discrimination he never forgot.

As he grew older, Lindeman did suggest that at times his family was a burden to him. "I, as the last functioning male of the 'great family of ten children,' " he wrote Dorothy, "came to be the main source in times of want and despair. Sometimes the burden is too great and I falter."[5] When his last surviving brother died, he wrote Dorothy in 1925 that he was greatly moved, "more so because of the gulf which has so separated me from all save one of my brothers and sisters. They all remained content with their status and resented my thirst for knowledge. When I at last set off for school, it was assumed that I was violating a family standard. Since that day our family began disintegrating until at last no real family feeling remained. It is as though we must bear a cross as the penalty for seeking truth."[6]

In actuality, the "great family" had begun to disintegrate as early as 1883, two years before Lindeman's birth, when the courthouse records showed that an older brother, George, died at age seven from peritonities. By January 1898 three Lindemann sons had died, each of an illness. Possibly two of Lindeman's brothers did die in accidents as he claimed throughout his life.

Lindeman persisted in calling himself an orphan, and indeed he may have felt like one. For him life may have seemed like an endless series of losses. It is not surprising then that at an early age he fancied himself an orphan and then actually came to believe it.

Other gnawing questions remained from the visit to the courthouse. Why did Lindeman's stories about his early life and heritage confuse fact with fiction? One plausible explanation was that his early life had consisted of grim reality, promising little in the way of a future. Breaking family tradition by leaving home and going away to college was so difficult and painful that it required a new identity. Did his only hope for the future lie in reshaping his past and creating a new personal mythology? When events in his childhood did not coincide with his aspirations for success in adulthood, did he simply alter them? I could only conclude that by distancing himself from his family and past he had found a way to provide coherence, a sense of continuity, and meaning to

13

his life. The new identity must have come, in time, to have more logic in a young man's mind than did harsh reality.

But puzzling questions still persisted for me, and I think for Lindeman as well. Did the fact that he concealed the truth about his past make him a less trustworthy father or a less authentic human being? In rare moments of intimacy, he confided in his daughters that he blamed himself for being such a poor father and for not spending enough time with his family. To his wife, he begged forgiveness for being an untrustworthy husband.

Uncovering the truth was not an easy or pleasant task. Things had been fine the way they were. My discoveries could upset family members and admirers, some of whom thought I should have left well enough alone. What is wrong with trying to create a better life? Nevertheless, the way in which he chose to cover up his past and to change his name, and the logic he used to create a new identity, posed a challenge for me. My responsibility, however, was not to try to make the facts come out right for admirers and our family, but rather to try to understand Lindeman's efforts to climb out of poverty and become somebody.

It is not likely that Lindeman could have transcended his past had it not been for his momentous decision to go to college. With almost no formal education and no encouragement from his family, going away to college must have been an essential and courageous first step for the young Lindeman. He had written to Dorothy one Christmas concerning the death of a brother, about which he felt so much guilt. Was he not saying that leaving home at age twenty-one to go to college was more than just a physical break with the family? It was a total break—physically, emotionally, and intellectually. Perhaps the break was made easier by what his mother had told him as a child, words he would never forget: "Someday you will read books and speak knowingly about important topics." Frederecka never lived to know how true her prophecy would one day become.

## Chapter 3

# College Days: From Laborer to Scholar

*I wonder if you can imagine the sensation of entering
a world of literature having already reached maturity.
I still feel a haunting sense in the presence of a book.*

Lindeman, 1950

Lindeman told different stories at different times about how
he happened to go to college. The facts vary slightly, but what
is important is how he himself viewed this experience.

One version was the story he told to Lucy Freeman, a *New
York Times* reporter, who interviewed him in July 1950 when he
retired from Columbia University after twenty-five years of teaching.
He told her that from age nine to twenty-one he earned his living
by hard manual labor. The introduction on a riveting job of the
pneumatic drill, to which he could not adapt, resulted in his return
to farming.

While working on a farm in Bowling Green, Ohio, a sympathetic farmer said, "Lindy, why don't you go to college?" Lindeman
replied that he had neither the money nor the education. The
farmer thought there might be a special program for people like
him and offered to send for the catalog. They soon learned that
he would be eligible for a subfreshman program at Michigan
Agricultural College (MAC) in East Lansing. So away he went in
the fall of 1906, with his total savings of $85.

Another version was told to me in 1974 by Sally Ringe Goldmark,
Lindeman's administrative assistant from the New Deal days. She
recalled a story he told his WPA colleagues about working in a
factory in Detroit, where his job was to hand a heavy sheet of
metal to a man who then put it through a press. One day the
press came down on the man's arm, crushing both his forearm
and his hand before he could remove them. The bell rang in the

15

factory, and the press came to a halt. The man was taken to a nearby hospital, and within four minutes another man replaced him. Lindeman was supposed to continue working as if nothing had happened. But "something flashed in my mind," he told Goldmark, "and I walked out of that factory and never went back." If any man could replace any other man on a job, then all men were alike. From that point on his spirit was in revolt against the machine. Then and there he decided to go to school.

Whatever his motivation for going to college, the "Edward Lindemann" who applied in person to the president of MAC in 1906 was, in the words of a former student, J. Roby Kidd, "large of frame, over six feet, hands powerful, shoulders broad, a shrewd, shambling and ignorant young man encumbered by a past of misfortune and failure, and doomed to further failure."[1] According to Gessner, Lindeman walked in a "rambling gait down the straight line of an imaginary furrow . . . searching for roots; the agrarian inheritance; the half-remembered mother; the inchoate affection between strangers; the road to righteousness"[2] Gessner felt that Lindeman had been emotionally sensitized by loss and loneliness and spiritually troubled by his religion, which he had come to identify with death, and that he was seeking blindly, but intuitively, an educational key to open up his new world.

Lindeman was accepted as a subfreshman in spite of his limited command of language and math. At first he was totally bewildered by what took place in the classroom. He told Freeman that his initiation to formal education, next to his inability to adjust to automatic machines, was the "most perplexing and baffling experience of my entire existence. I spent frantic hours poring over books which mystified and confused my mind. Nothing bore the remotest relationship to my own experience."

The first years were made more difficult because he was older than the other students, came from a poor background, and was frequently teased about his shabby clothes. The many years of hard manual labor had left an imprint that was to remain fresh in his mind as he made the transition from laborer to scholar.

By the end of the first term Lindeman was on the verge of expulsion, and he was also broke. According to Gessner, "He wandered in a daze from the President's office to a fence near the cattle barns, where he sat in the loneliest hour of his life."[3] He finally applied for a job, and the barn superintendent, impressed by some inner quality, secured him a second chance as a subfreshman.

It was during these years that Lindeman gradually began to change his name. Old records show that he was admitted in 1906 under the name given him by his parents. However, by the time he moved into Twait's Hall in 1907, he had become "*E. C. Lindemann*," the *C* having been added, and no clue as to what it stood for.

During the ensuing two years, college directories continued to list him as *E. C. Lindemann*. However, by 1910 the first use of the spelling *Eduard*, along with the full spelled-out middle name of *Christian*, appeared in the college yearbook. Curiously, it was also in 1910, as editor of the Eunomian Literary Society, that he had dropped the second *n* and became *E. C. Lindeman*. Two years later, residing in Dormitory 8D, he continued the use of that name.

Although the tales he told about his childhood appeared to be remarkably consistent, the spelling of his name was not. As editor-in-chief of the college weekly *The Holcad*, he was affectionately nicknamed "Lindy" by his friends. Letters to the Editor were addressed to Lindy. As author of his first book in 1912 and again in 1919 as author of a publication for the Michigan Department of Public Instruction, he had reverted to *Eduard C. Lindeman*.

Stewart speculates that dropping an *n* could be a response to frequent misspellings by others, especially in an anglicized society. Creating a middle name, I believe, could have been to add a note of distinction, setting off the first name from the last. The selection of *Christian* might indicate that he was not only active in the YMCA at the time but also taught a Sunday school class on the literature of the Bible. Stewart feels it was unlikely that he was aware when he changed the spelling of his first name to *Eduard* that it is the preferred spelling of *Edward* in Germany, or that he was actively seeking to hide his German heritage, as he would do later. He seemed also unaware at this point that people would and did misspell *Eduard*. Herbert Croly, for instance, once wrote to him as "Dear Edouard," and from 1922 to 1932, Dorothy Straight Elmhirst continued to address him as "Dear Edward."

On the surface there appeared to be no consistent pattern or logic to the process of altering his name or to the name changes themselves. What is clear is that they not only occurred throughout his college years but continued until sometime around 1919. And they may also alert us to other more profound changes occurring during his young adulthood.

Lindeman felt that his college experience had a profound and powerful influence over his intellectual and philosophical development, transforming him from laborer to scholar. His version of the difficulties and rewards of his college years is contained in the leather-bound volume *College Characters: Essays and Verse* (1912) published after graduation. There he writes fondly of his friends— the college librarian; the college secretary (a term used in those days for a person in charge of student affairs); the secretary's wife, who made it financially possible for him to remain in college; the judge; the gardener; and the English teacher who offered to tutor him after he was reinstated and who later became a friend. He wrote of "Our Librarian," "I love her as a Mother. . . . Friendship had to take the place of a mother, which you, who have had a mother's love through life, can never know." When Lindeman left college to assume his new post in Detroit, he carried with him a treasured gift from the librarian, a picture of Sir Galahad.

From *College Characters* it is evident that he not only believed he had been orphaned at an early age, but he wanted others to believe it also. The loneliness he experienced as a child had been reinforced in college. He writes that Sundays and holidays were especially lonely for him, and he was grateful for the warm hospitality of the secretary and his wife, the gardener, and the judge, "who invited me into their homes to share a meal and the warmth of their fireplace." Their friendship meant a great deal "to one without the comforts of a true home. . . . If college professors only knew how much their homes could influence students' lives, there would be more invitations extended to them." In this first book he cries out for a mother's love, affection, and a "true home," needs that he felt had not been met during his childhood.

Nature proved to be his best friend. "My greatest battles have been fought alone and in the quiet of nature's charm. Our greatest convictions come to us in solitude." When he felt cramped in his little study he would listen to the calls of his bird friends "who will entice me away from my books. The flowers will take the place of Emerson, the buds and cheering birds will quicken my step and brighten my eyes." There was a desperate cry for friendship, so evident in the poem "What I Ask of Friendship," in which he asks that friends not only share their worldly goods and bear

18

with him in sundry moods, but that "As long as I walk straight and to the right, / They believe me honest in my fight."[4]

In addition to these recurring themes, Lindeman began to express several ideas that continued to develop throughout his life. According to Konopka, these included the application of ethical principles to practice and the attempt to unify science and religion. In a short essay called "Science and Religion," he regarded the battle between Darwinism and religion as finished, and he was striving for a "religion without prejudice and with faith in science." A poem in his first book indicated the real conflict and unhappiness he was experiencing at age twenty-six:

Great God where canst thou be?
I ever search for thee.
In all mine eyes behold,
And thou dost yet withhold
From me thy tender hand.
How can I understand?[5]

Lindeman's college records indicate that during his first year he got A's in blacksmithing and carpentry, but sat through algebra without understanding a word. At first he majored in physical and biological sciences, but when his botany teacher sent him to Rochester, New York, to study the hickory tree, he began to drop in on community centers in the evenings and then decided he liked people better than hickories. He later changed his major to social science.

"Laboriously, inch by inch," according to Gessner, "he lifted himself up. He learned grammar, and improved his spelling. He acquired a love, which never left him, for the magic of words; the excitement of writing and the thrill of reading. He underlined what he read; his passion for books became fierce and tender. He was like a young Greek discovering the world afresh. He began his life-long habit of copying passages, of doodling intricate and colorful patterns; and a fascination with writing materials, pens, pencils, paper and inks. . . . A keen sense of continuous discovery became a part of his personality."[6]

Lindeman told Freeman that he immersed himself in a "sea of books," and after forty-five years of hungry reading, he still found "no greater delight. I wonder if you can imagine the sensation of entering a world of literature having already reached maturity. I still feel a haunting sense in the presence of a book."

Despite his reverence for books, Lindeman developed a trait that was to create a problem for him not only in college but throughout his entire life—an impatience with detail. Once he kept a library book beyond the time limit. "I faltered at the payment of 80 cents," he wrote, "for 80 cents had the appearance of a goodly portion of the world's wealth just then." The librarian, however, was determined to teach him one of life's important lessons. "She taught. I paid," he wrote.[7] Nevertheless, he continued to dislike details, and many years later as administrator of a New Deal program, this impatience placed a great burden on his assistants.

In spite of many adversities, Lindeman somehow found time to play football and even to become manager of the team his third year in college. By his senior year, he had found a niche for himself in various extracurricular activities, becoming a member of the Penman's Club (a literary club, and his favorite); president of the Cosmopolitan Club (an organization for foreign-born students); an active member of the Debater's Club; president of the campus YMCA; and editor of the weekly paper. In one of his scrapbooks he pasted an undated note from one of his encouraging teachers: "Perhaps you will not care to have me say this, but I am pleased to have you keep up your work. It has been said that you are a strong enough young man to keep up your work in spite of being a football player—that you have seriousness of purpose. Keep your standards up!" She was one of the many women in his life who gave him renewed faith in himself and in his purposes.

In addition to trying to keep up academic standards, Lindeman tried to keep up with finances as well—a problem throughout college. In spite of money he earned during the summer pitching for the semiprofessional Ontario team of the Michigan Baseball League, and some help from his sister Minnie, he became overwhelmed with financial obligations during his senior year. Bitterly disappointed and increasingly in debt, he decided to leave. It was another woman who took an interest in him and helped him to remain in school. Riding the bus from East Lansing to Lansing with his suitcase, he felt a gentle tap on his shoulder. It was the secretary's wife who, when she learned he was leaving, suggested that he see her husband. "I know he will want to help you," she said. As a result of this chance encounter, the secretary offered him financial aid that permitted him to complete his final year.[8]

In his last year Lindeman wrote *In the Hearts of the People,* a four-act play performed by the college dramatic club in March 1911. Gessner claims that "this raw play nakedly reveals much about the motivations which shaped his formative years." The play, he felt, would have amused the older Lindeman and is also important because it is the first example we have of Lindeman's writing.

The hero of the play discovers that he is not the true son of an oppressive, aristocratic "ward boss" but that his real father is of humble birth. Before he discovers this, he has fallen in love with a woman who, when she finds out he is not really from a wealthy family but rather the son of a common laborer, is willing to cross class lines to share her life with his at great sacrifice. Gessner suggests that "the evidence, though crude, is striking."[9] In actuality, it is even more striking than Gessner believed, now that we know Lindeman deliberately changed the humble origin of his mother to that of a noblewoman. It appears likely that it was sometime during his senior year that he began the process of creating his own personal mythology. Writing the play had been a very significant act for him, permitting him to indulge his imagination and then somehow to transform his life into something new and unique.

Although fraught with difficulties and challenges, Lindeman's college experience had been a profound one on many levels, providing him with an opportunity to rethink his own childhood and his experience as a laborer and to strengthen the ideas formed during those early years. His years as a laborer encouraged his natural instincts for fairness and his willingness to do battle against injustice, which characterized his entire life. Throughout his teaching career he would insist that students take a stand on politics at all levels. He had exemplified these beliefs in December of his senior year, when he called a mass meeting to protest the expulsion of two students from school. In those days this was a daring, risky thing to do. He clearly thought it was unjust, and at this meeting he gave a fiery speech on behalf of the students at the risk of being suspended himself.[10] Subsequently they were reinstated.

In the audience of this mass meeting a pretty, auburn-haired young lady sat in the front row. Lindeman recognized her as a student he had met at a Christmas party. She was impressed by the young Lindeman and did not seem to mind the fact that he was viewed as a rebel. Her name was Hazel Taft; she was later to become his wife.

The December meeting, along with other speeches he made and liberal articles he wrote for *The Holcad*, earned Lindeman the title of "campus rebel." He emerged from college as a radical convinced of the existence of a class struggle and also as "a complete product of adult education," Goldmark told me. "If there ever was a living example of what could be done, he was this to everyone: how to make oneself a person who counted among his fellow men."[11]

# Chapter 4

# A Career at Last: Many Beginnings

*The young man is a deep thinker, a logical reasoner*
*and intensely interested in agricultural and rural problems.*

The Gleaner, 1911

Although he had started out with serious disadvantages and it took him five years to finish, Lindeman graduated from MAC with high honors. He always looked back upon those years as "the most happy and fruitful years of my life."

Upon graduation he was offered many different job opportunities. He decided to accept the position of managing editor of *The Gleaner,* a liberal agricultural journal published in Detroit. During college Lindeman had been interested in the cooperative movement, which was gaining strength in the Midwest. Konopka speculates that *The Gleaner's* editor, Grant Slocum, for whom Lindeman had done some landscaping as a student, may have encouraged him to take the job. Lindeman also was attracted by the fact that *The Gleaner* had initiated one of the first insurance plans for farmers and was concerned with everyday problems of rural people. Also, Slocum was interested in young people and their advancement. In October 1911 Slocum introduced his new managing editor with these words:

> We are pleased this month to introduce Eduard C. Lindeman, who has accepted the position of Managing Editor of this publication. He comes to us well qualified . . . and brings the energy, enthusiasm and interest so necessary in carrying forward *The Gleaner's* progressive policies. . . . The young man is a deep thinker, a logical reasoner and intensely interested in agricultural and rural problems. . . . After an intense personal struggle, he chose *The Gleaner* as the best opportunity for the opening up of his life's work.[1]

And so the recent friendship with Hazel Taft was temporarily interrupted. Lindeman had first met Hazel around 1910 at the dean of women's home at a Christmas party for students who had no homes for the holidays. Her father, Levi Rawson Taft, had a distinguished career as professor of horticulture and landscape gardening at MAC, and as superintendent of farmers' institutes and state inspector of nurseries and orchards. He also owned Eveline Orchards, a vast cherry orchard near Lake Charlevoix in northern Michigan. Taft, with his handlebar mustache and dark hair parted in the middle, bore a striking resemblance to his first cousin William Howard Taft, twenty-seventh president of the United States.

Hazel's ancestry was deeply rooted in Puritan New England, dating back to Increase Mather, the first president of Harvard, and Rebecca Nourse, who was hanged as a witch. The Taft family was a serious lot, conservative and, some say, humorless, so it is not likely that Taft and his wife, Ella Maynard, understood the radical Lindeman, full of idealism and not bent on seeking the kind of career they might have approved of. It is not known if Lindeman had been a student of Taft's at some point, or why Taft was said to have resisted the attachment at first. What is clear is that the young Lindeman was not economically or socially in their class. But Ella Taft had liked him from the beginning, and soon he was welcome in their pleasant home on faculty row.

According to Stewart, Hazel was reserved, but popular on campus and a member of the college tennis team. She was an attractive young woman, with clear blue eyes and beautiful red hair. No snob, she had a practical approach to life. Hazel was a strong woman, with the brisk stride of an athlete. She, along with two other members of the tennis team, were chosen to represent MAC in the 1909 tennis match against Ypsilanti. As well as being a good tennis player, she could play the piano well enough to perform a solo of Schubert's *Minuet* in the parlor of the woman's building in 1909. She was also a good student, graduating in 1910 at age 20, a year ahead of Lindeman. In the fall after graduation, she took a job as a teacher in the public schools in Ionia, Michigan.

As editor of *The Holcad*, Lindeman kept track of Hazel's comings and goings, whether it be her return to East Lansing for a Eunomian party and football game with Notre Dame, or a visit to her family when school closed because of a county fair. In 1911 *The Holcad* noted that Hazel had resigned her position in Ionia

24

and had taken a new position as assistant registrar at MAC. No doubt her friendship with Lindeman contributed to her return to campus.

Not long after Hazel's return in October 1911, Lindeman left for Detroit to assume his new post. Their friendship would now have to continue by correspondence. From his cramped quarters in Detroit he wrote *College Characters, Essays and Verse.*

As editor of *The Gleaner*, Lindeman became involved in the first of many battles for social justice. He led and won the fight to extend the U.S. mail service to include parcel post, which would benefit the farmers in rural areas. His editorials showed sympathy for the struggle of the small truck farmers harassed by the middlemen, a concern for the soil, and conservation of natural resources. He also demonstrated an early interest in adult education for farmers. In one editorial written in 1913 called "The Attractive Farm House" and signed "E. C. Lindeman," he laid out simple plans for the design of a three-acre farmyard. He urged farmers to spend $60 to $100 over a period of two years to beautify their homes by landscaping. He warned farmers not to plant everything at once but to buy smaller shrubs and trees and wait for them to grow. "It seems to be the American idea to get complete and immediate planting at once, an expression of our unhealthy haste in everything."[2]

Although *The Gleaner* provided many outlets for his talents and his interest in farmers and cooperatives extended to include workers and unions, Lindeman was lonely in Detroit. He made one close friend during this short period, soon to become a lifelong friend of the family. Harriet Robinson McGraw (Mrs. William C.) was a wealthy supporter of liberal causes, intelligent and strong-willed. Like other older women who helped him in college, she believed in his purposes and encouraged him in his new career. She also knew he was lonely.

Perhaps because he missed Hazel or because he was not satisfied with journalism alone, by the end of the year Lindeman accepted the offer of assistant to the pastor of the Plymouth Congregational Church in Lansing.

Before assuming this new post on August 29, 1912, Eduard Christian Lindeman married Hazel Charlotte Taft in the Plymouth Congregational Church. An account in Lansing's *State Journal* described it as a beautiful wedding with one hundred guests. A large reception followed in the Tafts' home. The only Lindemans there were Minnie and the widow of Lindeman's brother William. His parents' names were not mentioned in the newspaper account. After the wedding the newlyweds left for Charlevoix, where the Taft family had several summer homes.

After the honeymoon the Lindemans returned to their first home in East Lansing. Lindeman became assistant in charge of church work, at a salary of $1,800, in September 1912. He and Hazel joined the church officially on January 15, 1913.[3]

Gessner's version of Lindeman's short tenure with the church was that on the one hand Lindeman had always cherished the special appeal of a church audience but, on the other hand, had always been opposed to the dogma and absolutism of organized religion. It was not long before he found himself in "misunderstood but stubborn opposition to religion in its traditional forms," which led to two fruitless battles with preachers. "He was seeking integration in activities—education, labor, and recreation."[4]

However, Stewart states that Lindeman seemed to have done a good job but the church was having financial problems. In February 1914, the board of trustees found it necessary to accept his resignation after trying to persuade him to stay on at a lower salary. Stewart speculates that his new job as state leader of the Boys' and Girls' Clubs with MAC's Division of Extension was undoubtedly a boost from his father-in-law.[5]

By October 1914 and now with one daughter, Doris, Lindeman began his new job as extension director. He was one of a number of special agents appointed to assist the various county agents. According to Stewart, the Cooperative Extension Service grew to become one of the largest adult education systems in the world. Lindeman's job was specifically with the youth arm of "this evolving adult education giant," though Stewart speculates that his involvement with the parents and adult leaders may have been "the initial locus of his lifelong interest in parent education." His new job would eventually evolve into the 4-H Club program. Stewart describes it as "wholesome, useful work, and Eduard was good at it." He suggests that the Service must have placed great confidence in him to charge him with the full statewide responsibility for this work. These were the war years and since food was essential to the war effort, Lindeman's boys and girls were prodded to do their share. "By 1916, there were 374 organized clubs with an enrollment of almost 6,000. By 1917 Eduard was hitting his stride; his programs

Hazel Taft Lindeman and children

looked good as they shipped some 456,873,430 bushels of corn as part of the war effort. Sugar-beet clubs and the pig clubs added to the war effort, making 1917 a peak year."[6]

Stewart says by 1918 Lindeman had what amounted almost to an empire. Under his leadership the total number of boys and girls for all projects had grown to 22,396. During this period Lindeman brought boys and girls to Lake Charlevoix and, according to Hazel's older sister Fucia, taught them how to build a bridge across the stream that ran between two Taft cottages.

Lindeman had begun now to write and lecture on farm cooperatives and recreation. He viewed recreation as "efforts to recapture the lost play impulses of youth." His first published article was "Thirty Selected Games," which appeared in *Playground* in July 1920. During his travels around Michigan he had also discovered that he liked to teach. He retained an interest in recreation and the recreation movement throughout his life and frequently linked its principles with those of adult education.

Lindeman's interests began to broaden, and he seldom missed an opportunity to present a paper at the National Conference of Social Work annual meeting. These early papers demonstrated his keen interest in rural recreation and education; topics included "Boys' and Girls' Clubs as Community Builders" and "Organization of Rural Social Forces."

By 1918 there were three more daughters—Ruth, Betty, and Barbara. He had wanted a red-headed son but had to be content with four girls, none of whom inherited their mother's red hair. He was present at all their births. In fact, in the negligent absence of both a doctor and nurse, Lindeman, Gessner said, delivered his second daughter, an experience he had not intended.

In the fall of 1918 the family moved into a crowded Chicago apartment, and Lindeman assumed his first teaching post as instructor in the YMCA's George Williams College. In addition to classes he did county social work and became active on an international committee working for the Dawes Plan, a plan to support U.S. allies in Europe. Soon he began to teach outside of Chicago at Y conferences in Wisconsin, New York, and Canada. In lieu of army service he worked for the War Camp Community College and later for naval disarmament. He was not eligible to serve in World War I because a physical examination alerted doctors that he had "Bright's disease"—a serious and chronic kidney condition

28

known today as glomerulon nephritis. Diagnosed in early 1917, it was to remain his inner foe and, in the end, one he could never conquer.

In the summer of 1919 Lindeman wrote Harriet McGraw in Detroit, "If I get much bluer I shall have to send for you to come." Then he told her that in writing to him she could use the title "E.C.L., Professor of Rural Sociology, YMCA College, Chicago, IL.," adding, "Now, does that look formidable enough?" Then he added that he was lonesome. "It is swimming time and as usual I am left alone. For that reason I dare not tap the facets of my real sentiment, hence you get a formal sort of letter. But you do know most of the things that I think."[7] Letters to McGraw indicate he was battling the YMCA officials, as we will soon see.

At the Adirondacks Training School at Silver Bay he wrote McGraw, "I am sure my spirits will rise with the shining sun. I have not felt strong enough to hike. I have been having fevers for the last 3 or 4 days and am perpetually tired. I taught my first class today and got along fairly well. You don't get the same response from these Eastern people that you get in our good old Middle West."[8] Later he wrote, "I just can't get interested in club work, somehow," implying he preferred to concentrate on teaching.

One day while teaching at the YMCA summer camp at Silver Bay, New York, Lindeman was called to New York City to be interviewed by President Julius Foust for a position as professor of sociology in the Department of Sociology and Economics at the North Carolina College for Women. We do not know how Foust happened to call Lindeman. We only know that Lindeman wrote McGraw shortly after his return from New York: "I have had an offer of a position in a women's college in Greensboro, N.C., at a salary of $4,000. That's the highest I've ever been offered. But, can you imagine me teaching in a women's college?"[9]

It was a tempting offer, and the move seemed to offer greater freedom than he was experiencing at George Williams College. Also, at a summer training camp in Lake Geneva he had encountered opposition to his identification with social action. "You would laugh if you could see my tent in the evening," he wrote McGraw. "The students have nicknamed it the 'Open Forum,' and we surely do have some hot discussions. Students like it better than classes. My Sunday speech has stirred up this place. The students want it published as a pamphlet, but there's no hope of that. The powers that be don't smile upon it." From Lake Geneva he wrote her again: "It is just as I expected; they, the administrators, have a nice, harmless job all lined up for me but I don't want to fall into their trap."[10] Even though he was experiencing the power and pleasure of teaching, he discovered it could be uncomfortable when too many restrictions prevented him from teaching what he wanted to teach and utilizing the more unorthodox methods he found so challenging to learners.

Stewart describes Lindeman's tenure with the YMCA College as "unexpectedly brief." After only one year of service, the college announced his resignation "on account of ill health." The newsletter praised Lindeman's work as one of "extraordinary brilliance," and the students presented him with a lamp "to one whose torch-like intellect had lighted their way with its flame." But according to Stewart the resignation was a cover-up designed to mask the fact that the young professor was too liberal for the conservative administrators, who were happy to see him resign. Stewart suggests that the anger Lindeman displayed toward the college officials during the 1919 summer session reached such intensity that "it may have been displaced anger, aimed at targets in the YMCA but stemming at its roots from individuals and events closer to Eduard's person and his past." Such an angry display, according to Stewart, was unlike Lindeman, and "while he never shrank from a battle, . . . he would never again provoke a fight in just the way that he had provoked these."[11]

Now a new world beckoned him—a world that included the lovely Carolina hills. When the job offer came, it seemed to promise potential for intellectual growth. But, above all, Foust had assured him he would help the Lindemans locate a house with a garden, appealing to his strong love of nature.

# Chapter 5

# The Ku Klux Klan: Greensboro, North Carolina

*And then, one day, without the slightest warning,*
*I became the target and not the observer.*

Lindeman, 1922

After spending their entire lives in the Midwest, the Lindeman family moved to Greensboro, North Carolina, in December 1919. Lindeman would now make a new life in this placid, easy-going southern college community. The rental house that Foust had found for them was modest but had a huge flower and vegetable garden, which delighted the young professor.

President Foust had immediately liked Lindeman, and students and faculty were not disappointed either. He taught a class to high school teachers and coedited a weekly journal in nearby Asheville with the college librarian, Charles Shaw. Shaw and his wife Dorothy soon became the Lindemans' closest friends — a friendship that lasted a lifetime. They quickly made other friends in the community. Because of Lindeman's experience with loneliness while in college, he and Hazel made a point of welcoming students into their home and for cook-outs in a nearby park.

In addition to teaching, he was also engaged in his own research on tobacco cooperatives in the South and in writing. In 1921 his first substantive book, *The Community: An Introduction to Community Leadership and Organization,* was published.[1] Based on ten years of contact with local communities in Michigan, it was his first attempt to produce both a philosophical framework and a technique for those engaged in community organization. The reviews were positive — "Some of the best material on principles of Community Organization ever to be published," said one. Another claimed that the book would "furnish the motivating power for democracy." With the publication of this book and his presentations at the

31

annual National Conference of Social Work, Lindeman was beginning to make a name for himself on the national scene.

It was not long before Foust showed his confidence in Lindeman by promoting him to head of the department. The outlook for his professional future indeed looked bright. This was his first teaching experience in a public institution, and more importantly, his salary met the needs of his growing family.

Meanwhile, the family found life in the South very agreeable. They loved the Carolina hills and vacationed in the Blue Ridge Mountains of Virginia. Life was pleasant—that is, until Lindeman's confrontation with the Ku Klux Klan.

The Klan was in its heydey in the 1920s. Reaching its peak both in numbers and in influence in 1924, "it was strong enough to block the nomination of Al Smith at the Democratic National Convention. It helped elect 16 United States Senators, many Congressmen and dozens of local officials. And in one of the most menacing events in the nation's history, the Klan inducted into its ranks a President of the U.S., Warren G. Harding, in a ceremony in the White House. According to historians, the Klan had "more than six million members."[2]

Lindeman later recalled that in North Carolina in the 1920s "the Klan was conducting a campaign in small communities to keep Catholics, Jews and Negroes in their places; that is, subservient to the Nordic-Protestant civilization of the South. The method of attack, the procedure for selecting victims, and the set of assumptions which motivated this curious organization" interested him as an observer. He had been "a persistent critic of many of the hypocrisies and anachronisms of that civilization." However, he had not known that "being a critic was tantamount to membership in all three groups. And then, one day, without the slightest warning, I became the target and not the observer."[3]

Dorothy Shaw, although not certain of the exact order of events or the nature of the threats, recalled the motivating incident—the Lindemans' cook's birthday party—and its ugly aftermath. From correspondence between Foust and the Klan and recollections of both Dorothy Shaw and Gessner, it is possible to reconstruct the events that led to Lindeman's forced resignation from his teaching post.

The story began on February 4, 1922, when the Lindeman's cook asked permission to have a birthday party. Hazel agreed it

32

would be all right and asked the cook how many friends she was expecting. The cook replied that she had invited nineteen but that she did not expect them all to come. Hazel said if they did all show up, it would be all right with her for them to use one of the back rooms. The cook, thinking it was unusual for a white lady to allow colored people in an upstairs room, immediately called another cook to tell her about Hazel's generosity. Soon word spread throughout Greensboro that the Lindemans were entertaining their colored cook.

The day before the party, Hazel received several anonymous phone calls, and two strange visitors inquired about the party. She thought someone was playing a joke and was rather amused. However, when she told Lindeman about the strange events of the day, he thought it more worrisome than funny. He concluded that they may have gone beyond the usual Southern customs, and he believed that the secrecy of the various inquiries indicated the activities of the Klan.

The actual party itself proved uneventful. According to a detailed account Lindeman wrote for Foust at his request, while the cook entertained her friends in the basement, the Lindemans entertained student visitors in the living room. By 10 p.m. the students had departed, the party in the basement was over, and the Lindemans retired for bed.

The next day Hazel received a phone call that the local paper had received information that she had given a party for her cook the night before. She informed the caller that the cook did have a party but that she had nothing to do with it. The caller said he thought there was nothing to the story and hung up.

A few days later the *Greensboro Daily News* reported that "By the time the sun had sunk in the west on the day following the 'party,' the report had been so magnified that one would have believed the Lindemans had actually entertained the entire Negro population of Greensboro."

The rumors did not die down, and by February 13 a colleague of Lindeman's reported to him that there was talk on campus that Hazel had entertained their cook. It was at this point that Lindeman decided to consult Foust, whose advice was "to remain silent for the present." By February 15 the rumors had grown and Lindeman knew that "some of the best citizens seemed inclined to believe them." Once again he spoke to Foust, who still preferred to remain silent. However, this time Foust made Lindeman vow not to act without consulting him first. Lindeman gave him this promise, and Foust in turn agreed not to act without conferring with Lindeman first. Both men were quite certain the Klan was spreading the rumors.

On February 16, nine days after the birthday party, Lindeman received a copy of a letter addressed to Foust, from the Gate City Klan #19 realm of North Carolina, Knights of the Ku Klux Klan, drawing attention to the fact that Lindeman "is a socialist who has even gone so far as to state that he sometimes is almost persuaded in the divinity of God." The letter then referred to "a social function given in his home for negroes in spite of requests not to do so" and to "indiscreet things in connection with certain students of the school."

The letter-writers went on to say it was none of their business "what a man does in his own home, nor what is his belief, . . . but that does not relieve the fact that such actions as he has displayed in your institution are not in keeping with our local and southern customs." The letter questioned whether a man "with as much influence as Lindeman" had belonged in a "Christian institution." Then it reassured Foust that the Klan was not attempting to interfere with his capability or duties, "but as 100% Americans" they felt that these matters needed to be called to his attention and that "it was with a spirit of cooperation and love for peace and harmony that we do so."

The letter concluded with a threat to bring the matter to the attention of the "state authorities, and unless some action was taken some might be tempted to go further." Finally, the Klan "respectfully" recommended the dismissal of Lindeman from the faculty.

Never before had anyone attempted to interfere with Foust's management of the college. He was stunned by this anonymous letter. Of course, right-minded people had no respect for the Klan, even referring to them as "white trash." As a Southerner, however, Foust was acutely aware of the potential terrorist nature of this outlaw group. Faced with this delicate matter, he decided to consult a board member, Judge J. D. Murphy, whose judgment he relied on in matters pertaining to the management of the college. He left Greensboro to visit Murphy, who lived twenty miles away in Asheville. He remained out of town and incommunicado for six days.

By the time Foust returned to Greensboro, there was no doubt in his mind about how he intended to handle the matter. As long as he was president, no attention would be paid to any suggestions from the Klan, unless some Klan member came out in the open and met him man-to-man. He planned to treat the whole incident with "silent indifference" and, above all, to avoid newspaper publicity. He did not care to dignify the Klan by paying any attention whatsoever to a communication from it.

When Lindeman received a copy of the letter, he too was stunned. The method used and the utter falseness of the statements shocked him so much that he later described himself as "unable to think clearly or act for some time." He could not have known that the next forty-eight hours and the succeeding months of his tenure would be a period of crucial testing, not merely of himself and his moral courage but also of his friends.

During Foust's six-day absence, Lindeman found it difficult to determine a right course of action. He was thirty-six years old, and this would be his first battle against bigotry—bigotry clothed in Christian righteousness. The fights he had waged growing up as a poor son of immigrants, even with the discrimination that had been so demeaning, had not prepared him for this. The small crusades he had launched against injustices on the campus while a student and on behalf of small truck farmers in Michigan were child's play compared to what he now faced.

In treating their black cook as a member of the family, the Lindemans clearly had violated Southern customs and tradition. Other charges of being too friendly with students were clearly false, a cover-up for the real violation of local custom—"being too friendly with colored people." He had to admit that the situation had gotten worse, for Gessner tells us that:

> Lindeman sat alone, lamps burning, his family in bed but awake, awaiting a threatened attack. Rocks were hurled, windows broken, and a cross burned on the front lawn of the Lindeman home. He sat in clear view, reading, and finally the Klan retreated.[4]

Lindeman would write in 1927 that, during Foust's absence, he had found himself "totally isolated, his only source of support, not the college or its president, but his friends, and labor."[5] Although he did feel honor-bound to keep his promise to the president "to ignore the acts of a terrorist group and treat them with 'silent indifference,' " at the same time he was talking to his friends who could take action, and did. They marshalled the forces of the community, especially the press, to take a stand. He admitted to Foust that he had called a few friends when he did not know what action to take and Foust was nowhere to be found. What upset Foust was that these few friends were influential people in the community with ties to the press.

Although in the beginning Lindeman believed Foust had confidence in him and appreciated the unfortunate situation in which he found himself, letters reveal that Foust was less than candid with him. While telling Lindeman he was confident that the charges of "atheism," "socialism," and "indiscreet and unconventional [behavior] in the classroom" could not be substantiated, Foust was at the same time writing a member of the board of directors that Lindeman was "a brilliant man, and someone who could have been a great asset to the college, if it had not been for the unfortunate incident." It soon became apparent that what Foust wrote and spoke to members of his board was not always what he told Lindeman and that the two men did not trust one another as much as their formal communications implied.

During his six-day absence, doubts about Lindeman were already building up in Foust's mind. He wrote a board member that things were in a "state of turmoil" and he was having difficulty keeping the story out of the newspapers. He also felt that Lindeman had already rocked the boat by consulting his friends during his absence, and he construed this as a breech of their agreement to act only in consultation with one another. Certainly Lindeman had shown lack of good judgment.

There are no letters or clippings about what happened in March or April 1922, but two and one-half months after the Klan's letter—on May 9, Lindeman's thirty-seventh birthday—the *Greensboro Daily News* morning headlines startled Greensboro residents, Foust, and the board of trustees of the college: "Warned of Klan Lindeman Quits." This was followed by a story that quoted Lindeman as saying that the Klan was one factor leading to his decision to resign.

What is puzzling is why the paper waited until May 9 to print the story if, in fact, Lindeman had tendered his resignation to Foust on April 4. There was no copy of the resignation among the papers sent to me by the university. There is no clue as to whether he resigned in writing, what was said, or if there had been some crucial, unrecorded conversation. Even more puzzling

36

is why Foust and the board waited eight weeks to take official action on his resignation. Perhaps they waited until Lindeman had found another position. It seems more likely that they waited until the school year was over because it would be less embarrassing for the college. One thing that is clear is that Lindeman did not have another position when he quit.

Once the news was released by the Associated Press wire, Foust was plagued with telephone calls, letters, and telegrams, and the situation was clearly beyond his control. *The Survey,* perhaps the most important social welfare periodical of the time, wired Foust on May 9, "PLEASE WIRE STATEMENT AT ONCE REGARDING PRESS REPORTS ON LINDEMAN'S RESIGNATION UNDER PRESSURE." Foust wired back, "SO FAR AS I KNOW KU KLUX HAD NOTHING TO DO WITH LINDEMAN'S RESIGNATION."

Meanwhile, the local newspapers told a different story. *The Observer* wrote:

> At the time of making the statement concerning his resignation, Dr. Lindeman recounted that he had been told to leave the city by the KKK. Some time ago he was told by the Klan to discontinue certain alleged practices, and later that the college was requested to ask for his resignation by the Klan.

Another North Carolina paper stated that he had been subject to persecution and that this was confirmed by a wire sent to *The Survey* by A. W. McAlister, president of the Southern Life and Trust Company and one of the leading citizens of Greensboro:

> President of college states Lindeman's resignation not forced by Klan. Charges by Klan not credited. Thinking people of Greensboro have confidence in Lindeman and have no patience with persecution that has been instituted.

*The Survey* published a short version of the story on May 10. In the preface it stated that the country was in a period of great conservatism, manifested by efforts to defeat the theory of evolution, and with strong activity on the part of the Klan.

> The KKK seems to have ladled out tar of a new brand. If the reports from the south are true—and there is good evidence for believing them to be—academic freedom, tarred and feathered, will have to

37

take its modest place at the end of the line of the Klan's pet aversions. Under the headline WARNED OF KLAN LINDEMAN QUITS, the *Charlotte Observer* states that E. C. Lindeman, Professor of Sociology and Political Economy at the North Carolina College for Women in Greensboro, has resigned largely under pressure of the Ku Klux Klan.

However, Foust persisted in vehemently denying that the Klan had any influence in the matter whatsoever. Thoughtful people of Greensboro seemed ashamed of the whole incident and wished it hushed up as quickly as possible. A large segment of the community knew about the Klan letter, including the two local daily newspapers, and the New York-based *Survey* had sent a reporter to Greensboro to try to get to the bottom of the matter. What Foust had wanted to treat with "silent indifference" had become a statewide issue. Some Greensboro citizens were indignant that the college was not taking a strong position in defense of the professor whom they felt was being viciously attacked. One member of the board, who felt the KKK was being allowed to run the college, wrote "It may even be that we need to get rid of the man—but we do not need to have a man driven out of the college by any gang of men."

The editor of *The Survey* wrote from New York on May 9 (after sending several unanswered wires to Foust) that it was apparent from the news clippings that Lindeman had been forced to resign under threats from the Klan, and he demanded to know the facts. "What action has the University taken in this matter? Is it the policy of the college to submit to outside pressure of this nature?"

Other universities in North Carolina took an interest in the case as well. On May 12 a faculty member from the University of North Carolina at Chapel Hill wrote Foust that it would be unfortunate if the Klan succeeded in forcing Lindeman's resignation or in forcing the college to get rid of him, saying, "Nor would it be any less fortunate if the public generally gets the impression that the college accepted the resignation under pressure." He concluded that the wisest choice would be to reconsider accepting Lindeman's resignation.

But it was too late. The board had already made up its mind. Accepting Lindeman's resignation on May 31, the board wrote that it had been voluntary, that he had made plans to accept other work, and that it was under these circumstances that the board accepted his resignation.

> The Board desires to state emphatically that the Ku Klux Klan had absolutely nothing to do with Professor Lindeman's resignation or its acceptance. . . . Furthermore, with regard to certain allegations or implied charges against Professor Lindeman, the Board brands them as false. . . . The Board cannot be too emphatic or explicit in its assertion that the members of the faculty of this college shall be sustained and protected in their unquestionable right of freedom of speech and conscience. But it should be clearly understood that neither the Ku Klux Klan nor any abridgement of this right is involved in this case.

It is puzzling why Lindeman felt obliged to respond to *The Survey's* article in a way that would not embarrass the college, saying in his letter to the editor:

> Knowing how difficult it is for people to rid themselves of first impressions, I am reluctant to offer further explanations. There are however several points your readers will need to know if this incident is to serve any useful purpose. The first is that the KKK attack upon me was based on only one . . . alleged fact; namely that colored people had been entertained in our home by us. This, of course, was untrue. It was, however, the only factual charge made against me. . . . The second point . . . is that my resignation took place several months following the incident.

It is also curious that Lindeman pointed out that his resignation did not take effect until September, and that it was his desire to have it accepted, "which renders nugatory your final paragraph of *The Survey* article."

He repeated Foust's words that the Klan had no influence upon him and that Foust had publicly stated that no organization of this type could influence him in the management of the college.

At the same time that he admitted to the "pernicious influence" of the Klan and their "cowardly, anonymous attacks" and acknowledged that they were "a dangerous factor in this hectic period of reaction," Lindeman stressed that if only the press would "ignore the Klan it would die a natural death." His final recommendation for extinguishing the Klan was for the press to publish the names of the members of the organization. Considering that the Klan had over six million members and was so influential politically, this suggestion appears peculiarly naive.

Not surprisingly, Foust was pleased with Lindeman's letter to the editor—so pleased, in fact, that he wrote immediately, "It seems to me that is a clear statement and should clear up matters. I certainly hope so."

In writing his letter, Lindeman had no doubt taken into consideration Foust's letter to him, which arrived as he was preparing his response to *The Survey's* article, and said, in part, "Remember, I shall stand firm with reference to any influence that may be exerted by the anonymous letter."

Considering Lindeman's predicament, it is difficult to understand why he chose to respond to *The Survey* article in such an uncharacteristic, waffling manner. There was no need to bail out Foust, who had not come to his aid or taken a stand on behalf of academic freedom. Why did he choose to refrain from calling attention to the academic freedom issue as *The Survey* had done?

It may have been due to a sense of loyalty to the college or to Foust. But it is strange that Lindeman would feel such fidelity to a man who had not shown any sympathy until one week before the board meeting, when he offered his assistance "in making the condition which has developed the least embarrassing possible for you."

Why did Lindeman bend over backward to deny that there was any influence by the Klan, or that there had been any abridgment of academic freedom? One can only speculate that his youth, concern for his family's safety, lack of a teaching position at the time, and perhaps threats from the college not to recommend him for future posts, may have played a role in his decision.

A few years ago, while visiting Greensboro, I stopped by the college library and asked to see the directory of professors from 1920 to 1922. I discovered Lindeman's name was missing, and I brought this to the librarian's attention. Several years later, my sister Ruth and her husband checked the faculty directory, and his name had reappeared.

Although Lindeman did not find another full-time teaching position for two years, he did find employment. Konopka writes that it was "Mary Follett's introduction of Lindeman to Herbert Croly and Dorothy Whitney Straight that resulted in Straight's offer to help finance Lindeman so that he could do free-lance writing and private research from 1922 to 1924."[5] Based on an interview with John Hader, Stewart confirmed that Mary Parker Follett had visited Lindeman in Greensboro in the spring of 1922 to meet and to exchange ideas with him. In the foreword of his book *Social Discovery*, Lindeman credited Follett's book *The New State* for setting off the trigger for "a new direction and new hope" to his own research.[6] Likewise, she had been deeply impressed by his book and was delighted by their similar theories about individuals in relation to groups.

During her visit with Lindeman, Follett realized how tenuous Lindeman's position in Greensboro had become. As a consequence she quickly arranged to meet with Straight and Croly in New York City. It was shortly thereafter that Straight offered to support Lindeman's research efforts for a two year period. Not long after, Lindeman submitted his resignation to the Board of Trustees of the NCCW.

When the Northern liberals got wind that Lindeman's life had been threatened at a Southern university and that he was under fire for the kind of liberalism that loves America, he soon became their fair-haired hero. On the wings of this publicity, Lindeman arrived in New York City to be welcomed by Alvin Johnson, Director of The New School for Social Research and a contributing editor of *The New Republic*. The liberal press was ready, willing, and eager to publish what he had to say.

Greystone 1930

# Chapter 6
# Life at Greystone

*For the first time I am the owner of something! . . . I am filled
with awe when I reflect on my relation to this bit of land. . . .
I think in terms of the children and their memories. There will
be a few years for me too, fascinating years of planning and bringing things to growth, and these I shall fully enjoy.*

Lindeman, 1929

In the midst of packing and farewells—prior to leaving
Greensboro in late July—Lindeman took time out to write to his
new benefactress, Dorothy Straight, to tell her of his plans. Hazel
and the children would take the train to Michigan to visit relatives
in East Lansing and Charlevoix while he would go alone to New
York to look for suitable housing for the family. Their furniture
would be shipped to a warehouse in New York so they could retrieve
it and settle quickly once a decision concerning a house had been
made. Until then his address would be The City Club in New
York City. In closing he told her how much he looked forward
to the two years of freedom which would enable him to do what
he so longed to do.

Lindeman was indebted also to Mary Parker Follett for having
arranged access to Straight and Croly, which resulted in Lindeman's
receiving financial backing for his work. It was not long before
Croly and Straight became very dear to him personally. Croly, in
fact, became his mentor almost immediately. Moreover, Follett also
introduced Lindeman to an organization called The Inquiry.[1] During
the next decade The Inquiry played an important role in Lindeman's
career. It would provide an important stimulus for the research for
his new book, *Social Discovery* (1924), and a later book, *Social
Education* (1933), was an interpretation of the work of The Inquiry.

Finding a house within commuting distance of the city to rent at an affordable price proved to be more difficult than Lindeman had ever imagined it would be. But in between meetings with Follett in Putney, Vermont, Boston and New York, and a second quick trip that summer to Europe, he continued to house hunt. Amazingly, by early fall he had located a home, "a beautiful stone house on a hilltop overlooking the Kittatinny Hills in the Land of Jersey," he wrote Shaw.[2] There he would spend many hours reading, reflecting and writing once Hazel efficiently had unpacked and put things into their proper place.

Meantime when Follett invited Lindeman to spent a week in September in her home in Putney, Vermont to plan a program of research, Lindeman accepted with pleasure. Because of Alfred Dwight Sheffield's expertise in group discussion, he was invited to join them. Sheffield was, according to Gessner, "a penetrating and gentle intellectual, professor at Wellesley College, and Executive Secretary of The Inquiry's Industrial Relations Commission. He taught classes for trade unionists in the practice of directed discussion, founded Boston's Trade Union College, and authored the book *Joining in Public Discussion*. Lindeman in his review of Sheffield's book in *The New Republic* (1922) called Sheffield's method "the abandonment of the methods of the crowd." Sheffield, himself, called it "the technique of democracy."[3]

Lindeman wrote Shaw that the visit to Vermont was most successful, "We worked from 8 a.m. to 1 p.m. . . . What a marvelous mind she has!"[4] In an atmosphere of "mountains, good food, woods, streams, and much good talk," they discussed among other topics the study of the constructive nature of conflict, the relation between compromise and integration, the nature of representatives, and distinctions between leaders and experts. To Lindeman, Follett wrote "The way our three minds work is extraordinary."[5] Years later Lindeman would refer to the Putney discussions as the most exciting intellectual event in his total experience.

Having found so many intellectual commonalites, especially their common interest in the concept of creative experience, Follett was eager for Lindeman to collaborate with her on a book. Age fifty-three and a graduate of Radcliffe College, she was a brilliant political scientist, lecturer and author. She had already published three books, and was then working on *Creative Experience*. It pleased her that she and Lindeman were each dealing with the problem

44

of social conflict and its resolution. Lindeman privately and publicly acknowledged Follett's assistance in the development of his ideas about adult education as a creative instrument within the democratic process, and other powerful ideas.[6] However, for several complex reasons, Lindeman—in the end—was reluctant to publish a joint book.

Stewart describes Follett and Lindeman as "an odd couple," and their joint experience as "wobbly from the start. . . . The exacting, sickly, maidenly, and severely neurotic Mary Follett, seventeen years older than Lindeman, did not always achieve good personal chemistry with the volatile, convivial, lusty, and often disorganized Lindeman. Though her own behavior could also be erratic, the ethereal Miss Follett required personal and professional surroundings that were predictable . . . very solid. She never learned that a predictable, ordered world was not possible for friends or close associates of Eduard Lindeman."[7] Privately, Lindeman confided in Shaw that Mary was "difficult to work with."

Even though Follett was deeply wounded by Lindeman's decision not to collaborate on a book, the two continued to hold conferences in Boston and New York. When Lindeman finished his book *Social Discovery* he wrote in the preface that "a continuing exchange of material . . . has brought our two approaches to similar problems into cooperative relationship. Just how far these two approaches interpenetrated as the result of diverse methods will be apparent to all who read her latest work called *Creative Experience.*"[8]

But it would be with Dorothy Straight, not with Mary Follett, that Eduard would develop a rare, idealistic, and mutually rewarding relationship which would last for many years. In Dorothy he found another woman whose faith in his mission was unswerving. Straight's initial support not only made possible his work for two years, it also enabled the Lindemans to take up residence in Greystone.

"It is too good to be true," Lindeman wrote Shaw, "with its four large bedrooms upstairs, two sleeping porches, two and a-half baths and servants quarters, a refrigerator in the basement, two riding horses, splendid furniture, and a two-car garage. . . . Its greatest charm is its thirty-four acres of gardens, beautifully landscaped, a sunken formal garden, and a vegetable garden as well. And all of that is surrounded by pastures and woodlands, and spring water from a nearby hillside."[9] For a man who all his life yearned for a farm, Greystone must have been at least a partial answer to a dream. Lindeman soon had visions of the tennis court and rock garden he would like to build one day.

It soon became apparent that the house and gardens were more than the Lindemans could handle by themselves. They were fortunate to find a live-in couple—Luvina, to help out with the house and the cooking, and Ben, with the gardens.

Even though Ben worked in the High Bridge steel plant in the winter, he could still drive the children to school in bad weather, and drive Lindeman to the railroad station every Monday morning.

The town of High Bridge, named after a lofty trestle spanning the south branch of the Raritan River, was a typical mill town. The Taylor Wharton Iron and Steel Company owned the entire town of over three thousand people and most of the surrounding land as well. The company owned Lake Solitude on the southern slope of the Musconetcong mountain, where the family swam in the summer and skated in the winter.

It is not surprising that Lindeman was viewed as unique, if not downright strange, for riding the train into New York every Monday and returning usually, but by no means always, on Wednesday evening. Unlike the other veteran ferryboat riders known as "the sad mariners of New Jersey," he enjoyed the trip, writing Dorothy that he found something "illuminating and excitingly romantic" about traveling from High Bridge to New York City.[10]

Soon after settling in Greystone, Lindeman chose two rooms in the attic as his workplace. Nicknamed "the crow's nest" by the family and friends, one room was ideally suited for study and writing. A small crescent-shaped window faced west with a magnificent view of the foothills of the Alleghenies and the tiny village of High Bridge with its church tower square in the middle, nestled in the valley two miles away. He designated the adjacent room as his library, which soon overflowed with books, periodicals, and papers. He worked there every morning until Hazel alerted him that lunch was ready. In the afternoon, weather permitting, he would work in the garden.

Roger Baldwin reflected that when Lindeman was at Greystone he was always studying, always had a book in his hand—that is, when he wasn't gardening or playing tennis.

He read widely and carefully, underlining and marking notes in the margins. When he finished with a book nobody else could use it.

46

Eduard was very attached to his books and his papers and loved being alone up there. . . . He was a slow and careful reader of philosophical and sociological books and journals, marking important passages, and taking out quotes and references for his little black notebook, which he carried around with him on his trips as a source for lectures and writing and teaching. I know he treasured these notebooks and used them constantly. I can't recall seeing him without one nearby."[11]

Baldwin was certain that Lindeman viewed Greystone increasingly as a retreat and that over the years it became of great importance to his physical and emotional well-being.

During the early years, life at Greystone tended to revolve around Lindeman's weekly trips to and from the city and longer journeys away from home. Or so it seemed to us children, who were nine, seven, six, and four at this time. Seeing his battered, old briefcase at the foot of the stairs every Sunday night was a sad reminder of another imminent departure. Although there were many joyous times, there was no doubt that our father's prolonged absences from home placed a strain on the family. As demands on his time, energy, and good nature grew over the years, Greystone became a special retreat for him. We viewed the time he did spend with us as very special.

One of the happiest moments was meeting our father's train every Wednesday at 6:30 p.m. sharp. You can't imagine our thrill as the Queen of the Valley rounded the corner and came to a screeching halt right in front of the tiny little station in High Bridge. The excitement mounted as Father stepped off the train onto the platform — handsome, smiling, his briefcase bulging with scrapbooks, students' papers, favorite books, presents for the children, and *The New York Times* tucked under his left arm. We would rush down the length of the platform to greet the nicest, friendliest father in the world.

Just as important as opening the presents was to have Father read aloud to us before bedtime. Tom Cotton was right when he recalled that the Rutabaga stories by Carl Sandburg were our favorite:

You had me out to Greystone some time that fall, after you all got settled. There were five steps: Doris, always the gorgeous one, Ruth the quiet one, Betty, the toughey, and Barbara with the long, brown curls, and then there was Zanthippy, who knew her place by the fireplace. The Rutabaga stories were read aloud around the fireplace after dinner and never ceased thereafter to influence my life.[12]

We also loved the times we gathered around the piano with Mother playing and singing spirituals and old college songs. It must have sounded pretty raucous because nobody could carry a tune; but it was fun. Sometimes Doris played the cello and I the violin.

Long walks with Father in the woods surrounding Greystone were another special treat, and of course our dog Zanthippy went along. In August the entire neighborhood was invited to enjoy the corn roasts, which we children viewed as festivals.

By 1928 our family, never a churchgoing bunch, had abandoned prayers at mealtime, and Lindeman wrote Dorothy that religion had gone from the Lindeman family for good. His reverence seemed to be more directed toward nature. More and more he grew to love the countryside, but especially his garden. With Ben's help, he plowed the soil and weeded, and we children planted our own vegetable garden. He put in a half-acre strawberry patch just for us. We were to take care of it and to keep whatever we could earn from the patch. We had other chores, which we did not mind too much, except for weeding. Picking cherries, strawberries, and grapes was not all that bad as you could nibble while you worked.

The Lindemans were a game-playing family, inside and outside the house. Not surprisingly, Lindeman had an intense interest in recreation and leisure time due to his early role as a recreation leader, boys' and girls' club leader, and, during World War I, a recreation worker for soldiers in a war community camp. Also, in 1919 he had published a book entitled *Thirty Selected Games*.

The sunken garden, rimmed by a high hedge, was redolent with flowers in the spring, summer, and fall. Phlox, goldenglows, gladiolas, and dozens of annuals provided cut flowers for the dining room table, living room, and the hall.

Lindeman could never rave enough about the fall. "The deep reds are already in the leaves and now the golds and browns creep in," he wrote Dorothy. "You can give me red sumac against an evergreen background, or the gold of the hard maples at the forest's edge, and Ziegfeld can have his Follies."[13]

Christmastime had always been a special occasion, but the first Christmas at Greystone was extra special. It was a new experience to cut our own tree from our very own woods and to go sledding down our own hills. Lindeman wrote Dorothy that the family was in the midst of great excitement as they painted the old dollhouse. Christmas Eve the family gathered around Mother at the piano to sing carols near the candle-lit tree. Under the tree would be a present for each daughter and a special package for the family from Dorothy. On one occasion it was an original Cézanne painting, which the family cherished.

But the Christmas of 1929 was one the family would never forget. Suddenly, thanks to Dorothy, the Lindemans were the proud owners of Greystone. After seven years of not knowing from year to year if Mrs. Knox Taylor would agree to sell Greystone or even allow us to continue renting year-round, the deed was delivered the day before Christmas. It was a grateful Lindeman who wrote Dorothy, "For the first time I am the owner of something! It seems very strange, and I am filled with awe when I reflect on my relation to this bit of land. . . . You must know how fine a thing you have done. Already I think in terms of the children and their memories. There will be a few years for me too, fascinating years of planning and bringing things to growth, and these I shall fully enjoy."[14]

It was not long before Greystone received a much needed face lift. The house was upset with painters and paperhangers, plumbers and electricians in every corner. "Nothing had been done to the house for twenty years," Lindeman wrote Dorothy. "Even the floors are all rotted out. . . . Hazel is doing a splendid job of redecorating."[15] He himself was soon hard at work developing a nursery and building a tennis court. He planted three hundred trees and set out three thousand young pine seedlings. He also put in a floor in the old barn with a plan to fix it up later so that it might be rented in the summer. (It never was.)

During the early years at Greystone Hazel had plenty to keep her busy managing the house, which she did skillfully and competently.

Despite the fact she had married the "campus rebel," a move that had not pleased her conservative Republican father, she very quickly fell into and enjoyed the role of homemaker, wife, and mother, organizer and board member of the local PTA, and parole board member of the state Clinton Farms Women's Reformatory.

Unlike Lindeman, Hazel was not gregarious and often gave the impression of taking a back seat to her husband. But she possessed an inner strength all her own and did not need the kind of adulation that her husband seemed to require. She went about her work, inside and outside the home, with quiet dignity. While Lindeman was prone to mischief, whimsy, and merrymaking, Hazel was by nature serious and literal. She had been raised to be frugal, conscientious, and orderly. By default she had to manage the family finances, since he clearly lived beyond their means and frequently had to borrow. Lindeman seemed unable to save money—and money, although he liked it, was not important to him.

Hazel did not pretend to be an intellectual, preferring a game of bridge or tennis to reading. For Lindeman reading was an essential ingredient of his day-to-day life. I don't know if she could share in his work, but I am quite certain she was proud of him and his accomplishments. Although she may not have appreciated some of his unique qualities—his imagination, creativeness, inquiring mind, sense of humor—he may not have appreciated some of hers either. It was Hazel's homemaking and parenting skills and the efficient way in which she ran Greystone that provided an ideal environment for Lindeman's professional success. Her confidante, Dorothy Shaw, wrote after Hazel's death that she had "the rare ability of letting Eduard do whatever he wanted to do, but being near when she was needed."[16]

Dinner at Greystone was served promptly at 6 p.m. except on Wednesdays when Lindeman came home—then it was at 7 p.m. Sunday dinner was often a special occasion, and there might be guests, especially during the tennis season. When Lindeman was home, meals were occasions for catching up with one another. He had a way of encouraging us to talk about what we had been doing, reading, thinking, and, hopefully, creating. He used to say with a big grin, "What do you have to say for yourself?" It was an open invitation for one and all to "show and tell," but for me it was a special challenge.

Lindeman loved guests—and there was a parade of guests in and out of Greystone. It was not until I grew older that I became aware of his "uncritical gregariousness" and its concomitant loneliness. His need to have people around him was more than just friendliness; it appeared that he craved companionship (almost any companion) to stave off the loneliness he felt ever since the death of his mother. Over the years visitors to Greystone included editors, social workers, educators, authors, poets, artists, colleagues, local school teachers, and friends and neighbors. Among these guests were Robert Frost, Carl Sandburg, Kurt Wiese, Robert Hallowell, Herbert Croly, Dorothy Straight, Roger Baldwin, Tom Cotton, and John and Mathilda Hader. After the Shaws moved to Swarthmore, Pennsylvania in 1927, they became frequent guests at Greystone. Other Michigan and North Carolina friends and their families were also guests. After 1930, especially in the summer, the tennis court was filled with tennis players from the surrounding area.

Like entertaining, travel was both stimulating and relaxing for Lindeman, and after moving to Greystone he began to travel more. During the 1920s and '30s his journeys took him to the Caribbean, Central America, Europe, Russia, India, Egypt, Canada, and almost every state in the U.S.A. "He was always dashing somewhere," Sally Ringe Goldmark recalled, "but I didn't feel he was running away from something, rather that he was running toward something."[17]

Hazel, on the other hand, was not an adventurer, and—with the exception of our six-month journey abroad in 1925 and a summer in Los Angeles in 1936—she did not join him. Her preference seemed to be to remain home. Nonetheless, his frequent and lengthy absences could not help but create a basic threat to the marriage relationship, which only a person with Hazel's patience and understanding could have survived.

Illusions of a happy life were as much a part of our family as they are of most. Part of the illusion was shattered, however, sometime in the early 1930s when the three youngest were still in high school. A letter was discovered by one of my sisters, soon to be shared by all—a letter from Lindeman to Hazel in which he begged her not to proceed with a divorce, saying he would refrain from seeing a certain "Mrs. C."

There is very little to indicate how he may have felt about his marriage, but there is an intriguing reference to infidelity— either his own or a quote—in one of his scrapbooks: "About infidelity—remorse is unnecessary if our infidelity remains hidden and we maneuver to taste the forbidden fruit without detection. We are indulgent for our sexual lapses." It is possible that he actually believed he could lead two separate lives without endangering the marriage. When I interviewed Ellen Cotton, Tom Cotton's wife, in 1975, she recalled that Tom had showed her a letter Lindeman had written to him from Italy in 1925, expressing some disillusion-ment with his marriage. She recalled a time early in her acquain-tance with Lindeman when she felt he was not a good influence for Tom and might lead him astray.

Our parents did not show their emotions, and if they quar-reled, we never knew it. Perhaps because raising one's voice was frowned upon, it never occurred to us to wonder why we never observed any overt display of anger or, for that matter, any spon-taneous affection between our parents. Whereas Lindeman wrote his daughter Doris and her husband in 1938 that his inability to express emotion was due to his "Scandinavian insulator," we believed it was Hazel's Puritan ancestry.

Maurice Connery, a former student of Lindeman's, told me in 1976 that he saw evidence of a lot of repressed hostility in Lindeman:

> When I had trouble with my supervisor, he took up my cause. It was then that I discovered that he had a great deal of bottled-up hostility—I think—an enormous amount. I once asked him what he did with his hostility and he said, "I play tennis. It's a kind of physical thing." He really did have a high amount of tension, and, in a way, he may have fostered some of it. That is, some of the causes he became so involved in were, in a sense, a way of sublimating that tension drive.[18]

It was not long before our parents moved into separate bedrooms. But it was not just Lindeman's absences from home, or other women, or the double life, that separated them. According to Roger Baldwin, their relationship was one of convenience:

> From what I observed of the two of them . . . there was no intimacy. Of course, there is always the fact that Eduard was away from home three or four days a week. I suppose he felt he had to sacrifice the companionship of his family for his professional work.

Baldwin may have been right. It is possible they could have been mismatched from the beginning.

We never heard Hazel admonish Lindeman for being gone so much of the time, but Lindeman himself did feel guilty about being a poor father. In 1938 when Doris and her husband criticized him for being a poor father, he countered:

52

I suppose you are referring to the weird "speakeasy epoch." Well, I've changed, and the change is not merely due to the fact that I have lived more than fifty years, but I see more clearly now what it is I have to do, and what my energies are to be conserved for.

In spite of the suffering Lindeman must have caused Hazel, he was devoted to her, and she to him. There was a lot of respect and affection that they both continued to feel for one another throughout the years. Stewart suggests that "from a contemporary feminist perspective, it was Hazel more than Herbert Croly, Dorothy Straight, or other suppliers of cognitive and material sustenance, who made possible Eduard's professional success."[19]

## Chapter 7

# Dear Dorothy, Dear Eduard

*I found new meaning for the prairie, for attachment
to the soil and for the eternal round of
seedtime until harvest.*

Lindeman, 1924

Although both Stewart and Dorothy Shaw suggest that Hazel
was responsible for Lindeman's professional success, it would be
hard to imagine how he would have fared without Dorothy Whitney
Straight, his benefactor. There is no doubt that Dorothy opened
many doors for Lindeman professionally during the years 1922 to
1925, as she had previously done for Willard Straight almost a decade
earlier. She introduced him to Herbert Croly, editor of *The New
Republic* where he would soon become a contributing editor, and
to Alvin Johnson, director of the New School for Social Research
where Lindeman went on to teach a course in worker's education.
Since Dorothy was the principal financial backer of The Inquiry,
it is likely that she also exposed him to The Inquiry crowd.

It was probably no coincidence that Lindeman accepted the
position at the New York School of Social Work (now Columbia
University) in 1924, since Dorothy was a member of the board
of trustees.

I also cannot imagine how the Lindeman family would have
fared without Dorothy. In addition to the many doors she opened
for Lindeman, she financed the Lindeman's six-month trip abroad
in 1925 to enable Lindeman to regain his health, and she made
it possible for them to own Greystone.

How did two such different individuals—Dorothy from a
background of fashionable wealth and splendor, and Lindeman with
his impoverished beginnings—become kindred spirits in such a short
time? Worlds apart, what did they have in common?

Both were orphaned at age seventeen. Both were in a sense self-educated, loved to read, and sought intellectual stimulation through discussions with knowledgeable persons. They both had a strong social conscience and a deep commitment to social reform and social justice. Promoted by Dorothy, Lindeman lectured to the Women's Trade Union League. Both were interested in the welfare of immigrants. They both had a strong religious orientation in their early years. They were, above all, ardent and critical observers of the life around them, and they both loved nature.

Dorothy was one year younger than Lindeman. She was born in 1886 to Flora Payne Whitney and William Collins Whitney. Her father had been secretary of the navy under President Cleveland. By the time she was twenty-one, she was an heiress to millions.

W. A. Swanberg in his book *Whitney Father, Whitney Heiress* described Dorothy as:

> easily the most remarkable of the Whitney children. Like her mother, she was born to wealth and social position, brimming with energy, hungry for learning, soon to be world traveler studying and commenting on the world as she traveled. Dorothy was so compellingly attractive in appearance and manner that she was to number her friends of both sexes in the hundreds. Her smile came easily and lighted her face. Her innate cordiality was guarded by an appropriate trace of reserve. . . . Her touch of shyness was not to be confused with any frailty of character. Dorothy had a compassion that was ultimately to be translated into "radicalism" displeasing to her set.

Swanberg also tells of her sense of independence, strong will, good sense, agreeableness, and intelligence. Before she was twenty she was her own hostess in a spacious house with a staff of servants. But aside from social gatherings and her work with the Junior League, Dorothy had a second existence. Remarkably, on her own initiative, she educated herself. Her official education as a fashionable young woman ended at age eighteen when she made her debut and became eligible for marriage, but she continued to attend lectures and read constantly. A keen observer of the world around her, she took a course at Columbia University in political economy. Surprisingly for a woman of her day, she also took a course in sex hygiene. She learned lace making, saved used clothing for the poor, helped Lillian Wald at the Henry Street Settlement House, and went to Bible class at Grace Church on Thursdays. She took piano lessons and loved the opera and theater.

In 1911 she married Willard Dickerson Straight, who was serving as advisor to railroad magnate E. H. Harriman and who had negotiated enormous banking transactions in Peking. During their seven-year marriage, they had three children.

Together in 1914 they founded *The New Republic (TNR)* with Dorothy's financial backing and enlisted Croly as editor. Dorothy was also instrumental in the founding and funding of the New School for Social Research, where she enjoyed listening to intellectual discussions of Professors James Harvey Robinson, Thorstein Veblen, and Charles Beard of Columbia. She attended the weekly luncheons of *TNR* where she would listen to Norman Angell, Ernest Poole, Lord Northcliffe, Walter Lippmann, and Charles Merz.

In 1918 Willard Straight died in France in the World War I flu epidemic. Dorothy herself had been extremely active in war work to the point of exhaustion. She also invested a million dollars in Liberty Loan.

Dorothy and Eleanor Roosevelt were, in Swanberg's words, "the most energetic female proponents of social reform to come from the highest echelons of society." It is not surprising that Eleanor and Dorothy became close friends.

Curiously, it was not until the mid-1960s, when Dorothy sent me Lindeman's letters, that I became aware of the intensity of their relationship and realized that he had looked upon Dorothy as a mother figure. Lindeman had fantasized that his mother was a Danish noblewoman. This new "mother" lived in a mansion on Fifth Avenue; owned a mansion in Old Westbury, Long Island, and another in Woods Hole, Massachusetts, plus a summer camp in the Adirondacks; and would soon become the owner of a Tudor castle in Devon, England. He had at last found a mother figure who was indeed a "noblewoman."

Reminded of his mother's prophecy as he wrote a Christmas Eve letter to Dorothy in 1923, he wanted her to know "how different my real purposes were until you came to believe in them. These are hopes and stirrings of the heart . . . prompted by your good self."

Dorothy responded on Christmas night, saying that his recent letters were like "a glimpse of a friendly ship on a rather solitary voyage across the Atlantic." She thanked him for sharing "poignant memories" of his mother and begged him not to call her "Mrs. Straight" anymore, saying she also wanted to call him something besides " 'Mr. Lindeman'. . . . I'm sure I will find the perfect name for you one day." Although she did suggest *Ned*, she never found a substitute for *Eduard*, and she frequently misspelled his name *Edward*.

But it was her sponsorship of "two years of freedom" that enabled Lindeman to continue the research that culminated in his book *Social Discovery*. When he wrote Dorothy that he wanted to dedicate his new book to her, she protested that it should be dedicated to his mother or to others whose thinking had influenced him. Nevertheless, she did accept the honor, saying that it "took her breath away" and gave her one of the "greatest moments" of her life. They eagerly awaited the reviews, both convinced that it was "a good book" that said "the few bold things which needed to be said."

It is not surprising that Lindeman and Dorothy's correspondence included frequent references to Croly, who visited the Lindemans at Greystone in June 1924. Lindeman wrote Dorothy of this visit, saying that his friendship with Croly "deepens continuously," and on at least one occasion "reached the heights of a spiritual experience." He was quite certain that their mutual devotion to Dorothy was responsible for "something exquisitely radiant" that happened as he read Croly's book, *The Life of Willard Straight*.[1]

Lindeman confided his philosophic yearnings to her, including his reflections on the meaning of life. Coming into Estes Park by train in the early sunlight,

> everything seemed to possess meaning . . . the stooping figures of women and children in the beetfields, the rows of indistinguishable houses of coal miners, the brilliant colors of the Japanese Pheasant standing by the roadside without alarm, the flamboyant magpies with their proletarian habits, and, always hovering silently to the left— those everlasting mountains. . . . And suddenly, out of the stillness came the piercing, resonant song of the prairie-lark . . . and I think I found new meaning for the prairie, for attachment to the soil and for the eternal round of seedtime unto harvest.

By 1924 Dorothy was insisting that Lindeman write his autobiography, but he was having trouble bringing "all that social theory of mine" into alignment with the "technique of self-revelation" and at the same time avoiding using chronological method. It is possible that it was not so much the avoidance of a chronological method or lining up his theory with a method that was causing the problem, but rather his newly evolving self-image.

In any event, he told her it would be "a life-time task . . . at least ten years." There is no evidence he went beyond defining the following categories: "What does one remember of youth?" "Death and many beginnings," "Labor and personality," "Individualism: The great illusion," "Citizenship: the great vocation," "Beyond religion and ethics," "The Good and the beautiful," "Logic and conflict," "Science, truth and the verities."

Perhaps because he was in Dorothy's employ he felt impelled to let her know what he was doing and thinking. He wrote her of a paper he and Baldwin had presented at the National Conference of Social Work in "Tory Toronto," "Sources of Power for Industrial Freedom," which was read and discussed "in the face of great opposition from the conservatives" but met with only "mild dissension from Jane Addams, Mary McDowell, and other radicals of the last generation. Miss Addams insists there is no class struggle in America." Apparently he lunched with Addams, who tried to persuade him to come to Hull House for a week in the autumn. He declined, writing, "I fear she wants to convert me."

From the Canadian Christian Training School in Lake Conchiching, Ontario, Lindeman wrote Dorothy that he was conducting a one-month course on "What the Thinkers Are Thinking" and that he had developed a real affection for the Canadians from his former training experience. Now he was striving for a form of teaching that "will reveal the 'living world.' It is surprising how much interest can be aroused by giving students an insight into characters and personalities of the too-remote thinkers." He continued to wonder if the teacher's purpose was "to precipitate discontent and to generate purpose." He was quite sure it was not "to impart knowledge or merely method." Whatever it was, he wished he had more of it.

He told Dorothy he was afraid he might have offended Croly in an open letter he wrote to *TNR* concerning La Follette's candidacy. (In 1924 Robert LaFollette was running for president on a third-party Progressive ticket.) He was afraid he might have spoken too frankly and unwisely in chastising *TNR* for not openly supporting LaFollette. "Herbert and I have so much to do together. Life must give us time as well as affection. And you, Dorothy, are the nexus of our unity."

In this letter the name of Leonard Elmhirst appeared for the first time: "Mr. Elmhirst approves of my proposed visit to India in the interest of rural life." It would appear that Lindeman had already met Leonard Elmhirst at this point, at least corresponded with him. In any event, he made other plans for a vacation with Baldwin in the wilds of British Columbia and did not go to India.

Soon his concern that he may have offended Croly was cleared up by a letter Croly sent Dorothy concerning his recent trip to Greystone. "I spent a weekend with Lindeman. He and I are more closely allied intellectually than I have been with any previous friend. I have more confidence in him and affection for him. His mind is expanding rapidly."

Dorothy continued to ponder Lindeman's letters and wondered if anyone had ever had such a friend. His letters had provided her "a beautiful vista into your mind and your work, a touch of affection and friendship which gives warmth to everything else." He had taught her the value of "candor, the absolute purity of notions, and uncompromising honesty." Somehow she had never learned how to observe or how to become interested in herself. "Alone, I find that my understanding of myself and of life is very meager, and that I don't grow unaided. You are always an example and I shall try to follow you."

September 1924 found Dorothy recuperating in the country from a thyroid condition, writing to Lindeman from Old Westbury, "I don't think you can have any conception of how badly I am going to miss you. You not only give me stimulus, but direction— and I shall be lost without you." She could not bear to throw any of his letters away and planned to keep and treasure them. (She did just that, and quite unexpectedly, I was the recipient of the letters in 1964.)

Over the next two decades they exchanged Christmas letters. In his 1924 letter Lindeman spoke of his disillusionment with organized Christianity. His philosophy had moved away from the strongly religious motivation of *The Community* to a concern for social ethics and social philosophy, so apparent in *Social Discovery*. "Creativeness was the essence of Jesus' life," he wrote, "and his life can never be found by imitation. We must live as fully in our time as he did in his. We must risk new sails as well as new routes. . . . To live in the modern world is to feel the pressure of innumerable other lives. They too must be released if our lives are to be free. We live, move, and have our being in others."

He apologized for the "sermonic" tone of the letter, but wanted her to know how much she "enlivened his hopes and powers" and "expanded his usefulness to others." Yesterday he had felt lonely and depressed. Then came a telephone message from Dorothy, "and suddenly life seemed filled with poignant sweetness. Comradeship with high souls and love of the dear earth, these sum up the best of life for me." His mood of loneliness passed away.

The "two years of freedom" officially ended in September 1924, when Lindeman began teaching social philosophy at the New York School of Social Work, a position he held until his retirement in 1950. Soon his relationship with Dorothy would undergo several significant changes. The first occurred in the spring of 1925 when Dorothy married Leonard Elmhirst. The second was triggered by a week-long conference at Dartington Hall in Devon, England, in the fall of 1926. Both of these events had a devastating effect on Lindeman, but their friendship, although significantly altered, endured.

Sometime in 1926, no longer in Dorothy's employ, Lindeman accepted a different financial arrangement in which Dorothy financed only his special projects. Stewart attributes this to Croly, who felt that Lindeman was becoming too dependent on his benefactress and was ready to stand on his own two feet.[2]

Throughout the first eight years of their friendship, they had in common a deep love for Croly. When Croly died in May 1930 after suffering a stroke in 1929, Lindeman once again turned to Dorothy for comfort. "I am overcome with grief . . . it needs to be said again between us. We did love him so. It is not too much to say that the entire direction of my life was altered by this contact, and to me, in this respect, you and Herbert stand apart." It was not so much that Lindeman's life was redirected, but that "Croly's devouring need to always be something more, something better, came, in the end to be the touchstone of my conduct. . . . How I long to see you. There is no one I can talk to about Herbert, save you. I've never been so lonely since childhood when I started forth to do battle against the world without my mother." He asked her forgiveness for leaning too heavily upon her. "Some brave day, we must talk. Now I can only think of days that are no more."

Another important aspect of Lindeman's life during the years 1924 to 1930 was the serious matter of his health. Although colleagues, students, friends, and Hazel were aware that he was frequently in pain, they were equally sure that he did not wish to talk about it. Frequent bouts with ill health could not help but interfere with his overall productivity, and they soon became an increasing burden to him.

In his 1924 Christmas letter to Dorothy he admitted that the last three months had not been fruitful as far as creative work was concerned. Teaching had taken so much out of him that he had very little energy left for other things. He promised her he would organize matters in a better fashion "once his health was restored."

From Lindeman's letters to Dorothy it is clear that he could be overwhelmed at times by a sense of tragedy, which he called "weltschmerz." The death of a family member or a close friend, his own ill health, or even the marriage of Dorothy to Leonard Elmhirst could and did trigger black moods. These feelings of weltschmerz may have also had a permanent effect on his ability to enjoy intimate relationships with women. His platonic relationship with Harriet McGraw, when he was thirty-four and the father of four small children, appears to be that of a child to a parent. "Please don't scold me," he pleads with her while teaching in the YMCA summer program.[3]

Lindeman countered these moods with thoughts of a rural life, which included his dream of one day owning a farm. He continued to find sustenance in nature. "I feel more at one with life," he wrote Dorothy in 1926, "when nature is included in my responses. . . . Just now I took a stroll in the pasture to the edge of the woods, and there I saw four belated blue birds flittering about. By all rules of migration they should have flown southward a long time ago, but here they are flashing their backs of blue against a foggy December day; somehow I returned to my study with new resolves of courage."

It may have been a letter Lindeman wrote to Leonard Elmhirst that triggered Dorothy's concern about his recently diagnosed health problem. His doctor had forbidden "any sustained and serious thought. . . . You will be interested to learn that my chief trouble is thyroid deficiency." Dorothy, who had known "the ravages of this wretched thyroid trouble," immediately tried to persuade him

61

to come to a New York hospital for a cure. She scolded him for wanting to go to the West Indies when instead he should be "under close observation for a month or two." Lindeman ignored her plea and instead tried to persuade Charles Shaw to join him in a quick trip to Puerto Rico, Bermuda, or Cuba. "Do you respond to duty? Then it is your duty [to come with me] since I, Eduardo, say it!"

Apparently there was a compromise, for it was not long before the Lindeman family was busy making plans for a trip to Italy. Realizing that Lindeman would not consider her plan for him to rest in a New York hospital, Dorothy may have proposed the alternative of six months abroad.

As it turned out, it is possible Dorothy may have had a very different reason for proposing a lengthy stay abroad.

## Chapter 8

# Sunny Days by the Ligurian Sea

*I cannot find words to fit the spell which Italy casts upon me.
Well you see, Charles, it has caught me—the scientist
who once scoffed at beauty and searched only for reality.*

Lindeman, 1925

On March 24, 1925 Lindeman sailed from New York Harbor on the *Conto Rosso* with his wife and four daughters. His destination was Naples, with the hope that Italian sunshine, a change of scenery, and a rest would restore his health. Although he had made two brief trips to Europe, his most memorable trip up to then had been to Puerto Rico with Charles Shaw in January of 1924. The trip to Italy would be the first and only time the entire family traveled together on a long journey, either outside or inside the United States. It was a wonderful adventure they would never forget.

Upon arriving in Naples, the Pisa Brothers, their travel agent, skillfully negotiated the family and their luggage through customs and then on to the Hotel Vesuvé, where everyone was delighted with the view of Mount Vesuvius and the Bay of Naples.

The next few days were spent sightseeing through the narrow and dusty streets of Naples, and up into the hills around the Castle St. Elmo for a breathtaking view of the city and the colorful bay. Side trips to Pompeii, Amalfi, Sorrento and Capri completed our short stay in southern Italy. We marveled at the blue of the water surrounding Capri and the fascinating ruins of Pompeii.

A few weeks after arriving in Naples Lindeman received a great shock. While exploring the city alone he bought a copy of the *London Daily Mail*. There, on the front page, was an announcement of Dorothy's marriage to Leonard Elmhirst. A few days later he wrote Dorothy of the huge surprise this news had brought.

63

"I read the *London Mail* and then walked up the hill of Via Santa Lucia with tears blinding my eyes."

He was all the more devastated because he had felt so confident of her friendship, which had flourished throughout the two and one-half years he had been in her employ. Her letters, encouragement, and extraordinary kindness to him and his family were evidence, he thought, of her deep feeling for him and of her interest in his projects. "You are capable of something that is the rarest thing on earth . . . ," he had told her, "original thought." Then she had once told him he had that rare combination of a personality that can "fire people's hearts as well as their minds."

Now he felt he had lost the two persons who had believed in him and his aspirations—first his mother and now Dorothy.

It is possible that Dorothy, knowing how upset Lindeman would be when he learned of her marriage to Elmhirst, had deliberately arranged for the family to travel to Europe to ease the blow. Of course Lindeman had known that she had met the young Englishman, seven years her junior, in 1920 when he was a student at Cornell University, and Dorothy was planning the dedication of the union building as a memorial to her husband. She had been eager to have Elmhirst meet "Eduard, of all people," and was pleased they did spend so many hours together. "He has your general point of view about rural life," she wrote Lindeman, "but is tackling the problem from the educational side solely. He needs more of your philosophic insights, discoveries about methods, and fuller comprehension of the whole social and economic structure." Elmhirst was thankful she had Lindeman as such a good friend, saying, "Thank God for Lindeman!"

It turned out that Lindeman was not the only one dumbfounded by the news of Dorothy's marriage. According to Swanberg in *Whitney Father, Whitney Heiress,* "Her marriage came as a complete surprise to the social world as well. . . . Moreover, it was a further surprise when they learned the Elmhirsts moved to England, bought the handsome but crumbling Dartington Hall in Devon, with two-thousand acres, and started a combined school and industrial-cultural center."

In addition to the profound shock of the news of Dorothy's marriage, Naples had not improved Lindeman's health. Traveling about and living in small hotel rooms with four children was not at all what he needed. He wrote Shaw that his health was about the same. "If anything, I feel less well than when we were in San Juan two years ago. . . . You were certainly the right companion. . . . The Bay of Naples has been our front yard and is entrancing. . . . The Italian sunshine is wonderful, but it would be improved by a long breezy letter from you."

Soon the family, not sorry to leave Naples where they could find nothing satisfactory in the way of a house or a pensione, climbed aboard a handsome Lancia touring car, driven by a Russian chauffeur, and began a thirteen-day journey to Rapallo.

Journeying over the mountains, they stopped in Rome, Perugia, Assisi, Florence, and Pisa. Rapallo was a great improvement over Naples, and they soon made themselves at home in the Hotel Bristol. There, for the first time in a month, they had a sitting room to themselves. Another bonus was that three bedrooms faced the sea.

Lindeman's spirits rose at once. He immediately wrote Shaw, "Was it Goethe who wrote, 'After visiting Rome, one can never again be wholly unhappy?' Well I'm not so sure of Rome, for it seemed to be less Italy than all the rest, but I am sure of this Ligurian shore. Florence won me completely, and I want to go back. Our room overlooked the Arno and the Ponte Vecchio, and . . . if I ever become despondent I shall want nothing so much as to run back to Florence."

His health seemed to improve rapidly. "I'm getting fat and saucy," he wrote Shaw. "I eat four meals a day, swim in the sea and take a sun bath each morning; I read about three hours; work on 'Egoism' and my new essay on 'Liberalism and the Scientific Spirit'; discuss Mussolini, Proust, Pirandello and Cal Coolidge with two American ladies of the grandmother age; play bridge with a British crowd and win on an average of four lire per night; in between, [the family] plays dominoes in our rooms and walks in the village."

But we children did not fare quite as well. Almost immediately, one after the other, we came down with the German measles. However, we soon recovered and the entire family began taking French lessons at the Berlitz school in preparation for a visit to Paris. "Mon Dieu," Lindeman wrote Shaw,

who could not be happy in Italy! Everywhere there is beauty. If you leave the Italians alone for a moment they break into song, and we are serenaded every evening by quartettes, soloists, harmonicas, accordions, and mandolins. Lately it has been past midnight before the revels begin.

The blue Ligurian sea lies at our feet, and terraces of olive trees roll away over the mountains to the rear. The bay is dotted with fishing smacks, and away off we see the larger ships bound to or from Genoa. At Portofino Vetta we can see Genoa on one side, and simply by turning around, the colorful lights of the coast of Levante. It was [on the rocks below our hotel window] that Shelley met his fate. What picturesque towns — Santa Margarita, Portofino Mare, San Michele, Zoaglili, Chiarari — each nestled in a cove by the rocky shores, and surrounded by hills of olive groves. And just beyond, as far as the eye can see, range upon range of snow-capped Apennines. Can you imagine a more picturesque combination?

San Michele is just a small cluster of houses from us across the bay. I cannot find the words to fit the spell which Italy casts upon me. . . . How often we wish you were here sharing it all with us. I feel sure that, were you here, you would at once mount Pegasus and be off over the hills. Well, you see, Charles, it has caught me — the scientist who once scoffed at beauty and searched only for reality.

(In actuality, Lindeman was always both a scientist and a romanticist.)

Despite Lindeman's improved spirits and health, he still had mixed feelings about Dorothy's marriage. On the one hand, he sent his blessings to her and Elmhirst, writing in April that he felt they had embarked upon "a spiritual venture" and that they shall be "ennobled by its lustre." He was thrilled by her "rebirth of youth and hope and intense life within," and he knew she would be ready with "her marvelous inner resources." On the other hand, he could not help but wonder how her marriage would affect her relationship to him. He wrote her that the time had come when they must discuss the discontinuance of her financial help. "I must also be true to my convictions in this region. Your interests now lie in other directions. The original plan has come to an end. You not only have carried out your promises but far exceeded them." He wrote that he was saying these things "with an air of coldness not consonant with my feelings. I could weep with every word. But you will understand."

Always he counted on her "understanding heart," saying that he wanted her to be free for her own experiments and that he was "one of those troublesome persons who demand a great deal from friends." In short, he told her he could not go on with his

66

projects and accept help from her "unless I can also have your interest, and under the present circumstances it would be unfair to ask for your interest."

Dorothy was shocked to think that Lindeman would feel that she had lost interest in him and his work. In spite of the fact that Dorothy and Elmhirst were immersed in restoring the grounds and gardens of Dartington Hall—"once so ravishingly beautiful"— she found time to write him a scolding letter. "How can you say my interest in your world will diminish? I could spank you for such a thought. Do you think that I could care one whit the less about America and her life and my friends? I think I care just about twice as much."

The Elmhirsts had been living in a hotel in Totnes while waiting to move into their quarters in Dartington Hall. Half the fun, Dorothy wrote, was the hard labor she was doing in the gardens. It was a job that would take all summer, and it was like a glorious adventure. However, she was puzzled by the English people, whom she found less than hospitable. "They are far less personal than Americans, rarely ask questions, and don't seem to care what one thinks or feels. It's going to take time to get on to them."

Over the next few months Lindeman's moods vacillated from periods of deep depression to elation. "I was told by a urologist that mood swings typically accompany both thyroid problems and nephritis."[1] In May, from Rapallo, he wrote Dorothy that he was living in an atmosphere of both extremes. "At times I feel sure that my efforts are futile and at other times I have been equally certain of what I was after. During the past few weeks I have been consistently buoyant." Never before had he been able to achieve such detachment from the externals of life and to begin to pay attention to his senses. "The faint sound of the bells of San Ambriogo," he wrote Dorothy in June, "are not differentiated as separate sounds, not the bird songs, nor the splashing of the sea against the rocks below. . . . I am immersed in this atmosphere."

The word of Lindeman's improvement brought "a secure inner joy" to Dorothy, who was also pleased that the Lindemans would be visiting Dartington Hall before departing for home.

Not too long after the family had settled into the Hotel Bristol, Martha Anderson, Lindeman's editor and translator, joined the family. He had met Anderson in the early 1920s when she was attending the Bryn Mawr School for Working Women. She continued to work for him for five years after their return, and they coauthored a monograph, *Education Through Experience*, published by the Worker's Education Bureau Press in 1927. The monograph contained a section on "Andragogy and Adult Learning," and it was the first time the now-popular term *andragogy* had been used in the United States. They worked on this material every morning on the beach or under the shade of the trees of the Hotel Bristol's spacious grounds, translating from German. Anderson's presence in Rapallo to assist Lindeman in his work was further evidence of Dorothy's generosity.

Halfway through his vacation Lindeman expressed some concern to Dorothy about his future in academia. The New York School would soon become affiliated with Columbia University, and it would not be long before all faculty would be expected to have an advanced degree. He wrote Dorothy, "Three more years at some university in order to get a Ph.D. would mean submission to hypocrisy, since I wholly disbelieve in the process of degree-getting." He had been attracted to the School because of its freedom from academic restrictions. Nor did he want to confine himself to research since "this would be a denial of my beliefs that these two functions — research and teaching — ought not to be separated, particularly in the social sciences."[2]

Due to illness, his teaching at the New York School had been limited to fall quarter and now he planned to return "to do a good year of teaching." After that he didn't know what he wanted to do. "My present feeling is I would like to buy a farm. [An idea Hazel did not approve of.] Then I would feel I was a part of a functional society." He confided in Dorothy that he was at times frightened by his responsibility for four children.

The Lindemans joined old friends from the United States for a pleasant tour of the Lake Country. At Lake Como Lindeman surprised Hazel with dinner, champagne, and a beautiful bar pin he had purchased in Milan for her thirty-fifth birthday.

With less than a week remaining of his tranquil life in Italy, Lindeman wrote Shaw that Max Beerbohm's villa was only a few meters away, and "he meets his confreres in the hotel every evening, when they all get gloriously drunk."[3]

After three and one-half months in Rapallo, the family sadly packed their belongings, said farewell to all their new friends, and departed for Paris.

Lindeman wrote Shaw that "when the burden again becomes heavy" he would look back with feeling to "those sunny, idle days by the sea. They were happy days, but with a quality of happiness I presume one can only have after youth is definitely abandoned." (Lindeman had turned forty on that May 9.)

However, by the first week of August, he was full of enthusiasm for Paris, a city he had once thought ugly; "its mongrel architecture, mock politeness, and post-war cynicism" had left him with negative impressions. But he wrote Dorothy, "This is a different Paris from the one I visited five years ago! But, perhaps I have changed more than the city. At least I feel a real affection for it now."

To Shaw he wrote that his favorite room in the Louvre was Monet's Impressionism and that his daily schedule included:

> debating with Floyd Dell, Dick Mount, Carl Chapman, Sislin, Bob Hallowell, and a few others on occasion. . . . Dell and I have taken a great liking to each other. He retains the odor of midwestern soil, the flavor of rural psychology, and consequently I understand him. . . . Scott Fitzgerald will be joining us today and he and Dell ought to liven things up a bit. . . . Leo Stein goes with us to the galleries. Our gang meets each day at 12:30 at the Café de la Paix, where the argument begins. We sometimes arrive at a decision about where to have lunch by one or two o'clock, and by five are back at Luigi's drinking beer and eating sandwiches: And, oh how often I wish for you! All you need to do is stand by the Place de l'Opéra and you'll see someone you've known before. They're all here. . . . And say, Carl [sic], about those eight-ounce wardrobes at the Folies Bergere, they aren't that heavy. They wouldn't even register an ounce if the entire company's wardrobe were placed on a scale. But to me, the human body has great advantages when it is slightly decorated.

Instead of going directly to Devon, the Lindemans spent a week in London. "London," Lindeman wrote Shaw, "is a vivid contrast to Paris, which is spritelier. . . . Pessimism seems to have pervaded all classes. I've come to feel that these British enjoy living in an atmosphere of doom. . . . The industrial situation grows worse day by day—and there is no leadership in the country."

While Hazel took the children to play in the park one day, Lindeman was at the tailor's being fitted for four new suits and an overcoat, which Dorothy—still mothering him—had insisted he buy. "Now you won't need to apologize for my appearance," he wrote Shaw, "at least not on the outside. You may have to remind me that my suit needs pressing, but at least I'll have some."

Next was a joyous week in Devon, exploring the beautiful grounds and old ruins waiting to be restored and the Devon countryside with its fascinating moors. The Elmhirsts were doing a splendid job of restoring the Tudor castle, originally dating back to 830 A.D.

Lindeman was equally impressed by the comprehensive and exciting plans for Dartington's future. A progressive school would open in the fall of 1926, and over the next few years farming, poultry, lumbering, weaving, glassblowing, and other cottage industries would be added. Dartington was more than a progressive school — it was a unique community involving not only students, faculty, visiting artists, writers, philosophers, actors, and dancers, but the townspeople as well.

It was the kind of experimental and imaginative project Lindeman could not refrain from becoming involved in. Already, Dorothy and Elmhirst wanted him to lead a conference in the fall of 1926 for the staff "to thrash out an educational philosophy."

On September 15 the Lindemans sailed out of Plymouth for home on the *Leviathan*. Just prior to sailing Lindeman wrote Dorothy:

> It has been a marvelous experience for us all! In Italy it was easy to let myself go and not take myself too seriously, and if only I can carry back a parcel of Italian ease, I shall have learned a great lesson. In the process of regaining my health, I have made some marvelous discoveries about myself. . . . Some of the hardness has melted from my spirit, and I am no longer ashamed to have beauty light my way.

He also carried back a pleasant picture of Dorothy "in her rural setting and newly-found joys," and he told her to "treasure it, for the Journey is not long."

For Hazel this first trip abroad — and longest time she had ever spent away from home — must have been one of the high points of her life. She had lived most of her life in the Midwest, with only a few brief years in North Carolina and New Jersey. I believe this was the only time she ever kept a diary. Unfortunately, there was very little in this leather-bound volume that revealed how she felt about her experience. It contains accurate descriptions of the

70

magnificent sights of the cities, theater, opera, art galleries, as well as the scenery of the countryside. She makes note of shopping sprees, swimming, and supervising the children at play. She looked forward to a visit from a college chum and to her trip with Lindeman and friends to the Lake Country. She does not say if she was homesick or lonely when he was working and curiously makes no mention of his health.

I cannot say if this trip brought Hazel and Lindeman any closer together. Living in such close proximity for six months may have highlighted their fundamental differences. I also wonder if Hazel was aware of Lindeman's total devastation at the news of Dorothy's marriage, or if she could share in his excitement about the book he was working on or in his concern about his academic future—if she knew about it.

Lindeman had wanted the trip to count in more ways than one—to gain some insight into the present political regime. Although Mussolini had only recently come to power, Lindeman was certain he was a pure dictator and not a democratic socialist, as some of his liberal friends preferred to believe. He was equally certain the man was as dangerous as he was unscrupulous.

But it was not until he received an urgent letter from Baldwin in mid-July that Lindeman was stimulated to take action. Baldwin appealed to him to get some reliable information regarding the status of political prisoners in Italy and also to learn the details of the recent press censorship bill. (Apparently the International Committee for Political Prisoners had found it impossible to secure this information.) Lindeman invited Benedetto Croce, an editor of the Milan liberal daily, author, and philosopher, to Rapallo for a few days, with the hope that he might give him some clues of fascist coercive measures. There is no record if Croce came. He also made plans to visit Mussolini in Rome, although he did not share this with his family. However, to Dorothy he wrote on July 18 that at the very last minute he decided not to go but that Anderson might go instead, and "she will do the job much better than I could. She has more nerve. As a detective my value might be measured by zeroes." He may also have felt that being such an outspoken antifascist would have created too much suspicion. As it turned out, neither Lindeman nor Anderson interviewed Mussolini.

71

On his return Lindeman planned to persuade Paul Kellogg, editor of *The Survey Graphic*, to publish a special issue alerting Americans to the danger of fascism abroad and, more importantly, to the possibility of fascism in America.

Lindeman would make his trip count in more ways than one. What he could not have known was that the one way he had wanted it to matter the most would not be possible, for no amount of sunshine, rest, or scenery could have restored his health. It would not be until 1931, after he had a thyroid operation at Johns Hopkins Hospital, that he would finally be free of pain for at least seven years.

# Chapter 9

# After Sunny Italy

*The only joy I have is here in the country with the children and in the garden. Somehow I need to get new reasons for living, and while these are in the making, I have no enthusiasm for the things I used to do and enjoy.*

Lindeman, November 1926

Lindeman returned from Europe feeling better and determined to teach for at least another year. He was also excited about the prospects for a special issue of *The Survey Graphic* on fascism—the first American journal to sound the alarm against fascism in America. When Kellogg asked him to be the principal editor, he set about at once to secure a passport for Gaetano Salvemini, an Italian scholar, author, and passionate exponent of liberalism, to come to New York to help. Putting together this issue was an enormous task involving many months of frustration and delays in locating American, Italian, and British authors. Finally, eighteen months later, it came out—introduced by Kellogg with a tribute to Lindeman: "In a sense, this issue grew out of the six months Professor Lindeman spent on the Italian Riviera in 1925. His human insight and grasp of the broad outlines of conflict in ideology have distinguished his work as a collaborating editor."

Lindeman's lead article, "A New Challenge to the Spirit of 1776," posed the question that confronts our civilization, even today: "Can we both organize creative energy and conserve liberty?" He was concerned that fascism could very easily be made compatible with large sectors of American thought and practice and thus "constitute the first realistic challenge to the spirit of freedom and democracy which emerged from the revolution of 1776." He pointed out that Mussolini was not joking when he told a representative

73

of the Associated Press in 1927 that he found more parallels for fascism in the United States than anywhere else in the world.[1]

In addition to working on the special issue, Lindeman resumed teaching after a six months absence at the New York School. There he soon started "a small insurrection" by volunteering to head a group to revise and integrate the school's curriculum, which he said "had grown just like topsy." He also resumed teaching at the New School and working with The Inquiry. He became the director of research for the Worker's Education Bureau, publishing a pamphlet on worker's education and the public libraries. One wonders how he also found time to publish numerous journal articles and to lecture at Bryn Mawr and in Richmond, Virginia.

Two private matters of concern remained unsettled, however. One was his future with the New York School. As far as he knew this could be his last year of teaching, and after that he had no definite plans. Also his relationship with Dorothy had undergone a significant change. Would she still retain an interest in his work? He made a point of staying in her Fifth Avenue home and eating breakfast with her three children, who remained in New York with a governess until the opening of the school in Devon. The children welcomed his visits, and Dorothy was grateful that he kept in touch with them. She was also pleased when Lindeman wrote that he liked the new Dartington statement, saying, "Leonard seems to have recovered the spirit of the venture, and it rings true." He had also not forgotten the Elmhirsts' invitation to visit Devon in the fall of 1926 and to lead a conference.

Unfortunately, with the return of cold weather Lindeman's health took a turn for the worse. By early December 1925, while in New York, a chronic sinus condition necessitating surgery sent him to Dorothy's home weeping and suffering. "I'm really as sensitive as a child about pain, and this quite unnerved me," he wrote her.

By March 1926 his health had become a constant source of irritation and disappointment. He wrote Elmhirst he not only had had the grippe but that he must have a radical operation on all five sinuses, and four or five teeth removed as well. The operation was scheduled for June, and the doctor had forbidden him to teach summer term.

Although he must have been told by the Army of the progressive and irreversible nature of his disease, the Lindemans behaved as if they did not know it. Every new symptom seemed to baffle them, and curiously the doctors as well. Stewart suggests that although Lindeman's hospitalizations or home-bound illnesses and other maladies bore other labels—a tonsillectomy with insufficient recovery time, grippe, influenza, gall bladder, heart attack, strep sinus, gastrointestinal problems, lymphatic infections—". . . it is likely that most of these were related in some way to problems brought on by his failing kidneys."[2] However, the family believed a thyroid deficiency was the cause of many problems—an alarming loss of weight between 1924 and 1931; wide mood swings; hyperactivity; nervousness; insomnia; and a tendency to feel overheated, causing him to head for the porch for a breath of fresh air. It was not until 1931 that doctors at Johns Hopkins Clinic clearly established that he had a hyperthyroid condition and not a thyroid deficiency. After his thyroid operation he gained weight, and most of the symptoms seemed to dramatically disappear for a few years.

Stewart reminds us that in spite of his perfectly healthy, even rugged, appearance, Lindeman was a very sick man who must have known that nephritis was incurable and that his blood would slowly be poisoned by waste products that his increasingly impaired kidneys could not remove. Today advanced medical science can save or prolong the lives of nephritis patients, but "during Eduard's lifetime, persons afflicted by the disease lived under an immutable sentence of death."[3]

I don't recall my parents openly discussing his health problems; instead they acted as if each new incident was unrelated to previous ones. Meanwhile, doctors continued to search for sources of possible infection—teeth, tonsils, sinuses. I do not recall any frank discussion of a kidney problem until he came under the care of Dr. Max Gerson in New York City in 1942. I suspect they may have preferred to ignore it. Lindeman himself blamed his health problems on "the little invisibles."

In May, one month before the June operation, Lindeman had to battle the "worst strep infection on record," but then he wrote Shaw that " 'the little invisibles' didn't do me in this time!" Once again he had fooled the doctors by improving so rapidly that the operation was performed on schedule and was a success.

It was typical of Lindeman to make light of his health and to be skeptical of doctors. However, soon after the sinus operation he did warn Elmer Scott, an old friend and director of the Dallas

Civic Federation, that his physical condition might make it impossible for him to come to Dallas for a month's engagement in November.

Nonetheless, by the first week in August he was off to Europe once again, illustrating his capability to recover from illnesses and operations rapidly. His recuperative powers amazed everybody. It is possible that he did not experience the full impact of many months of pain and suffering—culminating in a life-threatening operation—until after his return in September. Or perhaps what happened at Dartington, and its aftermath, contributed to a severe depression he experienced on his return.

He had been invited to be a delegate to the First World Congress on Adult Education in Copenhagen, after which he would proceed to Geneva to hear the debates on Germany's entry into the League of Nations, and then on to Devon for the conference. He hoped that Shaw would join him—"at least . . . to Rapallo for a few days, and save four or five for Paris and two or three for Berlin." Apparently Shaw couldn't, and Lindeman departed alone.

He wrote Shaw from Berlin that the meeting in Copenhagen had been a great success, and he had felt sad, as always, to leave Denmark. In Berlin he had begun to feel homesick when a letter from Shaw arrived "one rainy, dreary day and cheered me up." So much so, in fact, that he had to tell Shaw about an experience he had because he was "perhaps the only one to understand my mood." Oh, how he wished Shaw had been with him the night before when,

walking a mile or so along the Kurfurstendamm, I stopped to buy a hotdog from a little old lady hiding with her stove in the nook of a large building. Soon I found myself talking German, and, she, being a gay old lady, and I in a festive mood, the talk was boisterous, and a crowd soon gathered; two or three street girls, a taxidriver or two, some beggars and others. They called me the "Komische Amerikaner," and I had to live up to my reputation by showing off all my tricks.

I translated American jazz into German, and discovered I could do stunts, sing nonsense songs, and talk Platt-deutsch . . . But to do the Charleston at 3 a.m. on the Kurfurstendamm was too much! . . . The old lady was shrieking, "Ach, das tut weh in Magen, du Spitzbube," and all the time bent over with her hands holding her stomach.

It turned out to be the gayest time he had had in a long time, and he hadn't known he could act up so anymore. "Charles, you should have been there!"

This was a side of Lindeman few people saw. I knew he was a tease and full of mischief, but my father in the role of "comic," doing stunts and dancing in the streets. . . . Well, I was delighted that he could let go and have so much fun, and I wished I had been there to see it.

Before going on to Devon Lindeman met Croly in Geneva, where he had received confirmation from the Elmhirsts of the conference dates.

For many complex reasons Lindeman was no doubt eager to visit Devon again. Apart from wanting to see Dorothy, whom he had not seen for a year, he may have felt a need to be reassured of her continued interest in him and his work. He may have also been curious to see how the Elmhirsts were proceeding with their planned community. Their letters indicated that they had made an impressive start. Lindeman's letters had succeeded in reenforcing their belief that education should not be preparation for life but life itself.

Lindeman was also looking forward to leading the conference and making a contribution to Dorothy's school. She still looked upon him as an advisor on many matters. But there may have been another reason he was eager to participate, perhaps not so altruistic. He may have been harboring some resentment, even jealousy, toward Leonard Elmhirst.

Michael Young, referring to the conference in his book *The Elmhirsts at Dartington* (1982), wrote:

> . . . Reliance was placed upon a welcome visiting expert, an old admirer of Dorothy and a member of her New York Committee of Friends which administered grants on her behalf in the USA. Lindeman was invited to act as Chairman . . . Professor Lindeman came from the New York School of Social Work to advise on everything.[4]

Wyatt Rawson, one of Elmhirst's friends from Cambridge whom he had recently hired as staff psychologist, was another participant. Although Dorothy insisted that Lindeman was "integral" to Dartington, he was in fact the only outsider at this meeting.

If it had not been for Rawson, this conference would not have been too different from past conferences Lindeman had attended and played a key role in. Who was Rawson, and what happened at the conference and over the next year to change Lindeman's and Dorothy's relationship so drastically?

Lindeman undoubtedly led the conference, so it must have come a surprise to discover that Dorothy was expecting Elmhirst, as head of the estate, to play a primary role. Later correspondence indicates that people on both sides of the Atlantic were critical of Elmhirst, and thus he felt a greater need to make a good impression at the conference. There is also the possibility that he felt threatened by Lindeman's presence and fearful that he might not live up to Dorothy's expectations.

When the Elmhirsts first discussed the idea of a conference with Lindeman in September 1925, they believed the purpose was "to explore and define common policy and achieve a unity of mind with respect to educational goals and guiding principles." Lindeman viewed it as task-oriented, similar to the discussion groups he had led in Dorothy's Long Island home.

However, it was apparent from the very beginning that Rawson and Lindeman would not see eye-to-eye. On the one hand, Rawson believed that personality problems had to be cleared up before more substantive issues could be addressed. He planned to apply his new psychotherapeutic knowledge and skills gained from his own psychoanalysis. Lindeman, on the other hand, was more comfortable with objectivity than subjective examination of feelings and intimacy. If there were personality problems to be dealt with, then these could be solved later. I am sure he felt that, given reasonable people, any problems confronting Dartington could be handled rationally. It is no wonder, therefore, that disagreeing on goals, methods, and even ground rules, the conference got off to a poor start, and the staff was unable to arrive at any consensus for an agenda.

Unfortunately, the only record of what actually happened at the conference must be pieced together from letters written afterward. As far as I know, Lindeman never discussed the conference with his family, and in a letter to Shaw upon his return he made no reference whatsoever to the conference.

From the flurry of soul-searching letters in the aftermath of the conference, it appears that what happened *after* was more significant than what happened *during* the one-week meeting. The letters indicate that Rawson instigated a series of intensive "self-review" talks among Dorothy, Elmhirst, and himself in which each

78

exposed their most intimate feelings and reactions. Lindeman soon found himself embroiled in a whirlpool of emotions, accusations, intrigue, and collusion. "We looked at ourselves," Rawson wrote Lindeman in May 1927, "and saw the mistakes we had made. It was in this self-examination process that you came up in connection with Leonard's feelings." It soon became apparent to Lindeman that Rawson was having an extraordinary influence over both Dorothy and Elmhirst. After months of emotionally charged sessions and "gruelling self-investigations," they felt they must, in turn, be "perfect- ly honest about their relationship with Eduard." Under Rawson's influence, Dorothy had apparently spoken some bitter words about Lindeman. Rawson tried to soften the blow by writing Lindeman that it was really his doing because he, Rawson, had deliberately placed the blame on Lindeman, although he "hadn't meant to hurt you in her estimation. . . . And now Dorothy has upset you horribly—you felt you were drifting apart from her, and that I caused this to happen." Rawson apologized for saying anything intentionally "to hurt you with Dorothy or Leonard" and begged Lindeman to "understand."

There is no doubt in my mind that Rawson had deliberately set about to destroy the relationship Lindeman enjoyed with Dorothy over the past four years. As Rawson himself wrote in his May 16th letter, he was jealous of their relationship, and he seemed pleased to be able to report that "your old relationship is dead and now your unconscious vainly gnashes its teeth."

There is no record of Lindeman's replies, but from his and Dorothy's letters alone it is clear that the damage had already been done and their relationship would never be the same again. It was now up to Lindeman to pick up the pieces, or perhaps to try to create a new relationship on different terms.

Among the many mysteries about this conference, one of the most puzzling is the one letter of Lindeman's that did survive, written to all the participants immediately upon his return. In this letter he seemed totally unaware that anything had gone amiss, insisting the conference was a huge success.

> *Was it worth doing?* Nothing I've done in the last years since the war has seemed to me to be more worthwhile. *Did I learn by doing?* Heaps! Much more than you did, and when I speak of your ex- perience now to friends, a warm glow comes over me. I learned

something about the discussion method, but a great deal more about your various personalities—which is mostly more valuable.

He closed with a description of his "weird" departure and the "queer" feelings he experienced as "a heavy fog descended just as our tender started forth and we wandered about the Atlantic ocean until four a.m. before we found the large ship. . . . We stood huddled on the deck of the tender not knowing where we were and not able to see anything." This description may have symbolically represented a more accurate picture of the way he actually felt about the conference—lost, vulnerable, and unable to understand what was going on in the irrational realm. His initial upbeat mood may have been an attempt to rationalize what he could not understand. If the Dartington experience had been the most worthwhile thing he had done since World War I, why did he not refer to it in his letter to Shaw?

In a letter to Lindeman Rawson referred to "intimate confidences" Lindeman shared with him on "the eve of his departure."

> I felt you were battling something in yourself and I wished I could talk it out with you. It seemed so devastating for the moment. It must have something to do with the sudden flare-ups that you shared with me. . . . I feel they are in some way connected with your terrific desire for objectivity. Don't you think you should look into yourself over that?

Rawson may have felt that Lindeman was ignorant of the new psychoanalytic theory of Freud, Jung, and Adler, so prevalent at that time. "You may not have cared to study it, even may reject it," he wrote, in which case what he was about to say would seem foolish. In actuality, Lindeman had been exposed to the new psychology by virtue of being a faculty member of the New York School, and many of his Greenwich Village acquaintances were undergoing analysis. But it is also true that he had rejected the idea of becoming a dogmatic adherent of any one school of thought. "His concept of the individual human being was formed out of his acquaintance with the natural sciences, psychiatry, social psychology, and other disciplines."[5]

In one very long letter to Lindeman in July 1927, Rawson wrote they were happy that Lindeman directed the conference, and "spanked them all around." He also thanked him for telling me so sincerely about your relationship with Dorothy—but I think you both deceive and contradict yourselves when you say they are not subtle or complex, close and confidential. You say—"My relation to Dorothy has never been in any real sense confidential," and then you say—"It was in the garden of the Seymour Hotel that she first talked with me in a manner that implied she considered me to be a friend, in much the same sense that Louise Croly and Herbert were her friends."

Rawson's impression was that from the start Lindeman and Dorothy's relationship was "intimate, personal and confidential." He was quite sure that Dorothy supplied the place left vacant by Lindeman's dead mother, whom he had adored. "The interest in all your doings, the fine, personal touch of her letters, the motherly attitude of solicitude toward you in your illness, all combine to make you feel once again that which you had known in your childhood."

He stressed the similarities between Lindeman's mother and Dorothy, and he argued that it was this "unworked-out emotion" and its "undeception" that had upset Lindeman so much. "A mother does not criticize as a friend can and should! A critical Dorothy you were always afraid of because it would destroy your image of her as your mother. Now the criticisms are such that they must be met as challenges from a friend, not gentle admonitions from mother to child."

Rawson was not content to merely point out that Lindeman had always looked upon Dorothy as a mother figure; he next accused him of "failing to consider Dorothy's development as an independent being, with her own life to live, in which a friend might be interested, might encourage, inspire, and incite her to struggle and overcome." He accused Lindeman of taking more from her than he gave in return, saying, "Did you ever try to encourage her in her own work? This is what friendship demands from us. . . . Think of the occasions you expected her to take a mother's interest in you and yet you did not take a mother's interest in her—or even a friend's."

In spite of letters and face-to-face discussions misunderstandings persisted. A year after Lindeman returned from Dartington Dorothy wrote him that they were worried he had "taken amiss several of Wyatt's points in relation to her." She was especially concerned that the two of them "may have lost the spirituality of their friendship" because she frankly criticized him. In the past, she admitted, she had questioned certain things in relation to his work, "but that contained no element of moral judgment." She also puzzled over why he was so sensitive to criticism: "why does it knock you all to pieces?" She credited Rawson for pointing out her own need for "something more personal" and added that at the same time Lindeman was giving her "so very, very, much," she was, at heart, "desperately needing something more." She urged him to discover the origin of his fears and why he felt the element of intimacy was lacking in their relationship. "Can't we trust one another to take that further step? I certainly crave it from you."

As the Dartington conference faded into the background, the Elmhirsts continued to view Lindeman as integral to Dartington. My sister Doris and I were invited by Dorothy to attend the school, but only I could make it—and stayed two years. Lindeman visited there again in 1929 and 1930 and continued to offer helpful ideas about the school and the estate.

Rawson might have wished to undermine the relationships between Dorothy and Lindeman and between Dorothy and Elmhirst, but he may have coincidentally provided them with new insights into their own feelings and behavior, along with a greater appreciation of one another's needs. He may have been the first person to help Dorothy to better understand herself and her needs as a woman and a human being.

By the time October came Lindeman wrote Scott that he definitely could not honor his commitment to the Civic Federation. When a disappointed Scott accused Lindeman of placing his obligations in New York ahead of his commitment to the people of Dallas, Lindeman replied:

I haven't revealed myself so frankly to anyone else because in your case there is a personal factor of affection. . . . You are perfectly right in thinking that my obligations here stand in the way of a month's absence if I came to Dallas. But, there is something else of far greater importance: I have no zest for going. It is the same with other things. I feel quite well, although I tire quickly, and sometimes sink suddenly, but the difficulty is not, I believe primarily physical. It has been that way ever since June, when I spoke in Cleveland. I get through my work somehow, but always under a shadow of fear—fear that it doesn't amount to anything. And the only joy I have is here in the country with the children and in the garden. . . . Somehow I need to get new reasons for living and while these are in the making, I have no enthusiasm for the things I used to do and enjoy.

He added that his physician had told him that during the June operation he "actually passed beyond the margins of hope, and something within me passed out." He could not hope that Scott would understand since he did not understand it himself, but he asked for forgiveness. He had canceled three other engagements "with equally painful consequences," saying he "couldn't see what else to do."

A very perceptive student of Lindeman's told me that Lindeman had a few psychoanalytic sessions with Karen Horney,[6] and later with another psychiatrist, for a total of twenty sessions that he felt were not successful.[7] The Dartington episode, combined with some curiosity about this new psychoanalytic method (and the serious episode of depression in the fall of 1926), may have motivated him to seek help. It is unfortunate that no records exist today of these sessions. Such data might have provided valuable insights into Lindeman's complex personality, his difficulty in the area of intimacy, and a possible relationship between his kidney problem and his "black moods."

Chapter 10

# Social Philosopher, Social Work Educator

*I fully realize how important the trail is that we are now following and how long. There is no stopping for one who takes to it and it is full of extraordinary experiences.*

Herbert Croly, 1924

By the time Lindeman joined the Faculty of the New York School of Social Work (NYSSW) in 1924, the field of social work was in a state of ferment. Part of the problem was due to increasing specialization and professionalization, but another was confusion about what social work should and should not be. Bradley Buell summed it up in an interview with me in 1975: should it be a technologically oriented profession or a reform movement? "Social Work as Cause and Function" was the title of Porter Lee's[1] presidential address at the 1929 National Conference of Social Work, in which he stressed social work's continuing responsibility as a *cause*. "As long as man discovers new evils, each of these is a potential cause which looks for leadership in part to social work." According to Buell, "Lindeman came out of the reform tradition; he was a social theorist who blossomed into a social philosopher."[2]

At the 1922 meeting Lee, director of the NYSSW, and Walter Pettit, head of the Community Organization Division, heard Lindeman deliver a speech called "The Place of the Local Community in Organized Society." The speech was applauded by *The Survey* as "an incisive and genuine prophetic summons to return to the small village or neighborhood unit as a center of political, cultural, and moral reconstruction." Two years later Lindeman was hired to teach Community Organization, one of the areas of specialization at that time.

In 1924 the practice of social work was conceptually divided into five fields: community organization, criminology, public health, industry, and family and child welfare. However, with the growing influence of Freudian psychology during and after World War I, psychiatric social work was added and soon became an important and fast-growing practice. Lindeman wrote Shaw that his "class includes about twenty sophisticated young graduates of Barnard, Smith, Wellesley, and Bryn Mawr, their minds crammed full of modern jargon. Freud, behaviorism, and relativity are like so much Mellen's food, and they toss off Oedipus complexes and defense mechanisms as nonchalantly as—well, whatever you do nonchalantly. And you can start a fight about anything, anytime, which is, of course, the proper milieu for my teaching."[3]

Social work in those early years was almost entirely voluntary, with few public welfare departments. The core membership of the American Association of Social Workers consisted primarily of caseworkers in private agencies.

Although Lindeman never considered himself a social worker and in fact always felt something of an outsider in the profession, the bulk of his professional time was spent as professor in a school of social work. "Although not officially identified with the profession, he had always been excited about its powerful possibilities. He saw these as related to a dynamic society and an awareness of democratic values, democratic disciplines, and basic rules of conduct that must be applied if democratic values were not to become mere slogans and thereby meaningless."[4]

Actually, he had been on the fringe of the social work profession since 1917. His experience with boys' and girls' clubs and farmers' cooperatives in rural Michigan, and his work as recreation director in War Camp Community Services, no doubt predisposed him to view group work and community organization as the most promising of social work methods.

But neither his experience nor his writings was in the mainstream of social work in the 1920s. By the early 1920s, psychiatric social work occupied the top rung of the ladder of hierarchical status among social workers. Mary Richmond's *Social Diagnosis* had introduced a scientific base for casework as the basis for family diagnosis and treatment. Casework with individuals and families had become the mainstream of social work when Lindeman entered the field.

At times Lindeman was impatient with colleagues whose primary concern lay in the area of the individual's psyche and individual adjustment, arguing that "helping people adjust to the status quo

85

with all its inequities and social injustices was too narrow a focus." The challenge, he felt, was for professionals "skilled in conditioning human behavior . . . to become the instrument of social justice on its highest level and of social change on its lowest."[5]

In his course in social philosophy Lindeman probed the meaning of democracy. In the growth of American culture, in the educational system, and in current political and social activities, he sought the values that gave meaning to life and affirmed that only the use of means having integrity within themselves could accomplish good ends.

He prodded his students to look at the relationship between method and philosophy, which he later would call "means and ends," insisting that scientific, ethical, and philosophical methods and values must be integrated into social work practice. He felt his mission as teacher was to "assist students in developing a social philosophy, and to become social thinkers."[6]

Although Lindeman had been hired to teach community organization, he soon began to weave his two main preoccupations, adult education and social philosophy, into all his courses. He clearly had entered a new phase of his career, slowly evolving into a social philosopher, social reformer, and social work education reformer.

While he was becoming increasingly identified with the profession of social work, he was also a frequent critic—along with Owen Lovejoy, Gertrude Vaile, Grace Abbott, Julia Lathrop, and Jane Addams. He felt the field failed to live up to its promises by permitting shameful racial discrimination in some social agencies, by dispensing relief in ways that humiliated rather than preserved a sense of individual worth and dignity, and by allowing professionals to scoff at volunteers.[7]

Many of Lindeman's students went on to become prominent administrators, educators, social activists, and practitioners. One of these, Lester Granger, who became the director of the National Urban League, felt that Lindeman was responsible "more than anyone during the last quarter century, for what amounted to a complete revolution in the social philosophy of staff and board members of thousands of social agencies throughout the country."[8]

Roger Baldwin reminded me that Lindeman was influential in his field in a time "when he could be experimental and philosophical," but that today the "daring and bold approaches must come from outside the field." He felt the profession had became "too institutionalized, bureaucratic, and preoccupied with professionalism." He also thought it ironic that the profession waited until 1952 to bestow upon Lindeman the recognition he deserved.[9] It was one year before he died, and long after he had become a recognized authority within and outside the profession, that he was elected president of the National Conference of Social Work.

As absorbed as Lindeman was by his teaching, no single area of interest could claim his imagination and boundless energy. If the school was his professional home base, Greenwich Village soon became the center of his social life. Not long after arriving in New York City, he had found himself catapulted into the excitement of life in the Village. There he was drawn into the vortex of social and intellectual thought and action that would involve him in social activism and public service for the rest of his life.

It is easy to understand how anyone would have been beguiled by the Village. In his oral reminiscences, Bruno Lasker, a social researcher, author, associate editor of *The Survey*, and affiliate of The Inquiry, describes what Lindeman must have experienced in that frenetic and exciting milieu.

By 1922 the Village had already become a national symbol of the quest for newness and freedom. Artists and writers, lured by low rents, swarmed into the cramped and twisted streets, and slowly the Village became the Left Bank, everybody engaged in freeing themselves and the world. It had an air of excitement, and the air was emancipation. Some of it may have been eccentric, but, nevertheless, the ultra-respectable Walter Lippmann wrote his *Preface to Politics* in the Village. Eugene O'Neill kept the hours of a bank clerk; and Frances Perkins continued her family tradition of gracious living; and even the moralizing Herbert Croly had his few years in the Village and his hours at the Grapevine Bar on West 11th Street and Sixth Avenue. Every third Villager was being psychoanalyzed. There were tea and coffee houses where people just sat and talked.[10]

By 1928 Lindeman had decided to spend several nights a week in the Village as a roommate of Baldwin, who, like Lindeman, was an avid bird-watcher and nature lover. Baldwin recalled that the two of them blended into this bohemian counterculture readily and enthusiastically:

We first lived together at 21 Minetta Lane in a very small three-bedroom apartment in the heart of Greenwich Village. It was a pleasant place in surroundings we both liked, so bohemian and so neighborly, where nobody gave a damn about what anybody said or did.

Ed came and went as he pleased. We would walk up the Village streets to Alice McDougal's restaurant on 8th Street for breakfast. She catered to the intelligentsia, or pseudos, with an appetizing American fare like Mother used to serve: good hot cereal and hot corn bread. We would start our day with them and the *Times*, with appropriate comments on the day's news.

We rarely took other meals together; we both had our circle of friends, quite different ones, too. Some we shared. I think one of his closest friends then, and for many years, was Tom Cotton, who was devoting himself to adult education work. But Ed was so sociable he had many men and women devoted to him. He liked having people around [although] I think he was a very modest man, even shy. He did not assert himself in a group.

In 1930 Baldwin, Lindeman, and two male friends moved into a fifth-floor walkup on West 12th Street where their bachelorlike existence continued apace. There, Baldwin recalled,

I was often to hear his praises from his lady friends old and new, going way back to his Michigan days. . . . Mrs. McGraw and her daughter Kathleen Hendrie were proud of their part in his rise to so much recognition. There was also another devoted lady, Sue Hibbard of Winnetka, Illinois, a later friendship so intense that, when Ed needed a very expensive operation on his thyroid gland, Sue, then a widow, came to New York to be near him and pay the bills. Ed had young women friends, too, but he avoided involvement with his students; at least he said he tried to, and I suppose he succeeded. Ed had his admirers, too, among the wealthy ladies who supported dangerous reforms like mental health, peace, housing for the poor, adult education!

Ruth Morgan invited Ed to her evening salons, where earnest people made up their minds on social questions; and there was Mrs. Geraldine Thompson, her sister, lady of the manor in Red Bank, New Jersey, who asked Ed to lecture to her social work friends.

But the circle in which Lindeman moved was more than just a coffeehouse culture. These were political people living in an exciting, and disturbing era. "The times in which we lived," Baldwin reminisced, were turbulent and so difficult to appraise, and so surprising. Then the Russian Revolution broke out after the end of the First World War, and Fascism rose as a sort of answer to the Russian Revolution and dominated the 1920s and 30s, with the expansion of Germany and the Second World War. That was an awfully hard and trying time to test anyone's faith in what you call science or morality, or social stability. There was no stability and there were no guidelines. Everything was fluid, everything was changing, everything was a surprise. We were all confused.[11]

Baldwin reminded me that Lindeman played his part in the intellectual and political ferment of the times. Indeed, he was deeply committed to the activities of three foci of liberal thought: *TNR*, the New School for Social Research, and The Inquiry. Lindeman told Baldwin that in 1917 the librarian at George Williams College, knowing his reputation as campus rebel, placed a copy of *TNR* in his hands, saying, "There! This ought to suit you!"[12]

In an undated scrapbook Lindeman summed up what he liked about *TNR*'s philosophy: (a) belief in the utility and fruitfulness of fermenting public opinion, (b) faith in the latent regeneracy of human nature, and (c) belief in fairness in human relations and an allegiance to fundamental justice. Roger noted he was attracted by its "pragmatic, rather than doctrinaire, spirit." *TNR* advocated what Lindeman had been fighting for: "better conditions for labor, acceptance of labor unions, and worker representation in management." He was convinced that middle-class liberalism—a transformed liberalism—held the key to America's future. And the staff of *TNR* actively supported John Dewey's principle of "instrumentalism." They promoted "progressive education as a new force of liberation" and saw "industrial democracy as a desirable alternative to the tyranny of Bolshevism or the anarchy of pure capitalism."[13]

In fact, it suited him so much that Lindeman became a regular contributor and a participant in its famous Tuesday luncheons, where fine Italian and French cooking and wines earned it the reputation of the "best club in New York." Among *TNR*'s senior staff were Francis Hackett, George Soule, Edmund Wilson, Malcolm Cowley, Charles Merz, Stark Young, H. N. Brailsford, and Bruce Bliven, "who invited statesmen and foreign dignitaries, artists, literati and just about every luminary of U.S. culture and politics to discuss the pressing issues of the time."[14] Walter Lippmann, who in 1922 left *TNR* to become editor of the *New York World,* also occasionally attended the luncheons.[15]

Foremost among the editors was Herbert Croly, who presided over the proceedings from the head of the table. His book, *The Promise of American Life* (1909), inspired other major political movements such as Roosevelt's *New Nationalism* and Wilson's *New Freedom.*[16]

Although sixteen years older than Lindeman, Croly soon became the chief influence in Lindeman's life. By 1924 Lindeman had become profoundly committed to Croly's vision of liberalism, which *Time* magazine would describe in 1939 as "a great spiritual force to which a clear sense of mission was attached." The power of this messianic vision is evident in a letter Croly wrote to Lindeman in July 1924.

> I fully realize how important the trail is that we are now following and how long. There is no stopping for one who takes to it and it is full of extraordinary experiences. It is both dreary and exciting, both easy and immeasurably difficult, both inevitable and impossible, both utterly disheartening and enormously satisfactory. It converts life into an impenetrable secret which we are always (illegible) for the benefit of ourselves and others.

Croly made a point of writing weekly short notes reminding Lindeman of Tuesday luncheons. The two men saw each other at least once a week during the period 1924 to 1930. In 1926 they attended the League of Nations meeting in Geneva, returning on the same boat together. In 1928 Croly encouraged Lindeman to serve as editor of a special section on adult education published in February 1928, "Adult Education: A New Means for Liberals."

Richard Magat, Editor of *Foundation News,* suggests that it was under the influence of Croly that Lindeman first became interested in investigating private foundations. A decisive factor in Croly's and Lindeman's interest was that beginning in 1927 they were close advisors to Dorothy Straight Elmhirst on her own philanthropy. For many years Lindeman served as Chairman of the Advisory Committee of the William C. Whitney Foundation. Although she wanted to reimburse him for his services, he refused, saying not only did he enjoy it but it was one way he could repay her for her kindness to him.

Understandably, Lindeman was totally devastated when Croly died in 1930 after suffering a stroke a few months earlier. Croly had been central to Lindeman's relations with *TNR*, so it is no wonder that his interest in the journal dwindled after Croly's death. He wrote Shaw that *The Survey* had asked him to join their staff, "but I am afraid that they do not offer me the kind of channel I want and need for my kind of interpretation of American life." Nevertheless, Lindeman did continue to contribute regularly to both journals.

Lindeman was also active in a group that revolved around the New School for Social Research on West 12th Street in the Village, a unique adult educational institution. The school regarded the worker's experience as the resource of highest value—the equivalent of the learner's experience in adult education. Soon after arriving in New York Lindeman had begun to teach worker's education classes there. Working at the New School led to contacts with a variety of stimulating intellectuals—Charles Beard, James Harvey Robinson, Thorstein Veblen, John Dewey, Horace Kallen, Roger Baldwin, Alvin Johnson, Lewis Mumford, Sidney Cohen, Harry Elmer Barnes, and Charles Merz.

The New School was attempting to combine a research center and a school of adult education that would express a progressive, rational, and scientific outlook on society and its problems. It would provide freedom for a group of social scientists, untrammeled by grades, degrees, departments, and academic organization. Lindeman was one of many social scientists attracted to the school because of its emphasis on both research and teaching. Croly and Straight were the school's chief backers, providing both support and financing.

The school's golden era began with its founding in 1919, when historian James Harvey Robinson, philosopher Horace Kallen, sociologist Thorstein Veblen, and historian/sociologist Harry Elmer Barnes lived in the apartments for faculty, and Lewis Mumford gave the famous lectures about American architecture and civilization that became known as "Sticks and Stones."

Writing about the New School in *The New York Times*, Nathan Glazer alludes to the "remarkable group of scholars, many of whom were Jewish refugees, socialists and liberals who had been brought to the New School in the thirties by Director Alvin Johnson. Most had been dismissed from German universities by the Nazis. Many remained prominent on the faculty of the school for the next thirty years."[17]

In addition to writing, teaching at the New School, and working with numerous organizations, Lindeman spent much of the time between 1922 and 1930 working for The Inquiry, another unique project backed by Dorothy Straight. Bruno Lasker, secretary of The Inquiry from 1923 to 1928, associate editor of *The Survey* from 1917 to 1923, and lifelong friend and adviser to Lillian Wald of the Henry Street Settlement House, recalled the early days of The Inquiry:

> It was around 1923 when a number of people who had served overseas after World War I in the YMCA, or in social reconstruction, or had been a member of the government in some capacity or other, felt there was something fundamentally wrong in the American approach to problems in human relationships, in class relations. So they decided to set up an organization known as the National Conference on the Christian Way of Life, which later came to be known as The Inquiry.[18]

Not surprisingly, The Inquiry had a strong influence on Lindeman, because its members used newer methods embodying the lessons of recent experiences in adult education and the adjustment of group conflict. The Inquiry also provided Lindeman with a way to continue his research in the area of cooperatives and conflict resolution. Moreover, it was under the auspices of The Inquiry that Lindeman began his study of the adult education movement both in the United States and abroad. Associated with him in this effort were, among others, E. C. (Ned) Carter; Dwight Sheffield, described by Gessner as "a penetrating and gentle intellectual," professor at Wellesley College and executive secretary of The Inquiry's Industrial Relations Commission; Mary Parker Follett; Bruno Lasker; John Hader; John Dewey; Robert McIver; Rhoda McCullough; and Reinhold Niebuhr.[19]

John Hader credited Mary Follett with influencing Lindeman the most during The Inquiry years. She had pioneered the theory of "brainstorming," although the term, according to Hader, had been coined by Alex Oxborne. This was a vision of the committee process in which no negative ideas were recalled; only creative, new solutions based on the widest possible participation were generated. Lindeman joined in The Inquiry's work until 1929, and his 1934 book *Social Education* was a history of that remarkable organization.

During the years Lindeman was working with The Inquiry, it was clear that he was already overcommitted. In an interview with Stewart, Hader recalled that when Lindeman was chairman of the industrial commission he was often unavailable when needed for advice and guidance. On one occasion Hader complained to Croly that Lindeman was "not minding the ship" and that as a result The Inquiry was suffering. When Lindeman learned of this from Croly, he made it clear to Hader that he should have come directly to him with the complaint. Hader felt that Lindeman never stood still and allowed himself to get involved in too many things. "Maybe we'd meet some day passing from one train to another. We used to have to hold conferences in a taxi." If only Lindeman had been accessible, perhaps Hader would not have felt the need to speak to Croly.[20]

Perhaps the most important book Lindeman wrote during the first decade he was in New York was *The Meaning of Adult Education*, written in three weeks in June 1926. It was not long after this publication that adult educators claimed him as one of their own and he gained the reputation of "Father of Adult Education." Stewart suggests that this label may have been "overly broad," as this book was the only one Lindeman wrote on adult education. Strangely enough, though, it remains the only book on adult education written during the 1920s that is still commonly read and prized by American adult educators today. Stewart wrote, "It would be Lindeman, rather than his numerous and often eloquent contemporaries, who would set the mainstream course generally followed by American adult educators for the balance of the twentieth century."

In *The Meaning* Lindeman wrote: "A fresh hope is astir. From many quarters comes the call to a new kind of education with its initial assumption affirming that education is life . . . not a mere preparation for future living. . . . This new venture is called adult education not because it is confined to adults but because adulthood, maturity, defines its limits." As Stewart points out, "These were not the opening sentences, but followed one overlong and pedestrian paragraph and another, still drab and rambling, paragraph." There is not even a definition of adult education; the writing is uneven, "with ideas popping up" that appear to have no connection with the subject matter. Stewart calls it an "eccentric volume" with a "quirky style." What's more, the book did not even break new ground; the ideas were hardly original with Lindeman. Given these flaws, one wonders how to account for the "massive impact upon the nature and direction of adult education in the United States." The answer, Stewart suggests, lies in "creative synthesis. As a social philosopher he largely facilitated, rather than invented, adult education theory. His mind was fertile and quick, and he used it to popularize (in the best sense of the word) the concept of adult education." Stewart believes that Lindeman's four basic assumptions about adult learners "undergird much of mainstream thought and practice in America today" and that "contemporary empirical research tends to be the essence of his assumptions, and contemporary adult educators are challenging the established education order. Issues stemming from Lindeman's assumptions are prominent on the agendas at meetings of Adult Educators."[21]

Although *The Meaning* was his sole book on adult education, Lindeman published many articles and monographs on adult education throughout his lifetime. One of these was his article in a 1928 special *TNR* edition on adult education, which Stewart believes "heralded adult education as a new means of social change for liberals. . . . [Lindeman] took his cues from John Dewey, citing 'intelligence' and 'ideas' as the supreme force in the settlement of social issues."[22]

Considering the health and emotional problems Lindeman faced during this period, as well as a proliferation of responsibilities and commitments, it is difficult to comprehend how he could have been as productive as he was. The writing of *The Meaning* in such a short period was an amazing feat. In chapter 9 we saw that during the year 1926 alone, he was the principal editor for *The Survey's* special issue on fascism; and from September on, he was busy teaching at both the NYSSW and The New School. In addition to *The Meaning* he published two other books, *Today and Tomorrow*, which he dedicated to Porter Lee, and *The Future of Experts*. During this one-year period he also published articles and book reviews in *The New Republic, Journal of Applied Sociology, American Review, Homiletic Review, Rural America, Saturday Review of Literature, Social Forces, Cooperation, American Federationist, Worker's Education*, and, finally, *The Survey*.

In addition to his prolific writings of 1926, Lindeman traveled to North Carolina and Virginia, lectured at Bryn Mawr and in Cleveland, attended a conference in Washington, D.C., and was a delegate at both the World Congress on Adult Education in Copenhagen and the League of Nations in Geneva.

Judging by the quantity and quality of his work, the period 1922 to 1935 was easily the most productive of Lindeman's career. Despite the distractions of so many activities, the heavy commuting schedule, his inability to say "No" to organizations seeking his membership, and the setbacks due to ill health (between 1926 and 1930, especially), he published six books besides *Social Discovery* (1924) and *The Meaning of Adult Education* (1926). These are *Urban Sociology: An Introduction to the Study of Urban Communities,* coauthored with Nels Anderson (1928); *Dynamic Social Research,* coauthored with John Hader (1933); *Social Education: An Interpretation of the Principles and Methods Developed by The Inquiry—1922 to 1933* (1933); and *Wealth and Culture* (1936).

Such activity and productivity was not without its sacrifices, however. By living fifty-four miles away from New York, Lindeman had committed himself to twenty years of commuting and to leading a schizophrenic existence with the Hudson River symbolizing his two distinct lives. In a letter to Dorothy on July 21, 1923, he expressed the conflict he was experiencing by this double life: "New York has taken me in, but there is an unreal quality about it and I'm not sure I'll ever be an integral part of it. I feel I am destined to be *to* and not *of* city life and ways. I move in simple ways, and nature must be included in my responses." He loved it in the country when "the sharp winds blow across the hilltops, but therein lies the conflict. I still feel something illuminating and excitingly romantic about traveling from High Bridge to New York City." This conflict between country life at Greystone with his family and his "other life" in the city deepened as his life became more complex.

But not only was the weekly commuting and leading his "double life" taking a toll. Lindeman was also in great demand as a lecturer. He jokingly told Shaw that that was how he could afford to buy a car. Considering the ample time he spent away from home on lecture tours it was ironic that Lindeman was frequently invited to speak on family life. On these occasions he would stress a "habit of humor" as an important ingredient to a happy family life, as well as a condition of democracy. If one was going to live happily under the free conditions of a democracy, he would say, one needed a perspective of humor.

95

Lindeman proved to be a powerful speaker and an entertaining one as well. He had a captivating and irresistible sense of humor. He loved puns and clever witticisms, and he had an inexhaustible repertoire of jokes to fit almost any occasion. Chuckling as he told a story, his audience could not resist laughing along with him. He had formed the habit of jotting down jokes and bits of humor in a scrapbook of American humor, containing his favorite jokes of the nonsense and surrealistic variety. He planned to publish it one day. Unfortunately, the scrapbook was lost in a New York taxicab, and he tried frantically to retrieve it.

Lindeman introduced humor into his classes too. He was partial to the American humorists, and he stressed the relationship between humor and the democratic experience.

Meanwhile, by the early 1930s the United States was experiencing a severe depression. Even in the small village of High Bridge the only bank had closed its doors. John Dewey, alarmed by the prospects of another winter like that of 1931, wrote to Lindeman in June that he dreaded to think what would happen if nothing was done. He suggested a special appeal to Hoover as a humanitarian, stressing the terrible conditions of children.

Lindeman's concern for the country's bleak economic situation was growing steadily every day. By January 1932 he wrote the Elmhirsts, "Our economic situation does not improve. Our four largest cities are bankrupt and treasuries are in the hands of bankers. All around me the nation has collapsed, and I am anything but hopeful about our immediate future. This may be our hardest year." But even worse, the country was losing faith in itself, and its energies were all bottled up: ". . . and there we are, timid, weak, hesitant and filled with fear. What we need is the courage to experiment."[23]

According the Saul Pett, in 1932 "there were fifteen million Americans, one quarter of the work force, hunting for jobs that didn't exist. Middle-class people were knocking on back doors for handouts, and farmers with shotguns were fighting off deputies with foreclosure papers. By noon of March 4th, 1933, every last bank in the country had closed its doors. 'We are at the end of our string,' said the outgoing Herbert Hoover before yielding office."[24]

It was a great moment when Franklin Delano Roosevelt took command in March 1933 with the words, "This nation asks for action and action now!" The new president, standing for the swearing-in ceremony with his legs locked straight by steel braces, raised the hopes of every man and woman in the country. Lindeman was no exception. He watched FDR preside exuberantly over a nation in upheaval. As Pett wrote, FDR "entered people's homes with a style and a guile, cigarette holder tilted ever upward, with principles and expediency and a rare aplomb that delighted his adorers and outraged his enemies—unmatched since Lincoln."[25] FDR possessed the courage Lindeman had been saying the country so badly needed. Since he too was an improvisor and experimenter, he admired the pragmatic approach of the early FDR, who tried this and that, and if one approach failed, tried something else. When he saw that the poor could no longer remain the sole responsibility of voluntary social work, he welcomed the shift from the private to the public sector.

The country got action—unprecedented action—during the first one hundred days of FDR's administration. Lindeman focused his attention on the Civilian Conservation Corps (CCC) and the Tennessee Valley Authority (TVA) in particular—the CCC because he observed the youth at work in his own hometown, and the TVA because of its agricultural and recreational resources benefitting all the people in the region. He also watched with interest the enactment of the Works Progress Administration (WPA) legislation. He became increasingly concerned that a too-hasty transition from Federal Emergency Relief Administration (FERA) grants-to-states to WPA rolls was creating unnecessary suffering for needy families.

In June 1935, barely one month before Sally Ringe walked into Lindeman's office unannounced, a copy of a letter from an old friend from Texas, Valerie Keating, director of social services in Texas, had come to his attention. Keating, along with other state administrators, had been told by Aubrey Williams, assistant administrator of the FERA, to cut her caseload. When her June allotment had been slashed drastically, Keating wrote Williams:

> You have cut our budget so much that we cannot provide even minimum food to maintain health, let alone any of the other items FERA indicated as necessities for preservation of life, much less maintain a semblance of morale and decency. Our allocation for June was less than 45% of low-cost adequate food budget, with no allowance for medical aid, clothing, or emergency utilities, shelter, transportation, etc. I ask you, Mr. Williams, is this one of the social injustices against which you would have social workers raise their voices?

97

I appreciate the intense strain under which you are working. But I confess that I feel less regard for your physical or mental strain than I do for a certain one million Texans who are undergoing a strain much worse than yours and mine — hard and long though we may have worked — tense and nervous though we have become over the last two years.

After reading Keating's letter, Lindeman knew that he wanted to put his expertise to work to solve some of the nation's problems. But how?

# Chapter 11

# Lindeman and the New Deal

*The bells no longer ring for the New Deal,*
*at least I don't hear them, and I can't*
*stay long where there are no bells.*

Lindeman, 1938

When Sally Ringe called on Lindeman on a hot day in July 1935 to offer him the job of director of the Works Progress Administration's (WPA) White Collar Projects, she thought it unlikely that he would accept. Both Harry Hopkins, director of the WPA, and Eleanor Roosevelt had tried unsuccessfully to persuade him to come to Washington.

Ringe had first met Lindeman during an education seminar led by John Dewey in the Caribbean, and she knew his predeliction for bold and experimental adventures. She told him both Jake Baker[1] and Harry Hopkins wanted him to direct this exciting new WPA program involving recreation, adult education, and the arts. He was the only man—and the right man—for the job. Besides, if he did not accept, someone from the National Recreation Association without Lindeman's commitment to all three areas would get the job.

Lindeman hesitated. He had a full-time job teaching and was already overcommitted. He also had always avoided administration; he was no bureaucrat. Although a shrewd observer of politics, he thought he would be uncomfortable in a strictly political arena. Furthermore, working in Washington would increase his already heavy commuting schedule. Traveling to and from New York City, High Bridge, and Washington, D.C., every week would be an exhausting routine.

On the other hand, there were compelling reasons, stemming from a strong feeling of patriotism, to consider this job. Of all the New Deal programs, Lindeman found the WPA one of the most appealing. And he liked Hopkins, whom he had known since 1929 when the brusque, gangling idealist headed up the first state emergency relief program in New York state. Hopkins and Lindeman came from a similar background and experience with boys' and girls' clubs, and although neither had professional training in social work, they shared a similar philosophy concerning people in need. He especially liked what Hopkins had said in Detroit in June 1933 at the National Conference of Social Work — that relief was an obligation of the federal government to its citizens, a sacred right, not an act of charity.

The program Ringe described seemed tailor-made for him. He thought of himself as an applied social philosopher, living his philosophy and transmitting his ideas. Now he would have a chance to apply what he had been preaching most of his life. What's more, this position had an irresistible feature: a belief that work, any kind of work, was better than idleness, and it was the responsibilty of the government to furnish work when and if private enterprise was unable to do so. This was an exciting concept, and he accepted the job.

Lindeman's decision to join the ranks of the New Dealers was entirely consistent with the philosophy that had guided him in all of his earlier career decisions. First of all, his WPA job would involve adult education, a field about which he had been researching, writing, and teaching for thirteen years. Also, his early interest in recreation, dating back to 1915, had evolved into a concern for the role of leisure in a democratic society. In his book *Time On Their Hands,* Gilbert Wrenn credits Lindeman with an important role in the recreation movement for well over a decade.[2] Not only did Lindeman view leisure-time planning as an important part of social policy, he also saw its individual and cultural implications. Now, at the policy level, he would have an opportunity to design a program to meet both the need for gainful employment and the constructive use of leisure.

Additionally, he would bring to this new job a strong commitment to social planning, which he saw as the practical application of philosophy. He had long been interested in the relationship between planning and freedom. And along with other New Dealers, he had been encouraged by the philosophers of the 1920s — Thorstein

Veblen, Charles Beard, and John Dewey—to have faith in social planning.

When Lindeman arrived in Washington in November 1935, the New Deal had already changed considerably from the nature of its measures and underlying thought of 1933 to 34. Lindeman arrived in the midst of the New Deal's second phase, when it was riding high and Washington was reeling with excitement. The excitement peaked in January 1937 with the second inauguration of Roosevelt, characterized by his famous words, "I see one-third of a nation ill housed, ill clad, and ill nourished." According to Gertrude Wilson in her speech "Experiencing Living History," America was once again rediscovering its poor, as it does periodically "with a sense of shock."[3]

The New Deal attracted a new breed of dedicated public servant—idealistic men and women who were willing to work for miniscule salaries, thus earning the title of "Dollar-A-Year Men." Robert Sherwood describes them as "lawyers, economists, college professors and social workers who were prepared to use intelligence as an instrument of government." He credits Harry Hopkins, Frances Perkins, Frank Bane, and Lindeman, among others, with providing the social work profession a certain credibility it had not previously enjoyed. The New Dealers brought with them "a bravado, élan, cocky assurance and inexhaustible activism, which was infectious."[4]

And so it was that Lindeman, too, was swept up in the excitement. Barely one month on the job he wrote to Charles Shaw, "You won't believe this and neither do I, but I, who have consistently avoided administrative responsibilities because I thought myself lacking in the essential gifts, must now supervise 20,000 employees—leisure-time workers—and when I sign orders calling for the expenditure of millions of dollars, I often ask myself, is this fantasy or reality?" What fascinated him most was coordinating the four Federal Arts Projects—music, theater, art, and writing. "Both of my jobs—the leisure-time programs and the arts—strike at the heart of the American cultural dilemma," he wrote. "Of course we have our critics. The main thing is to get nationally known names to head up each project and then thunder back at the critics!"[5] Almost unwittingly, the New Deal, by the late summer of 1935, had launched the most extensive program of government support for the arts in the history of the nation.

101

At the same time, however, Lindeman faced a couple of problems. Concerning the confirmation of his appointment, Roosevelt and Hopkins were enthusiastic supporters, but others were not. "Mr. Randolph Hearst campaigns against me," Lindeman wrote Shaw in November 1935. "My appointment was supposed to go to the Senate, but because of partisan politics, Hopkins thought best to wait until the Senate adjourned for the holidays."[6] Therefore it wasn't until December, after Lindeman had been on the job one month, that Roosevelt personally approved his appointment.

Another embarrassing problem was deciding what to call his project. Lindeman originally suggested "Community Organization for Leisure," but when the U.S. Treasury nixed that name, he chose "Recreation and Education." "But that only led to another difficulty," Lindeman wrote Shaw, "because the Treasury insisted we make a sharp distinction between what was recreation and what was education. . . . I jokingly said that the easiest way to distinguish between them was this—'If the chairs are fastened to the floor, it is education; if the chairs are movable, it is recreation.' "[7] A legal advisor in the Treasury believed the definition serious, and, "with endless difficulty," Lindeman was obliged to correct the misunderstanding.

Lindeman's staff described the WPA in the fall of 1935 as a scene of intense activity and confusion. Men and women with sleeves rolled up worked over desks piled high with papers and placed wherever there was space. Messengers ran from one building to another among the nine buildings occupied entirely or partially by the WPA, and from office to office inside. The staff knew no set office hours; lights burned to the early morning hours, elevators ran all night, and telephones rang past midnight. Hopkin's colleagues believed it was his ability to get the most from his staff that made it into a working organization.

Despite the initial bureaucratic hangups, Lindeman enjoyed himself immensely, so much that by April 1936 he urged Shaw to join the WPA's Writer's Project, which was preparing an exhaustive travel guide. "You too might wish to be a Dollar-A-Year-Man! But," he cautioned,

> my external life is all action—with very little sense of direction yet. [But] I wanted this experience of working with a huge governmental mechanism, and it is grand discipline for me, but its satisfactions, as far as the inner life is concerned, are meagre. One's private life

disappears the moment one enters government service, and as I grow older, it seems to me that significance attaches primarily to thought and not to action.[8]

Nevertheless the action in Washington continued to absorb and challenge Lindeman for several months to come. Six months on the job he wrote Dorothy, "My Washington work grows more exacting and more satisfying. We now have 33,000 persons at work on leisure-time projects, and 39,000 in the various arts. Two nights before the President's vacation I dined with him and his family. . . . FDR wants me to go into politics, but I flatly refused. My present plan is to get out when the year is completed."

But by July 1936 he wrote Dorothy that Hopkins wanted him back the next year to supervise all educational as well as recreational projects. "I'd like to continue if it could be financially profitable. I know I shouldn't hesitate, but one's patriotism does get strained. I suppose I shall heed the call."[9]

Although Lindeman's entire staff was loyal and hard-working, the greatest share of the work load fell to his administrative assistant, Sally Ringe. In an interview forty years after the demise of the program, she tried to put her finger on what it was that had made the program so exciting and worthwhile.

If there was one deep influence attributable to Ed Lindeman, it would have to include both his philosophy of leisure and of community organization. You see, Ed understood what had to happen on the . . . community and neighborhood level to make the program work on such a grand scale, with local options and local participation. . . . He knew [the program's] broad educational value to individuals and communities in a democratic society. Just think of all the folk music and the slave histories we recorded that would have been lost to civilization. And the WPA Guides and Historical Surveys of the Writer's Projects that stimulated a renewed interest in America, in rediscovering American roots, and reaffirming a national identity and pride.

But the important thing here is that the program employed thousands of unemployed artists, writers, musicians, actors, and craftworkers; preserved skills that already existed; and created new skills where none existed before, thus generating a new potential employment field. We hired minorities, constructed facilities for blacks, conducted year-round training programs—but always, the focus was on

103

finding jobs for those, who, in turn, would help local communities set up programs to offer people a fuller and better life.[10]

Byron Mock, another staff member, recalled that Lindeman was a good friend of both Eleanor and Franklin Roosevelt and therefore had easy access to the White House. Mock remembered one special occasion when Lindeman was invited to dine at the White House as the Roosevelts' only guest. On the day of the dinner Lindeman told Mock to cancel the invitation because he suddenly remembered he had tickets for the baseball game. "Mr. Lindeman! You can't do that!" Mock said. "You're invited to dine with the President and his wife. You are the only guest!" But Lindeman told him to call the White House secretary and ask for a rain check. He did, but he never imagined anyone would do a thing like that. Mock felt Lindeman saw these occasions as purely social events and not as opportunities to further his own personal or political ambitions, stressing that he was far from being a political animal.

Mock was also fascinated watching Lindeman moderate a panel discussion, noting his ability to motivate commentary and summarize and synthesize points for effective dialogue. Lindeman's communication skills were evident in policy implementation as well.

He dictated policy and program without seeming to push his ideas, nor did he wish for credit personally. . . . Yet, he was instrumental in promoting a union for federal employees—a totally new concept at that time. But Ed Lindeman was a man who said what he thought and was not afraid of recriminations. He felt that if government was to become a primary employer of large numbers of people, then those employees must be protected against employers' abuses. Otherwise a bureaucracy could soon become one of the most unfair employers.

What Lindeman said was not always compatible with the backdrop of his time. He believed in democracy and the democratic process more than most people.[11]

As Mock stated, this was a very brave and dramatic period, critical in American history. He felt that the WPA's innovative, creative projects provided new energy sources, including Lindeman's projects in the arts, theater, music, and writing, that in some instances still enjoy success today. Lindeman himself summarized the WPA's influence by writing "Leisure—A National Issue: Planning for the Leisure of a Democratic Society," referred to by Wrenn as a "culmination of a decade of social thinking in the field."[12]

A similarly optimistic view was expressed in *Fortune* magazine's comprehensive appraisal of the WPA in its April 1937 issue. This article concluded that the lesson learned from WPA projects was that work relief was infinitely more popular than financial relief and that men and women need jobs fitting their training and experience. It also stressed that the federal government had made a commitment to the arts and to recreation for the first time in history. The government's experiments in music, theater, dance, literature, and arts created a revolution in America that brought audiences face-to-face for the first time with artists. The Federal Arts Projects had filled a vacuum.

This positive mood darkened, however, as this *Fortune* article reported that it was also quite clear that Roosevelt and Hopkins now had their minds elsewhere. Indeed, warning signs were emerging that trouble lay ahead for Lindeman's programs and the entire New Deal itself. Threats from inside and outside the New Deal contributed to its demise. Strong anti-New Deal forces capitalized on Roosevelt's abortive and divisive attack on the Supreme Court and on the 1937-38 recession, calling the art and theater projects "boondoggling" and ridiculing the notion that they were effective. Finally, the menace of war abroad coupled with the opinions at home of Texas Representative Martin Dies, chairman of the House Un-American Activities Committee forced the restructuring and eventual demise of the WPA. In June 1939 the Federal Arts Project was dismantled, and soon the theater project terminated in a flurry of criticism and controversy.

As Roosevelt and Hopkins turned their attention to the worsening international situation, some critics thought they had abandoned the New Deal programs. Certainly, those people who had labored long and enthusiastically for their programs felt they had been dealt a terrible blow—Lindeman included.

By December 1937 Lindeman's disillusionment with Washington politics, and specifically with Aubrey Williams (deputy WPA administrator under Hopkins) and Hopkins, was clear when he wrote Shaw that "the inner pull is gone and every decision a burden. I have been required to dismiss 20,000 employees, one half of my workers. Congress, at one stroke, has swept away half of our

105

program's accomplishments over the past four years." He was already thinking of leaving and suggested to Hopkins that he find a replacement. In notes entitled "A New Dealer Criticizes the New Deal" that he jotted down while lecturing around the country, he cited what he disliked most about the political arena:

> outsmarting the opposition, the hidden-ball tricks, the lack of forthrightness, the use of legalisms, the Machiavellian touch, the careless use of means (the end justifies the means), cynicisms re political machines, faulty political machines, faulty public information re bureaucracy, centralization, TVA, WPA, Federal Social Security Administration, and Taxation. Therefore, first class leadership cannot emerge, can only go just so far and no farther.[13]

Real disillusionment had set in when Lindeman wrote to Marion Beers in early 1938, "The bells no longer ring for the New Deal, at least I don't hear them, and I can't afford to stay long where there are no bells."

The White Collar programs died slowly and painfully, accompanied at times by bitter and vicious infighting. Lindeman chronicled his bitterness, sorrow, and pity in his correspondence.

> Aubrey[14] tells me you may be back in Washington after your long illness. I shall be very happy to see you and to feel that you are assuming leadership. Events move so rapidly these days and decision-making procedures become more and more complex. (Letter to Hopkins, March 1938)

> I must eliminate myself from this madhouse. My few brief hours last week left me confused and bewildered. Do I know the answers? (Letter to Beers, May 1938)

> I'm so glad the Reorganization bill passed at least one of its barriers. Now I feel I may wish to stay on in Washington for awhile; otherwise I shall leave as soon as Hopkins allows. (Letter to Beers, June 1938)

> I've resigned again. Harry has my resignation in his hands and I am wondering what he'll do. I imagine he'll say—"Well, if he wants to get out so badly, why in hell doesn't he just get out!", and that will be the end of that. My own date is December, 1938. (Letter to Beers, August 1938)

My last visit to Washington was almost fatal and now I'm not sure whether I'll come back again before my exile. (Letter to Beers, December, 1938)

Washington seems so very far away, almost unreal. It's queer how I come and I go, and it doesn't seem to make any difference. Everything is in such a terrible mess, I have the terrible feeling I have wasted four years of energy. I want to get as far away as possible, and as quickly as I can. (Letter to Beers, March 1939)

I came to Washington on the 16th and have the feeling this will be my last official visit. My services have ceased, although I have not resigned. I simply can't stomach the new bill, and everything that I wanted for the cultural projects is now impossible. I still believe that the problem of unemployment is our greatest problem, and our greatest danger. The WPA is lacking in statesmanship. (Letter to Hopkins, September 1939)

About the WPA, I am so sad I cannot talk. The collapse from within is too terrible. Has the New Deal been suspended until after the election? Is the disease which has struck the New Dealers chronic, malignant, or merely a rash? Is there any sound reason for me to ever revisit the Capitol again? (Letter to Beers, July 1940)

Lindeman was a sadder but wiser man for having participated in the agonizingly slow processes of government. Frustrating as the experience had been, he continued to devote his energies to the task of fostering a better democratic society. These words were written by a man who had literally "been through the mill" of a giant bureaucracy but who was not toally disillusioned: "Democracy represents an ideal which will never be realized. Imperfect individuals cannot build a perfect society. None of the democratic goals get fully realized. But—let this not be an argument for their abandonment!"[15]

And Lindeman in 1950, as chairman of Americans for Democratic Action, showed that his opinion of the New Deal experiment had mellowed even more over the years:

Those of us attracted by the spirit of the New Deal will be constantly tempted to revive both the spirit and the method of that daring adventure in progressivism. But we must remember that a new generation of voters has now come upon the scene. These younger citizens

107

must be given the opportunity to dream their own dreams. We cannot ask them to be loyal to something they have not experienced. Besides, the situation in the United States today is likely to call for an approach quite different from that of the New Deal.

In this same speech he summed up his experiences by saying, "I was privileged to serve in a program so unique, so new, so daring as to preclude all reliance upon precedent. One of those audacious, pioneering ventures which have characterized American life in its critical moments; so American, it grew right out of the American soil when climatic conditions were just right."[16]

Obviously Lindeman was proud of his programs—and no wonder. By 1939, 7,000 local communities had WPA recreation programs in 15,000 job locations, and over 6,000 of these had no other source of organized public recreation. Each had its own local advisory committee, providing a firm anchor in the community. At the height of its activity the recreation program employed 60,000 persons who conducted leisure-time activities and trained 140,000 relief clients for some type of recreation leadership.

One of Lindeman's admirers, A. S. Casgrain, wrote in a 1953 letter to Lindeman:

Your influence on public and private recreation through the WPA program has been so far-reaching that even today we see evidences of its influence as we tour the country. It took your leadership and your philosophy of education, recreation and planning—quite in conflict with professional recreationists—to channel such a program away from the traditional and into something more intensely a part of people's lives.[17]

Forty years later, members of Lindeman's staff remained convinced that the program, Community Organization for Leisure, had indeed made a lasting, significant contribution to the fields of adult education, recreation, art, music, writing and theater.

# Chapter 12

# Marion

*. . . so, Marion dear, keep vigil in*
*the long silences.*

Lindeman, 1937

Beginning with Paul Unger in 1973 and then four other of Lindeman's WPA colleagues over the next four years, I was told repeatedly that I had to look up Marion Beers "because she was a very good friend of Lindeman's." That was all I knew, except one colleague, Howard White, did say that Marion at one time was one of the most powerful women in Washington and that she and Supreme Court Justice Felix Frankfurter were good friends because of their common interest in the South.

I made a mental note to try to find out more about Marion Beers but had done nothing about it, when quite by accident I came across a copy of a letter from Robert Gessner addressed to Marion Beers Howden, dated August 10, 1954, in Columbia University's Butler Library. The letter inquired if she might have any correspondence or information that she would be willing to share with him. Marion replied a week later in a letter that when she married Colonel Howden in 1941, she had destroyed most of her letters from Lindeman, but she was sending Gessner about forty letters that happened to have been stored in a metal box and didn't get burned. She said she had carefully screened these and thought they might have publishable excerpts.

Responding to Gessner's request that she say something about Lindeman, Marion wrote, "What can one say? That ECL was the most admirable and deeply cherished person in my life? That it was a great shock, after the first delight of seeing his name on the cover of the *Saturday Review* in May, 1953, to open the magazine to his article, only to learn that he had died?"[1]

Marion's letter also mentioned that she had visited Lindeman in New York, had attended his stimulating classes, and that he epitomized for her "the ideal teacher, throwing out challenges to students, treating them as intelligent adults."

Gessner returned the letters a few weeks later, writing that he felt a vitality in the letters that was "typically and excitingly Lindeman." He assured her that in the editing process he would exercise discretion and judgment, "not too hard to do when one loved him as we do." In deference to Lindeman's family, he scarcely quoted from the letters at all.

Consequently, I had no idea of the content of the letters or of the nature of Marion's relationship with Lindeman when I telephoned her in San Francisco in October 1975, to ask if I might talk to her about Lindeman and to inquire about the letters. She was extremely cordial, informing me there would be no problem with letting me see the letters and inviting me to visit her at her home on Presidio Avenue.

I was, I thought, about to interview yet another in Lindeman's coterie of women admirers. But as I pondered her words to Gessner — "the most admirable and deeply cherished person in my life" — I wondered if this relationship had been different from the others.

Marion greeted me warmly at the door of her renovated Victorian townhouse and ushered me up the long, winding stairs to a second-floor living room where we were to talk. A striking woman in her early sixties, she wore her slightly bluish, grey-white hair swept back from her face into a chic French roll, dramatizing her smooth face with its high cheekbones and flawless complexion. (I found myself remembering that Lindeman had extremely high cheekbones and that he admired them in others.) She immediately put me at ease by speaking briefly of herself, then she abruptly asked if I would like to see the letters. As she handed them to me I asked her to relate how and when she had first met Lindeman.

In her soft, low voice Marion told me that they had met at the National Housing Conference held at the Mayflower Hotel in Washington in February or March 1935. In the early 1930s Lindeman had been both a member of the advisory committee to the National Housing Association and chairman of the educational committee of the New York Council on Housing. Marion had been in Washington since 1931, working for Nathan Strauss, an official in the U.S. Housing Authority.

110

"I looked up and found your father staring at me," she recalled. "Then I looked at him, and this went on throughout the evening." As soon as the meeting was adjourned Lindeman walked up to her and they started talking. A friend of hers who knew Lindeman asked, "Do you two know each other?" "We both said 'yes' at the same time, although of course we hadn't met — formally." Afterward the group went to dinner and danced. He brought her home, where they talked and read poetry until two or three in the morning. That was the beginning of a continuous relationship, sustained by telephone calls and lots of letters from 1935 to 1941.

After that they saw one another frequently in both Washington and New York. "We loved to go out to dinner. We loved to talk. He had a superb sense of humor and was a marvelous conversationalist. Always he had something interesting to talk about — like his Key West vacations where he met Ernest Hemingway, and bumping into Pauline Hemingway at the Union Station. And then he brought me some beautiful watercolor paintings of Key West done by Robert Hallowell of the WPA art project. (Hallowells had hung on the walls of Greystone for many years, and later in the Lindeman's New York apartment.)

"Sometimes we would just sit at the table and play games. One of our favorite pastimes was watching other couples dancing and speculating about their relationships. He loved to dance and was a marvelous dancer. I wasn't so bad myself.

"But much of the time we were together we read. He would read aloud. I loved to have him read because he had such a beautiful voice. I was touched when he read *The Yearling* to me when I was ill.[2] No one . . . could read Archibald MacLeish's poem 'America Was Promises' like your father. I felt very privileged."

"Did you ever hear him speak?" she asked. Not waiting for my answer, she continued, "He was so eloquent, a great deal of poetry in his prose. You could hear the alliteration in his speech, and it was natural to him, but the end result was very poetic, musical, and soothing. I don't know of anyone, of all the public speakers I've ever heard, who had that kind of precision and nuance, just right for a particular point he wanted to make." She said that a friend of hers, a professor at the University of Pennsylvania, had told her that Lindeman had the greatest platform presence in the United States.

111

She described Lindeman as a sort of Pygmalion who gradually became her mentor, molding her opinions in subtle ways and having a powerful influence over her unformed philosophy. He told her she had wisdom, even though she insisted this was not accurate. "I was anything but wise," she told me. "I was barely 22 and he was 50." She had gone to Washington from Montana at the age of 18, to seek her fortune "in Horatio Alger fashion." During her early years there she attended George Washington and American universities "in a desultory fashion" but never graduated.

She and Lindeman talked a lot about wisdom. "I think he had a real understanding of basic wisdom as distinguished from information. 'Anyone can have information,' he would say, 'but wisdom, no!' He had great respect for people who educated themselves, and not too much respect for the educational system, in the sense that he felt people were processed to get degrees, but were not necessarily educated. I guess that's because he grew up the hard way, educating himself." I nodded.

"Did he ever talk much about his favorite sage, Emerson?" I asked.

"He certainly did," she replied. "He saw Emerson as a very profound philosopher and a humble man. Emerson was one of his gods. The great goal of his life was to write a comprehensive book about Emerson." I nodded. "And when [his] small paperback came out on Emerson, the year he died, he inscribed a copy to me saying I would find a few goldfish among the ideas.[3] I felt he had a great deal to say about Emerson. It disappoints me that he was not able, as far as I know, to finish the [comprehensive] book." I told her that an incomplete manuscript had been found, with the last chapter missing. "What a shame, what a shame," she sighed, and paused a moment and then asked, "What was it like?"

"Actually, it was a very interesting and unique analysis of Emerson as a pragmatist, a realist, a radical democrat," I replied, "not the usual Emerson the transcendentalist." Her eyes lit up when I told her I had sent the manuscript to McGraw Hill and the editors there had thought it very beautiful. Unfortunately, despite thinking that it had relevance for today and offered a new view of Emerson, they declined to publish it. Revisions would be required, they said, and the last chapter would have to be found. However, they did feel it deserved to be published by someone. "Perhaps he never finished the last chapter," Marion said. We were both silent for a moment, wondering if this could have been the case, or if it somehow had been lost.

Marion broke the silence. "I think your father was one of the truly great people who had humility, and, as he always said, without humility you are not truly great."

Changing the subject, I asked her to comment on Lindeman and the New Deal. "Did he talk much about the WPA program, and how did he feel about what was happening in general in Washington?"

"Well, he quickly became disillusioned when Hopkins became Roosevelt's intimate confidante and representative abroad and got into that Mayflower social crowd, which your father felt was a contradiction to Hopkin's background in social work." Marion pointed out that in fact they had all shared in the disillusionment, just as they had all shared in a tremendous dedication. They felt they were not only contributing toward the economic recovery in this country, but also moving the country toward a more equal opportunity for all.

Marion had not been a part of the WPA, but she told me of her dedication to the housing movement. "I felt the home was the crux of everybody's life, and that if we could improve the living conditions of the poor, the chronically poor, those relegated to slums, it would mean we wouldn't have generation after generation consigned to poverty. That is, we would have a leg up, as it were—no more cold-water tenements or toilets shared by fifteen families. For many years of my life I continued to feel that housing was the most important thing there was, so I couldn't imagine a day of my life when it wouldn't be important."

She reminded me that by broadening the concept of mere shelter to include recreation and participation, Lindeman had actually made a very important contribution to housing. "When your father's program ended, many of his staff came to work for the housing program with me. They made an immense contribution because they had been trained in his philosophy—to understand the human factor, the need to set up all sorts of community relations programs within the local housing authorities."

I asked Marion if she thought that, as Lindeman became more and more disillusioned with the New Deal, some of his idealism also faded.

"Well, the feuding among the departments was very distressful to him. He was not a man who liked controversy at all, and he found it hard to be openly critical. He was too tolerant to be condemnatory; in fact, he would withdraw from a situation rather than try to correct it. I thought it was a rather singular approach," Marion commented. I had heard this from other of his WPA colleagues. Some resented that he would not fight to maintain his department.

Then very softly she said, "Of course, I knew him as a man, very warm, tender and intuitive. I did not know him as a colleague. I never thought of him as a fighter. But I did know that he knew what it was like to be cold and hungry and discriminated against."

By now it was late; we had talked for over two hours, and I did not want to tire her. I had already concluded that their relationship had been very intense and intimate for about six years. Now only one thing remained unanswered: how did their relationship end? "Did it, then, suddenly end in 1941 when you married Colonel Howden?" I asked. "Were you able to end it in such a way that you could remain friends?"

"Oh, we remained friends," Marion answered. "We communicated occasionally by phone and by correspondence, and when he was going to Texas he made a point to go by way of San Francisco so he could spend some time with me. My husband understood that Lindeman was a very important person in my life on a continuing basis, and he would get his mother to babysit so I could have dinner with Eduard alone."

She recalled vividly their last meeting when, in the summer of 1952, he had stopped in San Francisco on his way home from Oregon. "He was not well, but he never complained about his health. Always, he put on a good show. He came to my house and stayed about an hour. I think he came because he knew I had become estranged from my husband, and that I was going through a difficult time. He knew, because I had written him, that we had just about reached the stage of divorce. I was feeling that my marriage had been a mistake. I guess, between the lines, I was trying to tell him in my letters how sorry I was for having walked out on [our] relationship. I think he understood that it was a very difficult thing and that I wasn't equipped to handle it indefinitely. It was such a nebulous status, and I didn't know what to do. On the one hand this, and on the other hand that.

114

I think I spent most of my time during those five or six years talking soliloquies."

Her marriage to Howden had been an impulsive thing. She had seen her husband as a younger version of Lindeman, but she realized it had just been wishful thinking on her part—"the result of an inner despair. You see, when you care for someone so profoundly, you are always torn."

Marion was silent for a few minutes. I realized it must have been very hard for her. Then in a wistful tone she said, "But I did not see how he could have walked out on his marriage."

"Did [Lindeman] ever say anything about his wife?" I asked. She said it was curious, but it never bothered him; that is, he did not feel a sense of guilt because Hazel had a friend of her own who lived nearby, a male friend of the family with whom she played tennis frequently.[4] That was all Marion said, and I did not ask any more questions.

I thanked her for the interview and left. I visited Marion again in 1977 and 1979, then early in 1982 I learned she had died after her third heart operation.

I now had before me thirty letters Lindeman had sent Marion from 1935 to 1940—only a small sample, knowing he was a prolific letter writer. Letters during the first two years of their friendship, 1937 through 1939, are missing completely. We can assume that there may have been several hundred letters in all. Whether Marion actually did burn the letters she did not give to Gessner, or to me, we will never know. What we do know is that she felt those few letters she did share had "publishable excerpts," which may also mean that they were the least personal. In any event, the remaining letters constitute a believeable record of their relationship. They are sincere, tender, and loving reflections of a deep and long-lasting relationship. Viewed in the context of my interview with Marion in 1975, they appear to be an accurate testimonial.

The telephone, mail, and wire service served as the prime means of communication between Lindeman and Marion. Even their more intimate greetings and farewells took place in train stations or airports. By 1937 it was clear that lines of communication had broken down: "The phone rings," he wrote her, "but you don't answer." And, "If you feel inclined, drop me a note but don't feel under

115

any obligation." The messages are ambiguous. "I may come to Washington this week. If I do you will get a wire. But, don't let it interfere with your other plans." Marion wondered whether she should sit by the phone and wait for a call or make other plans. The sheer logistics of arranging meetings in New York or Washington constituted a common theme throughout the letters.

A paternal tone, much like that Lindeman used when addressing his children, pervades his letters. "Stay sweet, hear?"; "You're a dear, you know"; "No, I'm not scolding. I keep worrying about your health."; "Marion dear, do take a little care of yourself, hear?"; and "Be a good girl, Marion."

The letters also illustrate Lindeman's growing concern about his health. There can be no doubt that he was profoundly disappointed at the return of active pain and suffering. It is not certain whether the "imponderable black moods" he describes are caused by physical illness, or vice versa.

Loneliness is another persistent theme, as well as references to brooding and low spirits. Both Marion and Lindeman discuss the ups and downs of the relationship, and the conflict Lindeman feels about it. Never does he make reference to a permanent relationship, except once when he facetiously closes a letter by saying he wants to be a part of her "permanent collection." Meanwhile, Marion feels she is in a state of limbo and incapable of handling this indefinitely.

Finally, Lindeman's letters also reveal his concern with family matters (the cooks, fall, weddings, illnesses), the Spanish Civil War, and the welfare of his WPA programs. He is genuinely concerned about Marion's health and thinks she is working too hard and should take better care of herself. He frequently advises her to read a book that he has read, relating it to a particular event.

## 1937

There are only four letters written during the year 1937, including one in March from Buffalo, where he was giving a speech at the National Conference of Social Work on "New Patterns of Community organization." In this letter he apologizes for not coming to Washington after all, saying he was not coming next week either ". . . and that will make a long, long time." He asks her to please read *The Life and Death of a Spanish Town*,[5] saying it was her kind of book.

Another letter in March was written from Greystone, in which he tells her of his proposed western jaunt, saying he hates to be going off without seeing her and, in fact, does not want to go in any sense.

He is disturbed about the fate of the loyalists in Spain, saying ". . . Can it be true that the ruthless shall inherit the earth? There must be some honor for the resolute and free." He recommends that she read Borgese's *Goliath,* for she would then know more clearly "from what dark pools of history Fascism comes."[6]

A letter written April 9 from Greystone expresses how much he misses her and that Washington seems ". . . a very, very long way off." He had been ill with the flu and is still feeling "rocky." He is leaving for Boston and might come straight to Washington afterward, but it is uncertain. He hopes she would not postpone a trip to New York too long and would write him at the Gramercy Park Hotel and mark "HOLD." He is writing a book review of Mannheim's *Ideology and Utopia* and another on T. N. Whitehead's *Leadership in a Free Society.*

A fourth letter, also from Greystone, is dated December 23. In the midst of last-minute corrections and additions to his Indianapolis paper for the Conference of American Association of Advancement of Science on "The Utilizaton of Human Resources," he wants to wish her a Happy Christmas. "You are a dear, you know, and you do deserve happiness." He wants to buy her a little trinket as a token but prefers to wait until they can be together, ". . . when there will come one of those sudden impulses and I shall say 'Today is Christmas again!' "

As for his program, apparently he has made some sort of a compromise with Aubrey Williams, which has left him unhappy. "The inner pull is gone and now every decision is a burden." He urges her to come to New York, especially to El Chico's, offering to pay half the cost as "your impulsive Christmas present. Be tentatively happy, fractionally good, and completely loving all through the holiday season, hear?"

117

# 1938

There are ten letters written by Lindeman to Marion in 1938—from Chicago, the International House in Berkeley, Beth Israel Hospital in New York, the Gramercy Park Hotel in New York, and the Hotel Statler in Boston. This correspondence clearly indicates that he dislikes Washington more and more and has threatened to resign. He asks Marion why he should stay on "in this madhouse."

At this point it should be noted that Lindeman spent six weeks teaching at the University of California in Berkeley in the summer of 1938. He wrote his daughter Doris and her husband Robert Gessner that during this period he gave "two lectures a day to 200 students, gave 22 speeches before other audiences—especially unions, had daily conferences with graduate students averaging 12 a day, played 64 sets of tennis and drank 75 glasses of beer," saying that he had set a record and had "never worked so hard in all his life. At last it is all over, and now comes the let down."

It is interesting to observe that while Lindeman was writing to Marion from Berkeley how much he missed El Chico's, the New Yorker, and Johnny Shaw's dance platform, he was at the same time writing the Gessners that he had changed—that the "weird speakeasy epoch" was over. I believe that is further evidence of the ambivalence he may have felt about his relationship with Marion.

He wound up his western tour in San Francisco, writing Marion on August 23rd that he was making lots of speeches and "talking housing all over the lot. You know I do believe that housing is our most important single reform of the present."

By November he was in the hospital with a clogged vein that the doctors called thrombosis—or lymphatic infection caused by an infected blister—and was feeling miserable. He was in low spirits brooding about "my country and my world," but more than that he worried that he may be "slowed down indefinitely. It may mean that the two forms of movement that I love the most, dancing and tennis, will henceforth have to be enjoyed from the sidelines. (Although the thrombosis was serious, and he was in a great deal of pain, he was soon able to play tennis and dance again—for a few years, at least.) For the first time, he mentions Marion's "flares" and that he shouldn't be surprised when the "flares flare-up in my face." He then adds, "If I were capable of 'flares' myself,

118

I'd be much more sympathetic with other flarers." (This is a puzzling statement in view of Wyatt Rawson's letter to Lindeman in 1926, in which he mentioned that Lindeman had confided in him about his "flare-ups," and Rawson had advised him to get some help.) Apparently the relationship was not going smoothly, and Marion's outbursts may have indicated her increasing frustration with their arrangement.

## 1939

Nine letters were written during 1939, starting with a short note from Greystone prior to Lindeman's and Hazel's departure for what was to become their annual vacation in Key West and/or Bradenton Beach, Florida.

The 1939 letters indicate that the relationship had entered a new phase—a new direction—or at least they were working on it. The new phase had friendship as its base. It meant that from now on they would try to be friends and keep their hurts to themselves. Of course, it was not always possible. In one letter Lindeman admits he had already betrayed his own principles at breakfast with her. And if she were willing to forgive him, she could blame it all on the fact he was feeling miserable most of the time. Also, he tells her she "deserved happiness and ought to get married" and he "ought to have nothing to say about such a decision," nor should she "be influenced by [his] feelings or dispositions. . . . If you need to be a trifle abrupt in telling me, that's all right. I know this will come."

In June he scolds her for not taking better care of herself, noting that she had been in a bad mood lately, and when she is in one of her moods she takes it out by working harder and harder until she is exhausted.

Sooner or later the inevitable was bound to happen. Lindeman found he could not have it both ways forever, and Marion could not go on indefinitely in limbo.

## 1940

Of the six letters from 1940, one was written from Winnetka, Illinois, one from Kansas City, and four from Greystone.

By 1940, Lindeman was certain Marion was seeing someone else. He makes reference to the Colonel in one letter. He invites her to the World's Fair, speculating whether she would come and saying she may have "mortgaged a portion of her heart to someone else." He refers to their fateful "faux-pas" and says that he had never felt so unwanted. One can only speculate that their signals somehow got mixed, and when he arrived on the scene he found her with the Colonel. Nevertheless, he writes that he wants to preserve and honor their vow "to cling to friendship, natural and disinterested affection."

In the last letter, dated December 23rd, he tells her that she remains vividly in his heart and mind and that he hopes she is not working too hard, is having some fun and gaiety, and "retain[s] an enduring kindness for him."

In the fall of 1940, Lindeman announced his last official visit to the capital.

A few months later Marion married the Colonel and moved to San Francisco.


It is interesting to note that before the 1930s Lindeman's closest relationship with women, platonic or otherwise, tended to be with women his own age, or perhaps a little older (e.g., Harriet McGraw of Detroit, Sue Hibbard of Winnetka, Mrs. Caldwell of Montclair, New Jersey, possibly the Mrs. C. mentioned in chapter 6, and Dorothy Straight Elmhirst). I think it may have been during the 1930s that he began to seek out the company of younger women the age of his daughters; or perhaps they sought him out. Although Roger Baldwin was certain he did not have affairs with his students, John Hader thought otherwise, pointing to an occasion when Lindeman was using his apartment in New York during his absence. Hader unexpectedly came home a day early and, according to Hader, found Lindeman with a young woman who he was quite sure was a student. This remains another matter of conjecture. I did know that on occasion he took some of my college friends, those who lived in or near Greenwich Village, dancing in his favorite night clubs. I believe my sisters and I thought it was quite innocent, and I have no knowledge that it was not. We certainly did not suspect that he was having affairs (other than with Mrs. C.).

120

Eduard (portrait-type) sometime in the early 1940's

Now in retrospect I think it quite possible that it was because of Marion that Lindeman continued to come to Washington long after submitting several resignations, feeling like an exile and unhappy about Washington politics in general. It is also evident that he encountered problems in keeping the relationship a secret. Letters allude to attempts to avoid discovery by using the Gramercy Park Hotel as a delivery spot for Marion's letters. But this was not always possible, since one or another of his four daughters was living in New York City during some of those years. On one occasion, my sister Barbara was with a friend in a New York night club when she suddenly looked across the dance floor and saw Lindeman dancing with a young blonde woman. When he spotted her he came over and asked her to dance, later introducing her to his companion.

My contacts with my father in New York during the late 1930s were few. In view of the fact I lived in the Village not far from where they apparently spent some time together on West 23rd Street during several of those years, attended the World's Fair on numerous occasions, and dined and danced in Village night spots, it is strange that I did not happen to bump into him. But I do have one vivid memory.

Quite late one evening I received a telephone call from my father. He wanted a place to spend the night and asked if I minded if he came right over. I could tell by his voice that he was upset, but of course I had no idea why, and he did not want to talk. We were ill at ease with each other, partly because I had no bedroom and we had to sleep side by side on two beds that came out of the living room wall, and partly because he was too upset to talk.

Now that I know about Marion, I believe this must have been one of those times when things were not going well between them. He found himself unwanted and on his own, needing only to "crawl off by himself," but not be alone. As he had written Marion, there were times when he wanted to be with someone but did not want to talk. I was close by, and I was alone.

I am convinced that Lindeman's relationship with Marion was the most meaningful and long lasting of his love affairs; in fact, it was probably his last. I am equally certain that he never seriously considered divorcing Hazel. Marion, in a desperate attempt to extricate herself from an impossible situation, walked out on Lindeman.

# Chapter 13

# A Lifestyle Ends, A War Begins

*We—and our allies—are involved in a task for which there is no historical precedent or parallel—the occupation of a defeated nation with the avowed purpose of rebuilding that nation.*

Lindeman, 1945

Lindeman's life was to change profoundly during the 1940s. With the advent of World War II he and Hazel moved from Greystone—the only home they had ever owned and where they had spent the last twenty years—to New York City in 1942. The move itself was difficult enough, but it also signaled the end of a way of life. Lindeman was no longer the commuter, and the Hudson River no longer separated his two distinct lives. The end of his double life was also marked by Marion's marriage and abrupt departure to San Francisco in late 1940. These events put an end, I believe, to Lindeman's affairs with other women.

When gas and oil rationing went into effect after Pearl Harbor, Greystone was not only impossible to heat, but transportation to and from the station had become an insurmountable problem. I suspect there were other reasons for leaving as well. Greystone must have been lonely for Hazel with the children grown and gone and Lindeman away so much of the time. His health may have also been a factor, since his doctors were located in the city and he needed to see them more frequently.

"When they left Greystone just after Pearl Harbor," my sister Ruth told me, "Mother never showed her sorrow as much as Dad did. It was one of the few times I had ever seen him cry. I can still see him walking out alone to look at the garden . . . one last look. They threw out so many of their cherished belongings—even the oil portrait of Dad, which luckily I recovered. It was as if they were leaving the past behind and starting all over again."[1]

123

Eduard and Hazel Lindeman

The move to New York also marked the beginning of a new and different relationship between Lindeman and Hazel. "Soon after they moved," Ruth wrote, "I sensed a new kind of intimacy between them and they both seemed happier."[2] Hazel, who had seldom accompanied Lindeman on his trips around the country or abroad, now on occasion would join him.

Their new home in New York City, where they would live together for the next eleven years and where Hazel would remain until 1972, was an eleventh-floor, two-bedroom apartment located on East 22nd Street. With its several doormen, elevators, miniature courtyard, and traffic noise below, it was very different from quiet Greystone. But the apartment had several distinct advantages. It was only a short stroll to the New York School, historic Gramercy Park, and the Gramercy Park Hotel, where Lindeman enjoyed lingering over lunches with students, faculty, and friends. Their new quarters were also close to intracity transportation, as well as to a number of small, interesting ethnic neighborhood shops and restaurants.

They already had compatible friends in New York, and soon they made many more with whom they could play bridge, permitting Lindeman to continue his impetuous bidding. On the weekends they would ride the First Avenue bus to play several sets of doubles at "Rip's" congenial courts. (Gessner claims Lindeman was always self-conscious riding the bus in his tennis whites.) Lindeman's tennis was still steady, reliable, and forceful. They both enjoyed watching tennis matches in nearby Forest Hills, where Lindeman liked to sip a scotch and soda from the deck of the tennis club. Complete with pipe and beret, he soon became a familiar figure at both courts. Of course he and Hazel missed Greystone and the camaraderie of their own tennis court, but having Rip's courts and Forest Hills so accessible helped ease any homesickness. Lindeman still missed his landscaping, though yearning to work in his own garden.

Along with a significant change of residence were major shifts in Lindeman's intellectual life during this time as well. It is not surprising that Lindeman, who called himself a teacher, was slowly developing into a social philosopher. His relationship with John Dewey had flowered twenty years earlier, and he credited Dewey and Mary Follett for turning him into a pragmatist. Dewey and Lindeman shared winter vacations in Florida, and I know Lindeman had at least one invitation to Dewey's summer cabin in Nova Scotia.

Lindeman served as Dewey's best man at one of his weddings. Their relationship lasted until Dewey's death in 1952.

For Lindeman the move to the city was a reminder that he had only eight more years at Columbia before mandatory retirement. Now he had reached a point in his life where he no longer needed to travel in the same heady intellectual circles that marked the 1920s and '30s. The excitement of Village bohemian life was clearly behind him. His hair was thinning and almost white, and he was fast becoming the elder spokesman for educators and social scientists.

As his mouthpiece on social issues, Lindeman had begun to use *The Survey* and *The Graphic* more and more as *TNR* ceased to be the powerful influence it had been in the early years. He had an idea for a special issue on the arts, religion, education, and social welfare. "Even the President has promised me he will call a White House Conference on Art and Leisure some time next year," he wrote Kellogg, of *The Survey*. Moreover, FDR had even indicated to Lindeman that he was thinking of a separate government department to represent art and leisure. Excited about the prospects of a cultural awakening, Lindeman suggested to Kellogg that they act as "an evangel."[3]

The idea, typically Lindeman in its broad scope and originality, was greeted with enthusiasm by the editors of both *The Graphic* and *The Survey*. By 1937 Lindeman had spoken to FDR about the special issue. FDR encouraged him because he liked the idea of artists rubbing elbows with plain folk, and he wanted to take credit for the Federal Arts Project which had taken American art away from hushed galleries into post offices, courthouses, schools, hospitals, and city halls, and which had enabled music to be heard by farmers in Minnesota and laborers in Pennsylvania. Unfortunately, however, by the time "The Social Meaning of Art" finally emerged in the spring issue of *The Survey Graphic*, it was 1939, and the Federal Arts Program had already been dismantled. Lindeman's introduction, "Something Has Happened," addressed the questions, What was accomplished by the federal government's intervention into the arts? and, What did it mean to the artists, musicians, actors, writers, and American communities? In addition there were articles by Stuart Chase,[4] Robert Hallowell,[5] Lewis Mumford,[6] and John Dewey.

However, Lindeman's dream of a new cultural awakening in America did not come to pass, at least not in the form of a department to represent arts and leisure—an idea he had sold to FDR. Right-wing critics' accusation of "communism" had contributed to the downfall of Lindeman's program, and the impending world war took precedence over any internal programs. But *The Survey* and *The Graphic* continued to invite "Lindy," as he was affectionately called, to submit ideas because they felt he had his finger on the pulse of things throughout the country and because his ideas were fresh and creative.

Other dreams also never came to fruition. One was to write a book about Emerson portraying him as a modernist, even a radical democrat. Lindeman's absorption in Emerson, which began in the early 1930s, led to the incorporation of Emerson into his courses in philosophy and American culture. Over the years he had coerced his librarian friend Charles Shaw to send him rare editions of Emerson's journals and essays. Also, in 1934 he had stayed with Emerson's grandson, Raymond Emerson, in his home in Concord. His lectures on Emerson around the country were soon followed by articles, which in turn led to the publication of *Basic Writings of America's Sage*, published by Penguin in 1947. (Penguin Publishing Company soon became the New American Library.) He was especially pleased when Penguin's publisher, Victor Weybright, invited him to join their editorial staff, a position he thoroughly enjoyed.

Lindeman conceived of the idea of Mentor books—inexpensive, paperback volumes of philosophy, science, politics, and literature. In addition to his book on Emerson in 1947, he introduced *Science and the Moral Life* (Max Otto, 1949) and *Reconstruction in Philosophy* (John Dewey, 1950). In 1950 he edited *Plutarch's Lives* and co-wrote with T. V. Smith *The Democratic Way of Life*. Gessner thought that the mornings Lindeman dressed to attend editorial sessions at 501 Madison Avenue were happy mornings, ". . . as he sailed forth to select books which would be read by millions."[7]

The 1940s may have brought changes in Lindeman's life, but membership in several organizations was not one of them. At the time he left Greystone, he was president of the New Jersey State Conference of Social Work and the state's Social Planning Commission; advisor to the White House Conference on Children in a Democracy; member of the Birth Control Federation of America, the Child Study Association, the National Urban League, the

National Planning Association, and the American Civil Liberties Union, to name a few.

He had difficulty turning down organizations who wanted not only his name on their letterhead but his active participation as well. New Deal colleague Paul Unger wrote me that at times Lindeman would say he was going to resign, and he actually would. Then within three months, he would be back on the board again. Gessner wrote that when Lindeman's entry in *Who's Who* reached eighty lines, he pruned it to fifteen. Sally Ringe told me that when he discovered a committee didn't "commit," he would resign. "I won't stay in that kind of an organization," he told her.

By 1940 Lindeman was becoming increasingly alarmed by a world at war. Always concerned with freedom, with the rise of World War II he shifted his concern from the world of arms to the question of how to preserve freedom in a time of crisis. He feared for the future of democracy and the democratic way of life. He wrote the Elmhirsts in May that the trend in the East was for providing full aid to the Allies, but in the Midwest the isolationist movement was very strong. "Last week I was about to deliver a Commencement address at an engineering college in Cleveland when the President came up to me and said: 'For God's sake, Lindeman, don't say anything about the war tonight, will you?' Of course I refused his request."

He had also been rereading Nietzsche's *The Gospel of Superman* and Hegel's *Philosophy of Right,* telling the Elmhirsts that it appeared that Hegel's glorification of the state and Nietzsche's of the strong and the ruthless "have at last combined to form a new German ethos." What troubled him the most was the existence in Germany of a whole "generation of youth who know no other orientation to life." He could only assume that a "collective form of psychosis had gripped the world."

In closing he told them that Washington had some particular task selected for him in case the United States went to war. "I will do whatever is needed, of course, in spite of the fact that I see war as more futile than ever." Although no evidence has come to light that someone did in fact have in mind a job for him, Lindeman continued to visit Washington.

One week before Pearl Harbor he was invited to attend a public dinner at the White House. After dinner FDR invited him up to his study where he told him he did not trust the Japanese and did not believe the Japanese ambassador was serious in talking peace. He told Lindeman he had notified his generals and admirals to be on the alert, that they might be attacked either in Hawaii or in the Philippines, or even on the west coast. Lindeman asked him how long he thought the war would last. One half of the admirals thought it would last three months, the other half believed three years. FDR said, "I kinda believe the three-year fellas."[8]

Correspondence between Hopkins and Lindeman in 1942, preserved in the Hyde Park Library, indicated Lindeman's intense desire to serve his country in some capacity or another. He wrote:

> I get all sorts of frantic messages from Washington from some of our old WPA colleagues who think I ought to be there working on the plans for recreation in the communities near war camps and war industries. I did it during the last war, you may remember. Thus far, I felt no special urge to plunge into that field. On the other hand, I don't want to shirk any responsibilities which belong to me. I hope you will tell me if you think there is something I ought to do. I trust your judgment.

Hopkins's amusing response followed:

> I presume by this time you must be older than God and that may make it difficult, but I fancy there are some ways of getting over these hurdles. I don't know much about the professional guidance set-up in Army camps nor do I even know whether it is run through Hershey, but I would think you ought, if possible, to find a spot in the Army or the Navy where your experience would be useful. Do you know Osborn or Hershey?[9]

I don't know if anyone in the family was aware of Lindeman's interest in serving in the armed forces, or if he pursued it any further. But his desire to serve his country, at age fifty-five and in poor health, may have been partly due to a wish to experience something of the war, just as younger men felt. The fact that he had been turned down for service during World War I may have also been a factor. And, as the post-World War II years demonstrated, he sensed a gulf between himself and the returning soldiers who became his students. A former student and advisee of Lindeman's from 1946 to 1948 at Columbia felt that he was "hungry for the experience of what it meant to be in the service.

He had, in a sense, idealized what the soldiers had gone through and wanted to get in with this group—but they weren't willing. . . . I don't think those years after the war were particularly happy years for him."[10]

If Lindeman was unhappy that he had not been able to serve in the war, he must have been very glad to accept a postwar assignment in 1945 for the British Army.

Lindeman was to educate British troops in occupied Germany to understand American democracy and the democratic discipline of self-government. Such a grueling assignment leads one to wonder why, at age sixty and his health even more precarious than at the outbreak of the war, he accepted (or even perhaps sought out) the short but difficult post of special lecturer and consultant to the British Army.

The following quotation in Lindeman's notebook suggests that he may have viewed this assignment as a challenge in much the same way he had considered the New Deal a challenge: "We—and our allies—are involved in a task for which there is no historical precedent or parallel—the occupation of a defeated nation with the avowed purpose of rebuilding that nation."

But another notebook entry reveals that he viewed this assignment as something more: "As a citizen of one of the nations which conquered an aggressive, war-mad, authoritarian Germany, I share responsibilities for the creation of a future democratic Germany." Lindeman's strong sense of duty may have been intensified because of his German heritage and his hatred of the Prussians. The overseas assignment also provided an opportunity to bridge the gap between himself and the returning soldiers, one of whom was his own son-in-law.

Moreover, this assignment was unique—the first of its kind to be offered an American—and ideal for a man often referred to as "the democratic man."

And so, September 23, 1945, Hazel, daughter Barbara, and a few friends gathered at Pier 90 in New York to see Lindeman off as he boarded the troopship *Queen Elizabeth*. His first destination was London, then on to Germany.

Lindeman reflected on his fellow passengers in his ever present notebook. Of the military personnel aboard, the officers "seemed uncommunicative" and the Royal Air Force boys "bright but cynical." The businessmen seemed to be "on the make." Secretary of Labor

Frances Perkins and Lindeman took occasional walks together after breakfast. She was full of opinions: Pessimistic about the foreign minister's conference then in progress in London, and discouraged over the U.S. discontinuance of lend-lease.

With the exception of a burst pipe that flooded Lindeman's cabin with steam and the dangers of floating mines, the voyage proceeded uneventfully. Six days after setting sail the ship landed in Southampton, and Lindeman checked in the next morning at the Office of War Information billet in London to receive his orders. He was directed to go to Germany after an eleven-day stay in London.

The time in London permitted him to see some of his old British friends and to give two lectures—one an "off-the-cuff" talk to the Allied Circle, and the other an evening talk to faculty of a university in Shrivenham. While in the countryside there he managed two early-morning bird walks.

His once-intimate friend Dorothy Elmhirst had scheduled a two-hour visit with him in her London flat. Their correspondence had waned during the last decade, and over the years they had grown apart. Lindeman continued his practice of writing an annual letter to the Elmhirsts, usually around Christmastime, but they contained less and less of himself and more and more about his views of American public opinion. I recall him saying he did not understand Dorothy's persistent preoccupation with the mystical and occult—an area that held no interest for him. And it is possible that Dorothy may have been frustrated by Lindeman's lack of attention to detail, habitual disorganization, and overextended commitments, which she had heard about from her American friends.

Dorothy offered Lindeman the use of her car and chauffeur "Fleet" to drive him about London and into the country. This generosity on her part enabled him to go to Shrivenham and later to Braintree, Essex, to visit Harold Laski, who had written, "Will you please tell Mr. Lindeman that, old and decrepit though I am, I do not forget my American friends." Lindeman's notes of their conversation indicate that the two men enjoyed discussing diverse topics ranging from the Labour Party's program and Prime Minister Ernest Bevin's vanity, Felix Frankfurter, *TNR* and the excellence of U.S. historians. Both men could not have been more pleased when, at the end of several hours of conversation, they discovered they shared a similar view of Emerson as one of America's greatest.

No visit to London would be complete without a visit to the House of Commons, especially now that there was a socialist Parliament with a working majority for the first time. Lindeman watched with interest while Bevin gave an account of the foreign minister's conference, after which Winston Churchill rose to inquire when Parliament would be permitted to debate the nation's foreign policy. When Bevin responded that it would be at least two weeks, an irked Churchill sat down in a huff. The session ended with the Labour Party asking for a five-year continuation of war controls.

On October 11 Lindeman departed Croyden Airfield for Germany, after noting in his scrapbook that some of the old British humor was missing—the sallies and the quips that he had enjoyed so much on past visits.

Upon arrival in Bükeburg, Germany, he was met by military personnel and whisked away to the devastated city of Hanover. He wrote the Shaws that the city had been destroyed in a mere forty minutes, and of its half-million inhabitants "there are still about half living in cellars and God only knows where. Their sudden defeat and collapse has stunned them and they haven't started to think yet."

In his scrapbook he noted that the soldiers were "a sorry lot, sullen, not much like Herrenvolk." To the Shaws he wrote that every night "some 1500 to 2000 refugees filtered through the Russian lines into the ghost city of Hanover. In a small area of the city there are 30,000 displaced persons, mostly Poles, who seem to be preoccupied with stealing and raping. What a mess it is! Only the small children smile."

On October 12 in Brunswick Lindeman gave his first lecture to an audience of 450 British troops assembled in a cinema studio that had once been a Luftwaffe building. The only light came from "a pale blue reflection which appeared to emanate from blue walls and ceiling," and he could barely see the faces of the men in front of him.

His next lecture on October 14 was in the quaint, medieval town of Goslar in the Hartz mountains, and there were 350 soldiers present. On the way to Goslar, he had noticed posters in various towns that read, "Think always of this. 'Whatever evil in Germany you may thank Hitler and his National Socialists.' Think always of this."

Fighting a bad cold, Lindeman then journeyed through the ruins of Hitler's Third Reich. By the 16th he was forced to cancel his speech in Hanover. The next day, however, his fever was gone and he was feeling well enough to visit some German elementary and secondary schools in Hanover. "What a disappointment!" he wrote. He was appalled by what he saw and heard. "The schools were cold, dirty and unesthetic. Teachers were middle aged, unmotivated, and taught by rote."

From Hanover he moved on to Hankesbuttel, headquarters of the first Lothians. Along the road he noticed signs saying "Mines cleared to hedges." On October 21 Lindeman's party passed through Belsen, "now mostly burned," where he could "smell the decomposed flesh and watch little boys poke around in the remains of the camps." It was a "grisly, gruesome sight."

In Bustehude a few days later, Lindeman experienced firsthand some of the hostility Germans felt toward their occupiers. He discovered glass in his breakfast roll, but not until he had swallowed some. A doctor prescribed medicine that would coat over the glass as it passed through his system, and the German police investigated the baker.

At the end of October Lindeman arrived in Hamburg, a nearly ruined city whose shipyards still had submarines ready for launching. He was delighted to find mail from home and a teletype from the U.S. Embassy that he had reservations on the *Queen Mary* for November 4.

During the seventeen days Lindeman spent in Germany, he delivered eighteen lectures to the over 5,000 British troops stationed in North Western Germany Army Corps 30. The territory covered was approximately 13,000 square miles, lying between the Elbe and West rivers, stretching from Hamburg on the north to Göttingen on the south. All his lectures followed a similar format, lasting 30 to 35 minutes followed by a discussion period of 30 to 60 minutes. In deference to the British he always began with a remark about statesman William Gladstone, then he described his own background. What he said about himself, we do not know, but the following outline for introductory remarks about his native land is from his 1946 scrapbook.

**AMERICAN FACTS**

1. U. S. is a land of opportunity but the frontier is closed.
2. U. S. is a bad place to be poor in; good place to be well-off.
3. We found a new discipline in: (a) The Great Depression and (b) The War.
4. People are ashamed of what we have done and still do to Negroes, Mexicans, and Orientals.
5. We are pragmatic and experimental.

The subjects of the lectures were public opinion in the United States with respect to either foreign relations (chosen in all instances except three) or domestic issues.

The bare outline of these two lectures follows:

(A) U. S. and Foreign Affairs
   (1) Difficulties involved in interpreting American public opinion. (2) Isolationism and its decline. (3) The New Nationalism. (4) The Demand for World Organization. (5) The Dilemma created by the Soviet Union. (6) Programs for National Defense. (7) How is America to Interpret Itself to the World?
(B) U. S. and Domestic Issues
   (1) Defining the American Economy. (2) The Full Employment Bill. (3) Expanding Social Security. (4) Conflicting Educational Aims.

The most exciting part of this experience for Lindeman came during the question period. "I found the men exceedingly alert, very candid and, although not always well-informed concerning American affairs, invariably fair-minded in their attitudes." Among the questions the soldiers asked were the following: What do Americans think of the British as persons? Will America furnish credit for Great Britain and on what terms? Do American blacks receive a good education? If private enterprise fails, will America be willing to move toward nationalization of its industries? Is not Soviet Russia justified in suspecting both Great Britain and the United States? Do Americans realize how the cessation of lend-lease has affected the standard of living in Great Britain? What is the current attitude of the United States toward Canada? To what extent is the British economy dependent upon America?

In Lindeman's final report to the British Army he wrote:

The interest of the men is genuine. I think I have never observed a better attitude toward learning than that exhibited by the students at Wyvern College, and I am quite certain I have never spoken to better audiences than those comprising the British troops in Germany. These men were animated by a deep concern for world affairs, their interest in British-American relations was keen, and they were always prepared to enter into a discussion. It is my impression that they aim to be informed in order to take an active part in civic affairs.

In general, Lindeman's British soldier audiences were good ones. And he credited the British Army with impeccable arrangements for hospitality and travel; he was well looked after during his illness. In spite of the success of the lectures and warm hospitality, by the end of October Lindeman was looking forward to his annual winter holiday in Florida. "I'm glad I came," he wrote the Shaws, "but I'll enjoy the quiet of Gulf Terrace and the Shaws more than ever after this experience in human degradation."

He flew to London on October 30 and occupied himself with travel plans and completed a final report to His Majesty's forces. In his report he noted:

> There are certain elements involved in carrying out an educational program for an army of occupation which deserve consideration. In the first place, the task of occupation is in itself an onerous one, and this is especially true when one remembers that demobilization and occupation must somehow be integrated. Military units are dispersed throughout the area, the educational officer is frequently absent, and there are formidable difficulties with transportation. Facilities for large gatherings are not always available. Finally there exists the fact that not all commanding officers have an enthusiasm for army education. The disparities created by this fact are marked.

In closing, he made a few "random suggestions":

1. It would be advisable to have visiting lecturers meet with the same group two or three times.
2. It would be beneficial if other American lecturers were to be sent to the British troops to prepare the men in advance by furnishing them with reading matter on American history and politics.
3. The education officers might be given complete information about the visiting lecturer in advance. This would be helpful in making introductions, and establish a quicker and warmer feeling between audience and speaker.

4. It would be advisable to arrange for district conferences between the various education officers and the visiting lecturer at the close of such a series as I have just now completed. The experience could then be appraised and plans for future experiments formulated.

At this point Lindeman may have felt good about the success of his British assignment, but he was not optimistic about the overall prospects for the future of Germany. After returning to the United States, he did not quickly forget the horror of what he had observed in Germany. Addressing America's Town Meeting of the Air on January 3, 1946, he cited Germany as an example of what happened when a modern nation "eliminates its sensitive and humane leaders and the degenerates come to the top and control." When he landed in Germany he said he had looked for "good Germans" and had found them, but there were a whining, defeated, discouraged lot.

Lindeman listened to the shocking testimony of the officers of Camp Belsen ("that most efficient human slaugterhouse") as they were being tried at the courthouse in Lüneberg. He concluded that they lived in darkness too long and that in order to de-Nazify Germany, it would be necessary to stop trying to teach democracy directly because "there is no soil in the German mind in which democratic ideas can grow."

Later Lindeman published two articles about his 1945 visit that revealed his deep pessimism about the future of the German people: "Death of a German Generation" in *TNR* and "Inside the German Mind" in the *Saturday Review of Literature*. In the latter piece he wrote that he found not the "slightest shred of evidence that Germans feel any sense of responsibility for the present world chaos." Most Germans believed that Great Britain had started the war and Germany merely fought a war of defense. "Through hatred of themselves," he continued, "they had at last realized their collective death-wish. The corruption and degradation of living Germans is complete." He knew this was a harsh judgment, but "so it is meant to be."

Some of Lindeman's colleagues who also visited postwar Germany held different opinions. Clara Kaizer was much more optimistic about Germany's future. She attributed Lindeman's extreme pessimism to the fact that he was of German descent and that

136

his parents had experienced Prussian brutality. She added that their differences of opinion had alienated her from him for some time.[11] Gisela Konopka also felt such extreme pessimism was not warranted.[12]

It is unfortunate that Lindeman did not live long enough to see the full economic and even moral revival of democratic West Germany. He would have been pleasantly surprised to have been proven wrong.

It should be noted, however, that in spite of Lindeman's pessimism about the future of Germany, he did encourage Baldwin to accept a similar invitation to visit Germany in 1946. Baldwin went and found the experience gratifying. "We were determined to do it . . . to teach the Germans democracy. . . . We were really determined!"

# Chapter 14

## Trip to India: A Haunting Experience

*The most exciting teaching experience of my career.*
Lindeman, 1950

Ten months away from retirement in 1949, Lindeman and Hazel went to India where he was to be a visiting professor at the University of Delhi. It was a special trip in many ways. Not only was he the first visiting professor from the United States to visit India since its independence in 1947, but it was his first trip to the Middle East and to India. It was also special because Hazel would be going with him — their first trip together since their holiday in Italy in 1925.

Lindeman's trip was sponsored by the Watumull Foundation and the YWCA of New Delhi. His mission was to consult on the development of a social welfare program for the new state and to advise on programs of higher education. Duties involved teaching a three-month course at the University of Delhi School of Social Work; lecturing in Bombay, Benares, Bangalore, Ceylon, and Mysore; as well as speaking to numerous other schools, colleges, and organizations in and around Delhi.

In spite of a very serious illness requiring hospitalization in 1948 (symptomatic of later stages of nephritis) and the exhausting nature of the proposed schedule, Lindeman was as determined to go to India as he had been to travel to Germany. He and Hazel must have known about the poor sanitary and health conditions they would encounter and the enervating tropical climate, plus Lindeman's susceptibility to infections. They were certainly aware of his need for a special diet. Since 1943 Hazel had, with dedication and patience, prepared and monitored his strict diet of raw vegetables and fruit, whole wheat bread, yogurt, cottage cheese, and buttermilk.

138

What then would induce him to subject himself to such risks? Gessner speculates that it was because of Lindeman's preoccupation with democracy, beginning with World War II and continuing until his death. Another reason may have been that India was in the process of writing a constitution and he would be able to attend the Constitutent Assembly to observe the process. Gessner thought that Lindeman wanted India to understand democracy and that America needed to understand India.

Moreover, 1949 was a good time for Western scholars and observers to visit India, before things got too formalized. Relations between Indians and Americans were flexible and idealistic, and Americans were still regarded somewhat as a novelty. It was also an exciting time to visit India because the country was in the early, transitory stages of its independence. Two years had passed since Gandhi's death, and Nehru was at the peak of his intellectual powers—serving as head of both its party and the government. The Indian government was still a coalition government consisting of members of the Congress Party and other notables selected by Nehru to give it a consensual character. Gessner was certain Lindeman also wanted to meet Nehru. Nehru was planning to visit the United States at the exact time Lindeman was to be in India, but their paths eventually did cross in India.

The Lindeman's first stop was London, where they strolled in Hyde Park and spent an evening at the theater. During a brief stop-over in Paris, they hired a car, drove to Versailles, and in the evening dined in the Bois de Boulogne. The next day they flew to Cairo, stopping in Damascus for one night.

Lindeman planned to visit social work centers in Cairo and later in Beirut, Teheran, and Israel. He was especially eager to visit Israel because he had been a strong advocate of a Jewish homeland. Unfortunately, he was able to observe only a few social welfare programs and to interview a few social workers in Cairo before he contracted a severe case of dysentery. "Poor Dad," Hazel wrote, "he didn't get enough to eat in Cairo, and what food he did get was all the wrong kind." Apparently the raw fruits and vegetables were not safe to eat, and nowhere could he find any of the foods he needed. After one week he and Hazel reluctantly decided it was best to go directly to New Delhi, where dysentery would plague him intermittently throughout their entire stay.

Despite the fact their plane arrived in New Delhi four hours late, the Lindemans were greeted by the head of the School of Social Work with a warmth and friendliness extended to them throughout their entire stay in India. They settled in their apartment suite in the Maiden's Hotel in old Delhi—ten miles from New Delhi but only a ten-minute walk from the University. The hotel suite, plus three meals, cost $12 a day for two people.

Hazel wrote that their living arrangements could not be nicer for an extended stay like theirs: "a huge bedroom-living combination, a big dressing room and a large bath, opening onto a wide balcony overlooking a lovely green garden, colorful trees and flowers and birds. And what is best of all, two tennis courts belonging to the hotel are right below us."

The next day the head of the department hosted a large dinner party for them on the lawn of the school, where Hazel noted there were "forty Hindus and about ten Americans from the Embassy." The next day a woman from the Embassy entertained them at a big tea party where they met more interesting people.

Because of the heat Hazel did not join Lindeman on his lecture trip to Benares. She did meet him, however, for a week in Bombay, where he delivered four lectures—one before the Presidency Women's Council on "Human Welfare in a Democratic Society," another to the TATA Institute of Social Sciences on "Social Philosophy," later to the Progressive Club on "Democratic Disciplines," and at the Bombay University his favorite topic—"Strengths and Weaknesses of American Culture."

By mid-October he was ready for classes to begin. He was to teach on Mondays, Tuesdays, and Wednesdays from 8 to 10 a.m., for a total of twenty-seven sessions, ending on December 14 when the school closed for examinations.

On opening day of classes he got his first impression of his students' thinking when a student raised the first question: "Sir, my question is in three parts: 1. What are the similarities between Henry Wallace and Mahatma Gandhi? 2. Have you ever been close enough to Mr. Wallace to touch him? and 3. Will the wicked millionaires who conspire against Wallace ever be brought to trial?" After that introduction Lindeman decided it would be wise to request written questions.

He was to say later that such questions, and similar ones, did not arise from any particular communist indoctrination among

140

Indian students, but rather from their enormous ignorance of American life combined with an incomplete understanding of the few facts that did come their way. In his contact with Indian students, he came to the conclusion that "perhaps 5% or less might be active Communists who follow the party line in their hostility toward the United States and about 20% were vaguely anti-American." The large majority appeared confused but anxious to learn more about the United States. Lindeman felt that much of their confusion came from idealism, a lack of knowledge, and an inability to reconcile idealism with what they read about America through newspapers and journals.*

After the first week of teaching Lindeman decided to divide his class of fifty-seven students into seven small discussion groups. This was a method much preferred by Lindeman but totally unfamiliar to Indian students. His purpose was to acquaint students with various discussion methods and to offer them an opportunity to translate his lecture material into terms applicable to Indian conditions. The students' initial response was to engage in a heated debate. When one student made a statement, the instinctive response of the others was to refute it. There was also a noticeable lack of discipline, with as many as five or six persons talking at the same time. They did not understand the role of the discussion leader, who more often than not would find him or herself in the very center of the debate. It took a lot of patience, but before the semester was over the students were able to work within these small groups, which began to function as true workshops.

Lindeman was pleased when the students produced documents of graduate-level quality. One was a plan for introducing parent education into an Indian village, with an observation chart or guide to be used in the study of village life in India. The chart grew out of discussions in which it was obvious there was a great deal of difference of opinion concerning the nature of village life. Lindeman

---

*Lindeman's measure of the influence of Marxist doctrine in India was essentially correct according to anthropologist Harold A. Gould, Professor Emeritus from the University of Illinois—also expert on Indian politics and culture. Some of Lindeman's remarks about communism in India should be viewed in the context of the cold war, which was just beginning in 1949.

encouraged them to gather a large body of material, including fiction, anthropological and sociological studies, as well as each student's observations. The class attempted to achieve a master observation sheet that diverse observers might use over a period of time and hence furnish more reliable facts about village life.

Toward the end of the course, the students were able to conduct orderly discussions in larger groups as well. But what was most satisfying to Lindeman was that they began to see learning as a process in which they might help each other and make use of their own experiences. (The adult education concept of learning from your own and others' experiences had been totally foreign to them.) Most of the students had become inured to the instructional method of passive listening, taking notes, and learning by rote.

At the end of the course Lindeman's students wrote him a letter, signed "Your Grateful Students," that in a personal and intimate manner reveals that he had been an inspiration to each one of them. His story of his own life had touched them deeply. From "your stimulating lectures and friendly discussions" they gathered a "fresh insight into the nature of social work" and its role in India and the "larger perspective of human relations." But they were especially grateful to him for having initiated them into the "difficult art and mechanics of group thinking and group discussion," enabling them to realize that it is not the "rightness and the wrongness of an individual's opinion that matters, but the opportunity for its expression; a basic presupposition of the democratic way of life." They were pleased to have learned the "mechanics of group thinking and group discussion" and "the role of the scientific method in understanding the complex social relations of man." They pointed to the fact that adopting a "scientific attitude" does not mean either the "denial or abandonment of moral values." On the contrary, "the scientific method alone will enable man to achieve these basic moral values."

The students mentioned too that they enjoyed meeting Mrs. Lindeman. And they did not forget to add how much they also appreciated their professor's "quiet sense of humor."

Professor Harold Gould, an expert in Indian affairs, has told me that if Lindeman were to visit India today, it is unlikely that students would express this kind of exuberant gratitude. Their letter seems almost quaint today in the light of the changes that have occurred on campuses of Indian universities over four decades.

Letters from the United States provided the Lindemans with their only link to home during their three-month stay in India. However, news was slow in reaching them, and their letters mailed from India did not always reach their destination because postal employees were tempted to steal the stamps and sell them.

They wrote home that the weather proved to be "torrid and tropical" and that they had to wait for cooler weather to play tennis. The "squalor and filth" was much worse than anything they had ever imagined, but underneath Lindeman felt "there was a spirit of hope."

The side trips took a great deal out of him. He was picked up at 4:30 a.m. to catch a plane for Benares. He wrote his daughters that while in Benares he had stayed in a university hostel with no running water. He shared a room with a student who a few days earlier had been bitten by a snake that had apparently crawled into the bed. The bite proved to be fatal. Besides snakes this was also malaria country, so Lindeman slept with a mosquito net over him. There were some queer people in the hostel, including a California woman gone native and an American student who was spending three years studying the "variables in the analysis of the Absolute in Eastern and Western philosophy." Lindeman could not resist kidding him: "Why study the absolute, because if it is absolute, it's finished and nothing can be done about it."

The Lindemans were not at a loss for friends and socializing; in fact, they were entertained everywhere they went. By October 9, after a week in Bombay, Hazel wrote that she had had quite enough of a social whirl for one week "and was glad to get back to Delhi, which "seems like home to us now." She much preferred Bombay to Delhi because of its location by the Arabian Sea and its relatively cool and less humid climate. Also, its beautiful harbor reminded her of the Bay of Naples.

Lindeman praised Hazel in his letters, saying she was a "good traveller, stays well, is interested in everything, never complains about the inconveniences, the dirt and the smells, and has her own inner resources." Lindeman wrote his daughters that if Hazel was put off by the "indescribable squalor of the refugees living in cages lined up on the sides of the business district," she did not complain. She did find the beggars a nuisance, "who sometimes kidnap children and maim them to get more money." They prevented her from walking on the streets. But she was touched by the

143

"friendliness and generosity of the Indian people who tried to make them feel at home."

They were unable to locate the buttermilk, cottage cheese, and raw vegetables that Lindeman needed, but he was making do with beer and cooked vegetables, and he wrote Max Otto that with the discovery of a native kurd "dahi," he felt he was keeping "relatively well."

When Lindeman was gone on lecture tours, Hazel admitted to being "a bit lonesome," saying "It isn't too much fun walking on the streets with the badly controlled traffic, cows wandering all around, camels drawing trucks full of produce, in addition to all the busses, tongas and people galore."

By early November the Lindemans were playing tennis every afternoon. But near Thanksgiving they began feeling a bit homesick. Holidays had always been a family affair. After the children were grown holidays were spent with them and their families. Lindeman wrote Ruth that Thanksgiving in India found them having roast chicken, mashed sweet potatoes, beets, spinach, cranberry jelly, and pumpkin pie on the lawn of the home of the labor attaché of the American Embassy. It was "a bit of America transplanted to the very heart of India." There were fourteen Americans, "mostly Embassy folk," and a few businessmen and their wives." They played bridge afterward, but once back in their own quarters Lindeman had some wood brought in for the fireplace and built their first fire. "I even rearranged the furniture around the fireplace and it really looks quite cozy," he wrote Ruth, adding how much he and Hazel missed the many pleasant holiday dinners they had enjoyed at her home.

Already they were thinking about getting home in time for Christmas. "We have our passage from here to Honolulu—but the rest is in doubt," he wrote Ruth.

Lindeman wrote Otto that he had a "fascinating journey to Madras, Ceylon, Mysore and Bangalore." He found Ceylon to be a lush, tropical island, "a perfect paradise for anthroplogists and sociologists." In one village alone he had found three types of families living together in peace and harmony—"monogamous, polygamous, and polyandrous."

In Madras Lindeman was the guest of the Maharajah, who wanted to talk philosophy. Lindeman had now worked out a chart that he used every time his students started "going off on the mystical tangent." He interpreted it with these questions: "1. If contemplation does not lead to action, how will you know whether you are building a chain of cumulative errors? 2. If action is not preceded or accompanied by reflection, how will you ever be able to formulate any goals?"*

In December Lindeman was finally able to meet Nehru. He was invited to attend a garden luncheon at Nehru's home. The guests included a well-known Indian woman politician who had spent some time in jail, Kamala Kmladvi; the highest ranking untouchable and minister for labour, The Honorable Shri Jagjivan Ram; and The Honorable Dr. B. R. Ambedkar, minister for law and one of the main creators of the Untouchable Movement, which advocated that untouchables become Buddhists and reject the policy of untouchables. Also present were Dr. A. Appadorai, secretary general of the Indian Council of World Affairs and a prominent intellectual in India; David G. Mandelbaum, professor of anthropology from the University of California at Berkeley, one of the first to study India; Beatrice Pitney Lamb, a journalistic scholar then with the United Nations and author of a book on India; Shri C. P. Ramaswami Aiyar, a renowned Indian figure, mixture of scholar and politician; and Chancellor Arthur H. Compton, Nobel Prize physicist from Washington University, St. Louis.

Lindeman wrote Otto that he would have been greatly amused at the odd conversation that took place in the garden with Compton and Nehru.

Compton, as you know, has become very religious and at lunch he tried to involve Nehru in a religious discussion, but the Prime Minister dodged. In the garden, after lunch, I was talking to Nehru when Compton stepped up and a moment later a philosopher from the University of Calcutta joined our group. Compton began: "I can't

---

*According to Professor Gould, Lindeman's discussion about the Indians' preoccupation with the mystical in lieu of action does not take into consideration the fact that the art of contemplation is viewed in India as a kind of action; in fact it is action designed to transcend action. Hindus equate immortality with the annihilation of all attachment to mundane existence.

145

understand, Mr. Nehru, why you don't realize that we must depend upon God in the world's present condition." Nehru: "I wish you wouldn't use the word GOD. It is a bad word. It has no meaning for this time and age. It merely confuses issues." He then turned to me and said: "Lindeman, you teach philosophy. Do you tell your students to depend on God for solving today's problems?" Lindeman: "No, I'm not on familiar terms with the gentleman called GOD, and I agree with you that his name is a bad word." Nehru to the Indian philosopher: "How about you? Do you teach God to your students at Calcutta?" Indian philosopher: "Well, not exactly, but I do believe in the concept of GOD. God can have meaning for our time." At this point, Compton interrupted by saying: "What have you got to counter Russian communism with if you abandon GOD?" And then others, noting our heated discussion came over to listen, but that ended our talk because a messenger had arrived to inform Nehru that he was expected to participate in an important debate in the Constitutent Assembly and he had to move on.

Five days after the meeting with Nehru, the Lindemans left India. They were disappointed to have to decline a repeat invitation from the Prime Minister for dinner on December 20. The formal invitation had read: *The Prime Minister AT HOME on Tuesday, the 20th of December 1949, at 6:30 p.m. at the Prime Minister's House. RSVP Invitation Office, Government House, New Delhi.*

They stopped in Honolulu, where on December 20 Lindeman gave a report on his India trip to the YWCA. At a luncheon sponsored by the Watamull Foundation, at the country club on the 21st, he spoke on India's foreign policy. He also told them that of what he saw of India, this small school of social work seemed to him the most hopeful and constructive unit. "India needs technical assistance of all varieties, but perhaps none more poignantly than aid in dealing with complex social problems. Methods now in use are not merely outdated, but are of such a character as to perpetuate rather than diminish the problems." He praised the dedication of the faculty and the students of this pioneering school. Specifically, he recommended "high-grade, supervised field experience, training in research," and "more medical social workers, who must be trained quickly and in large numbers."

The Lindemans departed Hawaii on December 24, arriving in time to spend Christmas with their family. The next day Lindeman had an acute gall bladder infection and spent two weeks in the hospital, finally undergoing surgery on February 8. In letters to his family and to Otto, Lindeman had not mentioned a gall bladder attack he had had while in Madras. The first mention of it was not until his January 18, 1950, letter to Otto, when he wrote that in November a German doctor in Madras had diagnosed the attack as gall bladder, but the next morning he felt all right and hence distrusted the diagnosis. He had to admit now, "The doctor was evidently dead right."

He wrote Otto that he had returned home twenty pounds lighter, felt weak, and was not sleeping well. The Indian experience was "slowly falling into an impressionistic pattern. There is always something a bit frightening about it; the thought of those millions of Asiatics on the march and not knowing where. I keep striving to find the internal contradiction which torments them and I believe it lies somewhere in the region of pacifism vs. violence, but I'm not sure."

Lindeman wrote a number of articles, book reviews, and speeches over the next few years based on his Indian experience. In "The Moral Sense of India" (*The Survey Graphic*, September 1950), he predicted that if India could only solve its economic problems,

> it will become a powerful force for moral regeneration throughout the world. . . . This morality rests upon a simple but profound philosophical doctrine. This doctrine, stated in almost axiomatic form, has been repeated over and over by both Gandhi and Nehru. It is simply this: the basis of morality is adherence to the rule of compatibility between means and ends. Desirable goals never can be attained through undesirable methods. We become what we do. This maxim is not merely a sound basis for ethics; it is also inherent in the democratic ideal.

In his review of the book *God-driven Man of India* by Louis Fisher (*Saturday Review of Literature*, September 1950), Lindeman wrote that India had introduced a new note in world affairs. He spoke of a diplomacy "in a new key," meaning that relations between nations must be understood and resolved "only when regarded as instances of morality." This was what Gandhi had been saying for more than thirty years. It is a simple formula: "Do not ever assume that human problems may be resolved through the use of force and violence; when legalism itself enslaves you, practice

147

civil disobedience; and in all affairs keep your means as nearly as possible consonant with your ends."

He noted that since Gandhi was the person who invoked this method in our time (Socrates, Jesus, Tolstoy, and Thoreau held similar views) and became its international exemplar, it becomes necessary to understand how he had achieved such extraordinary power over his people, and finally "why he continues to be a haunting influence in the world." He pointed to the comparison of Nehru with Gandhi over the issue of Korea, saying that "Nehru viewed it as a moral equation—subject to discussion rather than force." Americans tend to be irritated with both Nehru and Gandhi, he said, because "morality when it is simple and actually practiced is invariably annoying."

On the whole Lindeman regarded the trip to India as "the most exciting teaching experience of [his] career." For Hazel it opened up a world she had never known and never knew existed. In spite of all the personal discomforts, the overwhelming sense of horror and pity she felt for the poor in India, and the periods of loneliness she felt in a strange country when Lindeman was away, she was glad she had gone. She must have been concerned about Lindeman's alarming loss of weight, the inadequate diet, and the way he drove his body mercilessly. I am quite sure she knew this was the way he wanted it to be. The bond between them that had grown stronger since their move to New York was invigorated even further by their common experience in India.

# Chapter 15

# Sage of Wisconsin

*Either philosophy is commonsense or it is nonsense.*
Lindeman, 1943

Being a pragmatist in the 1940s was a lonely battle. No wonder the two social philosophers Max Otto and Eduard Lindeman found support and joy in their mutual friendship. In Otto Lindeman found not only a kindred spirit, an ally, a man who loved nature and possessed a wonderful, whimsical sense of humor, but also someone willing to go to bat for pragmatism on American campuses.

Although Lindeman had quoted Otto in *The Meaning of Adult Education* as early as 1926, there is no clue as to how or when the two men became acquainted. Only two short letters from Otto to Lindeman from the 1930s have survived, showing that as early as 1931 the two philosophers were already supporters. Convinced that Lindeman should come to Madison, Otto wrote an imploring letter in May that year. "Why don't you write? I want to know when you can come, for how long, and how much we'd have to dig up out of our jeans. . . . Won't you help me to do a favor of immensity for this place?" Two accompanying cartoons show a man in obvious distress.

When Lindeman had to decline because he was participating in one of Dewey's educational seminars, Otto wished him a good trip and urged him to come back unchanged because "We need *you!*" Otto was getting a few things together for Lindeman to look at for a book, and, "Of course *you'd* be *the* one to write the introduction!"

The letters, most of them written between 1943 and 1953, reveal a rare relationship evolving between the two men, based on mutual respect and admiration as individuals and as fellow philosophers. Each provided the other with a forum for testing ideas. There was trust and affection and good-natured humor spilling over onto the pages of their correspondence.

Otto, one of the nation's leading philosophers, like Lindeman, was one of the most popular teachers at his institution. Also like Lindeman, he regarded philosophy as a base for the search for a better life. Due to their atheistic and pacifist convictions, they each became a target for religious and right-wing groups and were controversial figures on their respective campuses. Both men were in the latter years of their careers, possessed mature minds, and had no need to impress each other or to further their careers. It was not surprising then that their letters reveal an increasing concern with retirement. Otto was due to retire in 1947, and Lindeman three years later.

Lindeman resisted calling himself a philosopher, preferring (like Emerson) the title of teacher. However, he had been slowly evolving into a social philosopher, crediting Dewey and Follett with turning him into a pragmatist. He always credited William James for supplying the potent component of whatever philosophy emerges as "the new philosophy." He had already rejected the dogmatism of ultimate ends and static principles and sought to replace them by a "fluid and evolutionary concept of means—means which create their ends." He saw Man as "a behaving organism in a continuing process of adjustment to his physical and social environment; a process of interaction in which all factors undergo continual modification."

He viewed institutions not as ultimate objects of loyalty, but as "evolving means for individual fulfillment." He could not visualize a philosophy that was not concerned with the "application of the scientific method to the realm of human affairs and social action."

I cannot recall a time when Lindeman did not place an emphasis on values as well as on facts. It was this insistence on merging values with fact, I believe, that attracted him to pragmatism, along with a concern with means as well as ends. Lindeman, in common with Emerson, argued that ends and means must be consonant, that the ends pre-exist in the means, that "you become what you do." "Either philosophy is commonsense," he wrote Otto in August 1943, "or it is nonsense."

There were other reasons why Lindeman was attracted to Pragmatism, such as his infatuation with Emerson. Lindeman viewed Emerson as one of the early American pragmatists because of his concern with the issue of values. Also, I think he considered professional philosophy, practiced in American universities, as a form of self-indulgence. He could not understand why taxpayers would foot the bill for the "ivory tower philosophers" to "write footnotes to each other." His main objection was that their kind of philosophy bore only the slightest resemblance to life and action.

In the 1940s when Lindeman was formulating new applications for pragmatism in a democratic society, American universities were embracing logical positivism. Imported from Vienna in the early 1920s, logical positivism triggered controversial theories that shook the world. Its first proponents, known as "the Vienna Circle," sought a "purified" philosophy based on mathematics reduced to logic. Their concern was with pure logic, logical analysis, and the unity of science. Bertrand Russell became one of its most enthusiastic advocates in England, and it was not long before its influence had a profound effect on American universities. Whatever Lindeman and Otto may have thought about its uncongeniality with pragmatism, both were aware of its empirical, antimetaphysical and proscientific stance.

Lindeman also worried about certain American thinkers whom he thought were seeking to revive Hegelianism in 1943—"these new American absolutists who insisted that relativistic morality and progressive education [William James and John Dewey] are the twin evils of our time." He worried that education would revert back to "certainty and to an ethics which consists of rights and wrongs with nothing between—a parallel to the German philosophy." In spite of his fears, Hegel did not make much of a comeback.

Lindeman saw life as an unending series of experiments, saying that it was not our progressivism that endangers us but rather our timidity. For him a pragmatic or experimental stream of thought represented an effort to bring philosophy into harmony with science. Pragmatism was also consistent with his belief in pluralism, in diversity. Pluralism in practice presented a test for democracy, and democracy in turn was the appropriate environment for pluralistic experimentation. Lindeman saw the ultimate authority of science and of religion as experience, which he equated with pragmatism. In his speeches he loved to quote the famous pragmatic oath, which he saw as both humorous and truthful: "I swear to tell the approximate truth, the tentative truth, the relative truth, so help me, future experience."

151

When the bulk of the Lindeman/Otto correspondence resumed in August 1943, analytic logic was finding its way onto American campuses. Also there were idealists and some realists or critical realists, all of whom were antipragmatists. It is difficult to label the philosophers or philosophies that the letters talk about. What is certain is that Otto found himself fighting an uphill battle to maintain the foothold for pragmatism that he had worked so hard to establish at the University of Wisconsin. He feared that when he retired in 1947 pragmatism would come to an end on his campus. His fears proved to be justified. In effect analytic logic wiped out Deweyism and pragmatism for years.

And so it was no wonder that Otto was pleased that Lindeman spent three weeks in the summer of 1943 lecturing on the Madison campus. Professionally, it would do him no harm to have a fellow scholar and pragmatist of Lindeman's stature. And indeed, when Lindeman left, Otto wrote that he was "personally grateful" and "happy to get acquainted with the person he had watched and admired as he moved on the horizon of my vision."

Lindeman, too, had enjoyed his Madison visit and promised to return in October for a few days. Meanwhile, he told Otto he was working on his book on faith and function, "but it doesn't seem so good to me now. I find it necessary to summon every tiny shred of my own faith to believe that the results of this terrifying war will be anything but disastrous. But we must cling to whatever there is, don't you think? You will, I know."

Shortly after Lindeman's visit to Madison, both men were invited to serve on a commission to deal with philosophy in the postwar world. Fearful about the future of philosophy in general, Otto wrote Lindeman in August that he was specifically concerned about the difference of opinion between himself and the other members. He was eager to share these concerns with him and to find out if he and Lindeman were in agreement.

Although Lindeman and Otto had spent several weeks together on the Madison campus during the summer, they had not had enough time "to sit down and thrash out [their] views on the future of philosophy."

The other members of the commission thought of philosophy as something to be "designed by philosophers and brought down to men and women in general." Otto was convinced that if this was done, it would not "get down" to people but would get "stuck somewhere above the ground floor like an elevator between floors." Otto was having difficulty conceptualizing his own commonsense philosophy.

I can't get over the notion that the pattern of ends and means which we operate in is the commonsense level. In other words, this homegrown philosophy is absolutely essential to start with, that only by starting off with it do we get content and a sense of direction. So I keep yelling about the necessity of beginning with the wants and needs and aspirations of people. Now, how does all this strike you? I have to put the case before you because I know that you will say what you believe and think. And I certainly need to be illuminated.

Lindeman prefaced his response by insisting he never classified himself as a philosopher—"and for the very reasons you state. Whatever philosophy I have learned has come only incidentally from professional philosophers." He shared his own personal convictions: (a) One philosophical problem that all people understand is the question of means and ends, goals and methods. (b) Another problem they understand is that there are short-term and long-term ends. He felt it was necessary to harmonize these two types of goals. (c) And, people understand that there is something very queer going on in our world with respect to the existence of "individual differences and our common requirements or needs." He asked Otto to let him know if he wanted more of this commonsense approach, and if so he would tell him how he taught his introductory course in philosophy to graduate students whose only use for philosophy will be in social practice.

By 1944 it was apparent that the two philosophers were not only in fundamental agreement but were reveling in their shared convictions about the role of philosophy and democratic institutions in the postwar world. They also had the same hopes and fears for academia and their brethren philosophers.

This increasing concern about the "steady misrepresentation of pragmatic philosophy" became an important common bond between them. When James and Dewey were being cited as the "twin evils" of the day, their concern grew into alarm. Lindeman suggested an all-out offensive that he called his "Manifesto Pragma,"

153

which would "give the other boys something to do." Otto was only too happy to join in such a project.

We do not know what happened to the Manifesto, but in October Otto wrote to Lindeman asking for his help in formulating some ideas for a chapter he had been asked to write for the commission on what philosphy can do in the community. This was a tailor-made challenge for Lindeman, who felt the primary task was to bring philosophy "out of the chair and put it to work in the midst of human affairs."

In his response, Lindeman warned Otto that what he was about to say was "off the top of [his] head." Having taught in adult institutes the major portion of his life, he knew "how lively and exciting philosophy can be for men and women faced with important practical decisions. The major question they have is with respect to ends." He saw philosophy as being useful to luncheon clubs, women's organizations, chambers of commerce, and trade unions, "for these are the decision-making centers in American communities." But he also warned Otto that "action without direction could lead to catastrophe."

Lindeman described a discussion group that he had been involved with for over a decade, which met in individuals' homes in a New York suburb. The group met prior to the large forum, and each group was furnished with a discussion outline. "A forum by itself is a poor instrument for enhancing reflective insight," he pointed out, "but when supplemented by small discussion groups, where there is time to test ideas and acts, it moved to a much higher level. Even the lecturers at the forum were surprised by the quality of the discussions, and, more precisely, by the philosophic character of their contributions."

It was Lindeman's turn to invite Otto to New York in May 1945. He wondered what it would take to "lure him from his Wisconsin lair" to come and expose himself to the "confused pagans of New York." He had in mind a "season of lectures, perhaps at The New School." He closed by boasting to Otto that while on a holiday he had "an excellent chance to watch two birds he had never seen before — an oyster-catcher and a water turkey. Funny guys, both of them, but I'll tell you more about them some day."

But Otto had an alternative plan: Lindeman must come to Madison again. He wrote in June that he was "super enthusiastic to bring this about" and wondered how much it would cost.

At the same time he told Lindeman that he had just heard it was the end of the war in Europe. "What a day! . . . And my mind goes out to the big jobs that have to be done—not only in the East, but here at home—and that makes me think of you and the necessity of spreading your light everywhere we can."

As their friendship deepened they began to sound like a mutual admiration society. Otto wrote Lindeman in 1944 that he had a way of presenting issues that was "clear, direct, put so it could be grasped at once, and such a telling argument, yet without any nastiness. Power, brother, and more power to you!"

Asked by a Unitarian minister in 1945 to name the philosopher he could most identify with, Lindeman unhesitatingly cited Otto. By 1946 Lindeman wrote Otto that he had a much deeper influence over him than he had realized and that it had deepened tremendously "since we have come to know and love each other."

Otto likewise told Lindeman, "If there is any one 'essence' of the democratic way of life, and if there is anybody who knows what this is, his name is Eduard Lindeman." Lindeman should think of himself "as among the noble," Otto believed.

The first hint of even a minor disagreement between the two men was sparked by an article Lindeman wrote for the *Christian Science Monitor* (August 25, 1945) in which he disapproved of peacetime conscription. Otto responded to the July 24th advance carbon copy of the article sent to him by Lindeman, saying that it was a magnificent article, and that Lindeman had an uncanny way of "clearing a path through ambiguous ideas and phrases." But although Lindeman had been one of the early interventionists with respect to the current war, Otto had not been. At the same time, he wanted his friend to know that he had not been an isolationist either. "It is possible that you had more faith than I had in supporting every effort on the part of FDR to aid our allies and prepare our own defenses." What seemed important to Otto was that they both had refused to be isolationist when it came to "the general human welfare."

Otto was also pleased with Lindeman's suggestion to include him in the New American Library series on philosophy: "No less so since you think of including Otto along with James and Dewey. . . . I am aware that the royalty flowing to me from these 25 cent books would not exactly be at flood tide, but any little addition to the $1500 a year on which we shall have to be getting along in two years would be helpful." (Otto was referring to his retirement in 1947.)

When Lindeman returned from his assignment in Germany in October 1945, there was a letter from Otto scolding him for not letting him know where he was and inviting him to join the University of Wisconsin faculty to teach two courses during summer session, one in philosophy and one in education. Lindeman had to turn down the offer because he was already scheduled to teach a summer course at Columbia. He told Otto that was the penalty he had to pay for being away in the winter.

By March 1946 Otto was more eager than ever to bring Lindeman to his campus "for one illuminating season before I quit." This time he wanted him for an entire semester, saying, "Couldn't you get away from the N.Y. School for a stretch? We need light out here too!"

Concluding on a philosophical note, Otto wrote, "If I can't say or sing 'And only man is vile' it would simplify matters, but I guess I'll have to get on with a more complex philosophy than that. I don't respond to this emphasis on the rediscovery of sinful man. Some of them are pretty low down, but some of them seem to me higher than the angels, though wingless and housed in bodies."

Lindeman could not give a whole semester, so they settled for the month of February 1947—four months before Otto's retirement.

Meanwhile, the plan to publish Otto's work as a part of a Penguin series on philosophy was delayed because of a slump in the publishing business. Frederick Burkhardt, younger colleague of Otto's from the University of Wisconsin, was already in the process of making selections from Otto's work and writing his biographical sketch. Through Otto Lindeman was able to form close intellectual and friendship ties with Frederick Burkhardt, Harold Taylor, and Horace Fries, all from the University of Wisconsin philosophy department and all fellow pragmatists—the last of a dying breed.

Lindeman discovered he was enjoying the summer session at Columbia after all. He had a heavy enrollment, he wrote Otto in June, "and fortunately I have some excellent students. Teaching is a disease, isn't it? One would think at my age the romance of it would have been dulled, but somehow or other a new class always seem as exciting as ever." Meanwhile, Otto was teaching in the philosophy department at the University of Minnesota in

June and feeling gloomier than ever about his academic brothers. Fortunately, he happened upon one of Lindeman's books—*Selections on Emerson*—in the university bookstore. "Just reading the foreword to this little book lifted my spirits. . . . Emerson is a perennial, a hardy perennial, with roots so deep in the American soil that there are flowers and seeds for thoughtful people everywhere." He also liked what Lindeman said about Emerson being a philosopher, even though he did not display "a baggage of technical ideas or talk jargon."

There is no record of Lindeman visiting the Madison campus in February 1947, but we do know that Otto retired in June that year. He wrote Lindeman afterward from Laguna Beach, California, inviting him to visit. He and his wife Rhoda were spending the winter in California where Otto was teaching at UCLA. Steps had been taken at UCLA, he wrote, to "wipe out all traces of the kind of philosophy we have been trying to develop there. They want 'real philosophy.' Social philosophy, so called, is not philosophy." Otto was delighted to learn in January 1948, that Lindeman would visit them in Laguna Beach very soon. "What good news! We can have some talks. I need them, brother! No—we don't have a telephone. No car, either, alas. We only have a village post office, not even a telegraph station. (No, it's not New York City.)"

Also eager for this visit, Lindeman wrote, "Well dear Max, help me stretch—until I reach the Pacific Coast and find you."

By all accounts they had a splendid visit in Otto's winter home; so much so that after Lindeman's departure, Otto wrote, "The spirit of one E. L. haunts this place. Good Heavens, can't you be satisfied to leave a place after you go away!"

When the Ottos returned to Madison in the fall, Otto read Lindeman's article "The Professionals" in the *Antioch Review* (1945).

He must have read it before, "but still it spoke to me so forcefully on this second reading. Of course your commitment to the democratic profession movement would have won my heart in any case, but there is your detailed practical application, so commonly lacking in what one reads, and that comes home to me about equally with your humanity and dedicated spirit. What a good job you did! (Always do.)" He had needed badly to hear that message about "us professionals. One thing we do know, however, and that is this: American professionals are a big asset to the American historic profession movement. And if we think of philosophic professionals, they are a liability."

Otto referred to correspondence with people at Northwestern University, where they intended to expand their department of philosophy by three or four men, and stated that what they want is "technical philosophers, experts in symbolic logic, and such! Good God! Is the whole human venture in danger or not! Or is it more important that we provide this opportunity for a few men to play this game with each other than that students in college be introduced to a will and a way to lead themselves and their fellows toward a little more sanity and humaneness!"

Lindeman thanked Otto for his words of encouragement, then told him he had been brooding over a serious conversation they had at Laguna Beach in regard to Lindeman's essay on morality.

> I want you to know that you left a question in my mind which we shall need to thrash out. It is this: What is the relation between tolerance and conviction? In my case I think I have over-stressed the former primarily because I have been motivated by the diversity theory of democracy, and by the underlying assumption of inclusiveness which has always seemed to me inherent in the pragmatic movement. This is all, probably, a neat little rationalization emanating from my temperamental dislike of contentiousness. But, rationalization or not, I seem always to strive for avoidance of "either-or" thinking. Now, this gets me into trouble, as you so clearly pointed out. I don't mind being in trouble but I certainly abhor getting into trouble of the kind that troubles you. . . . So, put this on your agenda for that unhurried visit we shall have one of these days.

He also told Otto that there had been a complete split between the British and American branches of Penguin Books and that "we now have a new name, a terrifying name—*the New American Library of World Literature*." He assured Otto that his book would again be put in production and told him to be patient.

In closing he said he planned to visit Burkhardt at Bennington College, Vermont, in May, and "that ought to be fun." Burkhardt had been installed as the new president of Bennington College in 1948, and both Lindeman and Otto wished him well in his new enterprise. "I hope with you," Otto wrote, "that he may put his superb mind to work on educational philosophy and procedure, and not be bogged down with housekeeping chores. He's really an extraordinarily gifted youth and a fine character. I'm glad you visited with him and worked with the students. It would please us if we could feel you are around within reach to help Fred."

In this letter Otto referred to Lindeman's "avoidance of administration jobs," saying he does not know why people desire that kind of task. "If someone must do it let it be someone who has not your unusual ability to teach." Lindeman had apparently accepted an offer to teach once again on the Madison campus, and Otto was having mixed feelings about that. On the one hand he felt it was the "first hopeful news from this quarter for a long time." But he did not have confidence in either the dean of the College of Education or in the president of the University, "especially the former. They don't deserve to have you accept." On the other hand, Otto knew there were large numbers of students to be considered.

After pressuring Otto for five years to lecture at the New School for Social Research, Otto finally agreed to enlighten the 'pagans' in New York. Lindeman warned him that he would be "feted by the big shots" but hoped he would manage "so that the Lindemans will at least get a glimpse" of him.

But Otto had some trepidations. He had struggled in writing his lecture and now was afraid that Lindeman and his students would "tear him to bits." Just the thought that Lindeman planned to meet with his class after Otto's lecture "makes me rise to the defence of the Lecture. And how I wish I could attend your attempted destruction. Well, I hope you'll see me in the flesh. I'm beginning to fear that I'll be nothing but a ghost when I have to walk up to the podium and announce 'My name is not Eduard Lindeman, alas.' " Max planned to see Dewey also while he was in town and attend a dinner in his honor at the New School.

In the meantime, Lindeman wrote Otto he was working on a problem of basic issues, namely:

How does one know when an issue in American life is basic or secondary or derivative? And how does one relate, in education, the derivative issues to the basic issues? I have a clue, but it seems too simple. A basic issue, under our peculiar form of government, is one which recurrently appears before the Supreme Court. *Basic issue:* to what extent shall the federal government assume responsibility for the economy and for the general welfare? *Secondary issue:* Housing, Social Security, etc. Think it over and let me have an insight or two, please.

159

Because there was a lull in their correspondence over the next five months, we do not know how the "pagans" received Otto's lecture. In April 1949 Lindeman wrote that "something seems to have happened to our system of communication. What is it?"

Meanwhile, Lindeman had an important decision to make and needed to consult with Otto. He had been invited by T. V. Smith to collaborate with him on a book *The Democratic Way of Life*. Lindeman had agreed to do so, but had many misgivings, saying that Smith "was so facile that I wonder at times whether he is fooling himself. He seems to have weakened on the civil rights issue, and that bothers me. Whenever I have any choice among values of which freedom is one, I instinctively choose freedom, feeling that if I have freedom I can use it for the purpose of pursuing the other values, and if I sacrifice freedom, where can I go?" He asked Otto to please tell him what he knew about Smith.

Lindeman was also apparently thinking ahead to his own retirement in 1950. He had recently written a paper for the Academy of Medicine on the "problems of retirement for aging professional persons." He asked Otto what was happening to the philosophy department and to the university. And "What are you reading and what sense does it make? And what do you chuckle over? What do you get saucy about?"

He wrote Otto in the end of June that he was coming to Wisconsin to lecture in Eau Claire in July; "that is, I think I'm coming but some citizen of that community, a Legionnaire I believe, has started a campaign to keep me from coming. It seems I have been too outspoken on behalf of Negroes and against Fascists and my name appears in an appendix of the Dies Committee report." In spite of the fuss he intended to come and also to visit the Ottos in Madison. He hoped as he moved westward there would be less hysteria. (As it turned out, he actually found more.) He added that Dewey came out in *The New York Times* with a fine statement on communists as teachers, which said "they're not fit to teach but an attempt to suppress them is a much worse disease. That's my position. There must be a better way to fight Communism."

When Lindeman finally announced to Otto in August that *The New American Library* had at least agreed to publish Otto's book, Otto responded by saying he would believe it when he saw it. However, he would make sure there was a window display, although he doubted if his influence would amount to much.

160

**Eduard Lindeman, about 1950**
*Volpe Studios, 145 West 57th St., New York*

Outwardly cynical, inwardly he knew "that the book will be used by some of our friends here."

Otto concluded with a verse from the poem "history of the world," subtitled 10,000 B.C. to A.D. 1941 (no author mentioned):

> Today tho there's a change of pace
> And individuals and place,
> Josephus and Herodotus
> Would were a knowing nod at us;
> For still we boast the cultured mind
> To all the suckers we can find
> And while they lend attentive ears
> We kick their unsuspecting rears
> Lay by your books my studious friend;
> You've learned the substance and the trend
> For here's your history, pulp and core,
> It's all there is . . . there ain't no more!

From an April 1950 letter from Lindeman we learn that Otto once again wanted him to come to Wisconsin for a semester. Burkhardt was also urging him to come to Bennington for a weekend when Otto would also be there, but unfortunately Lindeman could not make it because of an important committee meeting of the President's White House Conference on Children (of which he was a member). We also learn that Lindeman began teaching again in early April, his first class since his gall bladder attack, with only two terms to go before retirement. "Like an old fire horse I was greatly stimulated by the smell of chalk. Of course my voice gave out near the end of the second hour, but otherwise, no bad effects."

His health had miraculously (but only temporarily) improved. "I feel so good right now," he wrote Otto on April 8, 1950, "I can scarcely restrain myself from plunging into all sorts of activities. But, the doctors are watching me, and I have to behave." He told Otto that New York was becoming a "queerer place than ever. Nothing but pessimism and fright. Courage is lacking everywhere. . . . I refuse to become infected, but there are moments when I truly wish I were living on a farm."

With retirement only a few months away, Lindeman was beginning to be swamped with invitations for postretirement teaching and lecturing. Fisk University in Nashville; the universities in Florida,

Kansas City, and Wisconsin-Madison; and Bennington College all wanted him to teach for at least a semester. Meanwhile, he told Otto in May that his only intellectual work, aside from teaching, was collecting Plutarch's "Lives" for paperback publication. He had selected Pericles, Solon, Alexander, Alcibiades, Lycurgus, and Cicero.

He was reading Charles Morris's new book *The Open Self* and liked what he said very much, but his style bothered him. "Why do the younger philosophers have to use so many big and awkward words? I shouldn't ask that question because I did the same thing once. It was because my ideas weren't clear. It takes experience, obviously, to gain simplicity."

By June Lindeman was proud to report to Otto that he had gained almost twenty pounds since he left the hospital and that he was playing three sets of tennis on Saturdays and Sundays. He had begun his last term of teaching at Columbia, "where I have now taught for twenty-six years. I really feel 'out of it,' as if I didn't really belong. It's a curious business, this retiring. I've spent hours with an insurance specialist to determine exactly how much we'll have to live on after September 1st. It turns out to be about one-half of the previous income."

When the invitation to teach one semester at Madison fell through, Lindeman accepted the post at the University of Kansas City, to start in September. He had turned down the invitation to come to Fisk because he heard that the atmosphere "was thick with pietism and that's what I'm not much in need of at the moment."

The closer Lindeman came to retirement, the more he found himself "passing through the most peculiar moods." He wrote Otto, "Issues which seem important to my colleagues leave me completely disinterested. In spirit I've already left. It is only when I am teaching that I feel at home. What a funny profession this teaching business is!"

He was finding himself in a minority "with respect to the Korean affair. Everybody seems to think it means a general war, but I don't. War, it seems to me, is the costliest and riskiest instrument the Communists could use for their expansion, and I don't believe they are dumb enough to use it."

There is a gap in their correspondence from July to December 1950, when Otto wrote, "we hear every now and then of a speech you have made, here, there, elsewhere, what with dinners, classes. . . . But here's hoping you will take Christmas day off! . . . The world isn't encouraging us to be merry or to think of Peace, but I'm all for keeping up these intimate spirit-reviving occasions as we can. Best Wishes!" Otto included a cartoon he drew of himself carrying a Christmas tree.

There is then another gap in their correspondence, until July 1951 when Lindeman reported to Otto that his health had not been good, but he had managed "to keep some work going. Right now I am wrestling with an important decision: should I attempt a regular teaching schedule this coming year? At Bennington they want me to head up that American Values course with which you had something to do at the outset. Teaching is what I like most of all but I hesitate to commit myself." He asked Otto for advice and ended by saying how happy he was to learn that Otto would be mounting the rostrum again at Madison. "I can't think of anything pleasanter than the sight of you in a college classroom."

Apparently Otto had allowed himself to be persuaded to teach for one semester, but in an undated letter in the fall of 1951 he told Lindeman he already regretted it. As for Lindeman teaching at Bennington for a full year, Otto thought it was too much. On the one hand, "You'd have colleagues to your liking and assume that Fred [Burkhardt] will be back." But on the other hand he felt that a year would be a long time "with time contracting." But he had to admit that Lindeman would "jump at a chance to get out of N.Y.C. But you will decide."

Otto reassured himself and Lindeman that they are "traveling in the same ship headed for the same harbor. Moreover, I'm proud to be in that ship and am glad you are in your big town where there's a better chance to be heard widely when some news of ports of call are announced."

In September Otto wrote Lindeman that he had just heard news from Bennington that Lindeman was not in the best of health. "I'm terribly sorry to hear it. The only ray of hope I get out of it is the probably unreasonable one that you will decide to take things easy." Otto had been uneasy for a long time because Lindeman "insisted upon going at a pace that no human being can stand. You've done several men's work all along. You've done enough! How about agreeing to retire? Let's meditate and read and observe and look on."

By late fall both men were aware that their communication was not good. "No, we mustn't drift apart," Otto wrote Lindeman. "The little army to which we belong is being pushed around these days. Aside from personal considerations, we need to help one another professionally. Philosophic orthodoxy these days is *sad.*"

Again, Otto admonished Lindeman about his health. "Why must you work so hard?" He had long wanted to read him a sermon on the way he works, ". . . so this is nothing brought on by your illness. Do be sensible. Do a little coasting." But a short note to Lindeman in September 1951 confirmed the fact that Lindeman did indeed go to Bennington, with his health deteriorating badly. Once more Otto scolded Lindeman for not taking things easy.

Correspondence between the two friends did not resume again until April 12, 1952, when Otto was both delighted and concerned about the news that Lindeman was in better shape: "And so now you did go to Bennington! Does that show good sense? It must be because of your spotty schooling. If you had only been educated regularly!"

A month later Otto wrote Lindeman that every night as he dropped off to sleep, "I say to myself, 'Tomorrow I must write to Eduard and find out what's become of him.' " The last he had heard was that they were waiting for him at Bennington. Then, a few weeks later, Otto was suddenly called to New York City for Dewey's funeral service. (Dewey died on June 1, 1952).

> We were hoping you might come down from Bennington, as we hoped Frederick Burkhardt would, but alas neither of you did. . . . But all I want to do this morning is to ask where y-- are? how y-- are?, and what you are doing. . . . So John Dewey has gone from us. He was of course never more needed. The ranks of those who were once active in the pragmatic movement are getting thinner all the time, aren't they? Well, that's life. It looks to me as if young men and women are coming along to carry on the spirit of that movement, who will give a good account of themselves. (What a sentence!)

A couple months later Otto wrote that he regretted that he had not known Lindeman was in New York when he came for Dewey's funeral. It puzzled him why Lindeman, knowing that Otto was to give a speech at Dewey's memorial service, had not gotten in touch with him.

What Otto did not know was that Lindeman was too sick to go to Dewey's memorial service, too sick even to see his dear old friend from Wisconsin, for he wrote that he was glad to hear that Lindeman was *reasonably* well, at least. "I worry a lot about you. There's a personal reason, of course, but also 'professional.' You're needed in the case which is dear to me." Knowing it was useless, Otto nevertheless could not resist scolding Lindeman: "Why in hell don't you take things easier? There are other things to do rather than running around talking. I have told you this before — you take on too much of the talking, discussion, work when you should be loafing." Moreover he was distressed about Lindeman's six-week-long trip to Oregon to teach, feeling he should not have undertaken this long trip.

In November Otto wrote that he too had gone down with Adlai Stevenson, adding, "And *we* had McCarthy to take! As for Eisenhower, he'll have plenty of trouble in his life from here on. I wish we didn't have to take Nixon along with Eisenhower. That may bring us calamity. We must learn to live with decisions that have gone against us, you said when you were here. Quite an art, isn't it? And with all this spreading talk about Dewey and the rest being done for — there's call to arms brother!"

The end was drawing near.

Throughout their long friendship the two men had rarely disagreed, but an incident arose in November 1952 that was never satisfactorily cleared up before Lindeman's death five months later. It all began when Otto wrote to Lindeman criticizing Lindeman's recent chapter "Social Philosophy: Its Method and Purpose" in *Cleavage in Our Culture: Studies in Scientific Humanism* (1952). The book was edited by Burkhardt and dedicated to Otto. In a roundabout way Otto let Lindeman know that he was not pleased by what he wrote. Rereading Otto's letter today fails to clarify exactly what it was that Otto objected to.

> If that book gets any reading a lot of people will soon know more than they now do about social philosophy as I have seen it developed. The characteristics which you enumerate and illustrate will help any one who cares to be informed, what philosophy so conceived comes to. And you lean over backward to be fair to the pure scholarship boys. Of course, I myself don't believe in them or, should I rather say, their pretensions, nevertheless it becomes us to be decent even in talking or thinking about them. It seems to me that these gents, at any rate the present day representatives of real philosophy, rare social philosophers too, although they would deny it, the difference being that their society is narrowly conceived and is limited to a

166

small circle of academic cronies. I haven't been able to make sure what type you had in mind when you spoke of our profiting from contact with the scholarly philosopher, these specialized specialists who contend that they alone are philosophers, or men like Whitehead who, in spite of their scholarly attainments are social philosophers too. Royce also—not to speak of earlier philosophers.

Otto felt Lindeman needed to do a lot more work on the chapter before he would be satisfied that he knew Lindeman's number—his number as an expositor of social philosophy. The chapter stirred Otto to think, he said, but his final words seem faint in praise for the job Lindeman set out to do: "I am respectfully grateful to you for making the effort, for putting in the time, and of course I'm glad you had the goods to deliver."

As far as Otto himself was concerned, he was anxious to contribute a little more before "I hang up my fiddle." He wanted to say something about philosophy, and he wanted Lindeman to know that he will be "tougher on the smart-chicks and their camp followers. Well, I don't live in New York City."

In December 1952 Lindeman wrote Otto that he felt "impelled" to give him a report on his "present condition and state of mind. That heart attack I had in early September was more serious than we thought. I have had a long term in the hospital and as a convalescent at home."* He was now able to function only minimally, and he felt the enforced idleness was good for him. "I'm not sure that it has left me any wiser but I do see some things about myself more clearly." He recalled that after Emerson's long illness he had written in his journal: "He has seen but half the Universe who never has been shown the house of Pain."

Lindeman had spent some of his enforced idleness trying to figure out a satisfactory explanation for the ultimate failure of the ancient Greeks:

---

*I discuss Lindeman's deterioriating health in further detail in chapter 17.

(a) They became provincial, isolationist in temper.

(b) They were unable to curb corruption.

(c) They developed a fear concerning non-conformists.

(d) They were not able to form a federal union.

(e) They lost faith in their humanist tradition and sought escape in religious and mystical cults.

(f) They didn't know how to stop war.

He added, "These are all manifestations with us as well. I suppose I was too influenced by the contemporary scene. In any case, this had been my preoccupation during the last three trying months."

It was evident that Lindeman was distressed by Otto's response to his chapter in Burkhardt's volume.

> You seem to infer that there was some lack of clarity, that there may have been some concealed meanings. This disturbed me because I do so much value your opinion. I re-read my piece and it seemed to me that if it fails, it is on the side of its plainness, but authors are the poorest judges of their own work. I wanted very much to do a good job because of my love for you. So, please do tell me if you have found something in it which is not wholly clear or straightforward. I should feel very badly if I did not feel I was traveling in your ship and headed toward your harbor.

Their long correspondence ended with a letter from Otto in December 1952, four months before Lindeman's death. In this letter Otto attempted to respond to his friend's distress about Lindeman's chapter in *The Cleavage*.

> I wanted to go all out for this chapter and I know I didn't. It wasn't that I objected to something specifically and didn't want to tell you and also didn't want to lie. Of course we needn't agree. But I can't think of any views we disagree upon. I doubt if we differ on basic principles at all. Anyway, my failure to write freely and with verve — which is what I take it you missed, wasn't disagreement, none that I was aware of, in our views. Had that been it, I'm sure you would have found me vocal and specific. Well, what was it? That's what I want to make more sense of than I can tonight.

I am not certain if the following lines are, in fact, part of Otto's attempt to make sense out of his own remarks. They are from a missing page of a letter, undated, with no beginning or ending pages. What is important is that they indicate an attempt on his part to end it all on a positive note. They express the way Otto typically felt about Lindeman—personally and professionally. They also express a need, in the few remaining days, to reassure Lindeman that no matter what he may have said about his chapter, he still admired the fact that he had something to say.

> You do say it: and believe me I happen to know that the mere saying is a job. And you say *something*. If it's time that people won't listen, that they don't care, then we are in for a bad time—all of us. But what greater cause can there be than the one to which you are giving yourself? I'm sure that you are not in a position to judge how much good you've done in keeping alive and giving body to the best idealism of the country in which we live—still live.

Otto may have known when he wrote those words that he was, in fact, delivering a eulogy for his friend. He knew Lindeman was dying; he had known it for some time.

# Chapter 16

# Bigotry in the City of Roses

*It looks as if we are in for a disagreeable summer. . . . We may have an unhappy time of it. It might even transpire that there would be no workshop if you are to be the consultant.*

Odell, 1952

I will never forget the summer of 1952. Lindeman's final stand against bigotry was about to take place in Portland, Oregon, the City of Roses.

The Lindemans had come to Portland for a six-week visit, and Lindeman was also planning to conduct two graduate workshops at nearby Lewis and Clark College, a private liberal arts school. They arrived June 7, the same day as the start of the annual Rose Festival.

I had not seen my parents since the summer of 1949, before their trip to India. Lindeman had written me in March 1952, saying that his retirement was proving to be a rather peculiar experience. "Everyone seems to think I have nothing to do and hence expect more of me than ever. If I am to get any writing done I shall have to get out of New York. My publishers are pressing me for my autobiography, and I still have over half my book on social philosophy." (Neither Gessner nor I found evidence that he had been working on either of these two books.)

His agreeing to accept Lewis and Clark's invitation was typical. He had found it impossible to say no to anything exciting and innovative, and the two workshops certainly promised to be that. One of them was called "Like Life Itself." But at age 67 he did not need this additional drain on his time and energy, or the added stress he was about to encounter in the final months of his life.

If his agreeing to come was typical, so was the controversy his visit aroused. Although Lindeman was not a man to seek controversy, it had followed him throughout his career. He had lost his first teaching job in North Carolina for being too sympathetic to blacks. He had been dismissed from a library commission in 1941 in New Jersey—one he had helped to found—because his ideas were too "liberal." He had been booed in Dallas, Texas, and heckled in Chicago, Eau Claire, and Los Angeles. And now, with the growing hysteria of the McCarthy era, it was happening again.

Over the years he had grown more philosophical about personal attacks, saying he would know he had reached the stage of "unworthy, irresponsible old age" when the *Chicago Tribune* ceased to call him "a Communist."

He always enjoyed telling the story about George Bernard Shaw, who over the years had become accustomed to public and personal attacks. Shaw was speaking at Albert Hall when a lone member of the audience in the gallery began hissing him. Shaw stopped speaking, looked up at the gallery, and said, "My friend, I agree with you, but what are we to do against the multitude?"

The first hint I had that trouble was brewing came in early May when Lindeman sent me some correspondence between himself and Morgan Odell, president of Lewis and Clark College. He was informing me as gently as he could that the workshops might be in trouble. Early in the correspondence Odell had taken a somewhat philosophical position concerning the controversy that had been stirred up by a local woman's accusation that Lindeman was a communist.

The woman, Louise Gronnert, tried to substantiate her charge by quoting the Tenney Report, which listed a large number of communist "front" organizations, then naming the organizations that Lindeman had joined over the years.

The Tenney Report was compiled in 1951 by Congressman Jack Tenney of California, who had received his information from the U.S. attorney general's list. This list was by now notorious as well as ominous. It was a checklist of organizations with four kinds of ties—to communists, to fascists, to totalitarian groups, and to those with "subversive" views. Membership in any one of the organizations listed was enough to warrant an investigation. It was meant to be an internal document to assist in implementing President Truman's loyalty tests.

The publication of that list became the basis for all kinds of civil rights violations by Congress, individual employers, and

171

entrepreneurial blacklisters. Without charging any illegal acts, supplying the ground for its proscription, or offering any mechanisms for individual reply, the government could brand as disloyal any citizen who belonged to any of a large number of organizations. In the public mind this was extended to include those who had given money to an organization or who had attended one or more of its meetings. So now any private citizen, armed with the list, could impugn another citizen's loyalty with what appeared to be the authorization of the U.S. government.

Odell referred to Gronnert as "a most reactionary amateur politician who has written extensively to the chairman of our Board of Trustees protesting your coming to the college this summer." He had responded to these accusations by expressing confidence in Lindeman "as an idealist American citizen who might have been affiliated with organizations in which Communist strategy developed infiltration, but who had not been nor was now a Communist." He attempted to reassure a retired University of Oregon professor who was concerned about Lindeman's visit:

> We have been informed by those who know him quite well that he is on the Communists' list of Number One enemies because he is concerned to bring about the amelioration of human difficulties in our country and thus do away with misery and frustrations upon which Communism feeds. . . . Dr. Lindeman comes to us as a good American citizen and educator despite the fact that he has been labeled otherwise through "guilt by association."

"Written in the highest of American tradition!" Lindeman congratulated him. He hoped at the same time that the matter would end there.

The controversy continued, however, and Odell, somewhat apologetically, wrote Lindeman asking for reassurance:

> This controversy is evidence of one of the tensions in which we presently move and I seek your help on the problem. My Board of Trustees represents the general run of average, decent, Christian, and somewhat conservative businessmen. I would like to be able to meet their inquiries with adequate reassurance.

Lindeman informed him that the Tenney Report had been thoroughly discredited:

172

. . . so far, as a matter of fact, that the Associated Press will give no attention to its claims. . . . But we are not dealing with reasonable people, and I despair of satisfying them by re-iterating the statement that I have been for long a well-known anti-communist.

Clearly, Odell hoped he would hear no more of the matter, even though he was aware that Gronnert was bombarding the trustees of the college on the matter.

By April Odell wrote Lindeman that the chairwoman of the Eugene, Oregon, Parent's Council for Education was threatening to take the information to the Presbyterian ministers in Portland. "I hope you can do somethat about Eduard C. Lindeman, who was not permitted to speak in Texas. It seems too bad," she wrote Odell, "to let the record of Lewis and Clark be spoiled, perhaps because of lack of information about Eduard Lindeman." She had always thought that Lewis and Clark was one of the few colleges with a "good record" as far as leftist teaching was concerned. (This same woman had attempted to have the book *Races of Mankind,* by Ruth Benedict and Gene Weltfish, banned from the Eugene public high schools.)

In response, Lindeman made an effort to express his position vis á vis political ideologies so that President Odell could allay the fears of all concerned once and for all. "I belong to that school of philosophy," he wrote on April 23,

which is committed to experimentalism, and hence have been consistently opposed to all forms of absolutism and dogmatism—and this certainly includes Marxism. A reading of any of my books makes this clear. My position with respect to communism was so clear that I was made the first president of the New York State Americans for Democratic Action. I am a trustee of the ACLU, one of the first national organizations to disbar communists.

I have never seen the California Tenney report, but understand that I, along with many other American liberals, am there recorded as having been a member of a large number of so called "front" organizations. There is this much truth: in the thirties I still held the hope that there might be some way of getting along with Soviet Russia without resort to force. I believed that if this were possible, it would come about by means of organizations purporting to promote such understanding. In each instance I soon found that these pretensions were not genuine, that there was no sincere desire to

173

gain objective insight, but these were in fact propaganda agencies. I never attended any such meeting more than twice, and I never gave permission to use my name.

Another item of truth: I, along with a number of well known anti-communists, signed the petition to request the President to reduce Earl Browder's prison term; we did this with the belief that a maximum sentence would tend to make a martyr out of him. I believe now that this was a mistake. In short, I have never knowingly belonged to any organization which followed the Communist "line," and if at any time my name was thus used, it was without my knowledge or consent. As to my most recent book, *The Democratic Way of Life,* * I have just been informed that the State Department has arranged for this book to be translated into Turkish, and other foreign languages.

Lindeman had been forced throughout the McCarthy era to defend himself against attacks of being a communist. His defense was generally on four grounds:

1. *Philosophical.* He belonged to the American tradition of which William James and John Dewey were the chief exponents— experimental and nonauthoritarian, opposed to the dogma that led to Marxism.

2. *Moral.* He felt that communism taught the immoral doctrine that good ends can come from evil means.

3. *Cultural pluralism.* Whereas communism advocates cultural uniformity, he believed in diversity because he believed in freedom.

4. *Judeo-Christian ethics.* He believed in human brotherhood and love. "My loyalty to the bill of rights is unwavering." Communism teaches hate and conflict.

In early May Odell wrote Lindeman:

It looks as if we are in for a disagreeable summer. The real awkwardness of the situation is the fact that our workshops are not offered by the college alone. We are tied into the Chamber of Commerce, the Board of Education, the City Council, the PTA, the Kiwanis Club and other community organizations in Oregon City. We are

---

*The Democratic Way of Life: An American Interpretation* was co-authored by T. V. Smith and E. C. Lindeman. (1951) New York: New American Library.

having a conference with the Superintendent of Schools in Oregon City in order to apprise him of the attacks on you which are directed toward undermining the desire of Oregon City to carry through with the community workshop. We may have an unhappy time of it. It might even transpire that there would be no workshop if you are to be the consultant.

He referred to the protestors as a "zealous" group and to the situation as "unfortunate" and "awkward," but he hoped that "understanding" would prevail.

On May 7, one month before his arrival in Portland, Lindeman wrote the following letter to Odell:

Your very disturbing letter of May 3rd arrived just as I was leaving my home to address a meeting at Christ Church. I read it in Dr. Stockman's study as I was waiting for the audience to gather, and it seemed to me at that moment unbelievable that I should be attacked in far-off Portland and so thoroughly accepted by the people who know me best in the community where I have lived and worked for more than thirty years. . . .

What are the alternatives? I presume the simplest solution would be to have me withdraw. This seems to me an unworthy, even a cowardly choice. If these charges are made public, I presume there is a good case for libel, a course I should dislike to pursue. The American Civil Liberties Union would no doubt lend its resources for such a procedure and this might in the long run do the most good for the future. The other alternative is to go ahead proudly and bear the brunt of the attack in the hope that reasonable citizens would, after coming to know me, see the absurdity of these charges. In choosing alternatives we must keep in mind the welfare of the college. . . . I wish, therefore, that you could tell me with complete candor what you think I ought to do.

Lindeman wrote to me in May that he felt we ought to "see this through, distasteful though it is. We must go ahead and refuse to be drawn into an open defense. This way it may all fade after my arrival on the scene. But," he added, "I don't like the temper of the times."

Now, sick though he was, he chose to do battle. He was not a man to compromise his principles, even in the face of personal threats or economic reprisals. This was intellectual and academic cowardice at its worst. He would fight if he had to.

The contract had already been signed back in March. At this point Odell had only one alternative, and that was to try to persuade Lindeman to withdraw voluntarily. My husband and I received an invitation to attend a formal tea at the college on a Sunday afternoon in April—"just to get acquainted." Since we had no connections with the college and were newcomers to the community, we suspected the college wanted us to use our influence to persuade Lindeman not to come.

During the tea Odell handed me a packet of letters saying they were written to him, with a copy to each member of the college board of trustees, from a local woman, Louise Gronnert. I had already seen copies of some of the correspondence, but Lindeman had refrained from showing me the most provocative letters, not wanting to upset me. I told him that I thought the community viewed her as a fanatic and that even the newspapers refused to publish her letters to the editor anymore. As we parted he was polite but grim, saying, "You may not take her seriously, but my Board does."

More to the point, Odell knew I would not use my influence to persuade Lindeman not to come. The future looked even more ominous.

What I did not know then was that a proposed gift to the college was at stake—over a million dollars from the owner of a large lumber company, also a trustee of the college. The donor had threatened to withdraw the offer if Lindeman set foot on the Lewis and Clark campus.

With my parents' arrival imminent, I was increasingly apprehensive about what lay ahead and especially concerned about Lindeman's health. He tried to play down the seriousness of his illness, saying his doctor assured him he would be able to make the trip. He was not about to give up at this late date, even though if he violated his salt-free diet, "moisture quickly accumulates in my body, and I become short of breath and quite unable to function." He had just had two nasty dehydration treatments.

One morning that May my telephone rang as I was getting dressed to go to work. It was President Odell. His voice was trembling and he sounded very upset. He had to see me right away, he said. I had not seen or heard from him since the faculty tea. We agreed that I would come to his office after work.

When I hung up I had just a few minutes left in which to call Dr. Richard Steiner, a Unitarian minister, active in the ACLU and president of the City Club. He was acquainted with the community, whereas I at that point was not. I did not know him well but I was a member of his church, and he and his wife knew who Lindeman was and had heard him speak. They knew what he stood for.

I told him briefly about my conversation with Odell. Steiner was about to leave for Colorado for summer vacation but said he would make a few calls that day. He would put pressure on the board of trustees and on the college, saying, "If they renege on that contract of your father's, Lewis and Clark will never hear the end of it."

It was late that day when I arrived at Odell's very formal office. Behind an enormous desk sat a man as white as the proverbial ghost. I saw his hand trembling as he handed me a sheaf of letters, saying, "Read these! I didn't want to show you these before, and I gather your father didn't want you to see them because he didn't want to upset you. But this is the correspondence we've been carrying on since March."

As I read these letters the phone rang. I heard Odell say, "Yes, Rabbi. No, Rabbi." There was more conversation and then, "Thank you very much, Rabbi, for your concern. Good-bye." As he hung up, he explained. "That was Rabbi Nodel. That won't make any difference, you know, because he's Jewish."

Intermittently, while I was reading there were more calls. One of them was the wife of a very prominent citizen who had heard Lindeman speak, had read his books, and knew he was a fine person. Odell laid the phone down, saying, "That won't help. E. B. McNaughton is known as a pink."

Incredible, I thought. I couldn't believe what I was hearing. Cheryl McNaughton was highly respected in her own right. Her husband was the publisher of *The Oregonian*, a conservative paper, president of the First National Bank, and temporarily president of Reed College.

Then Odell asked, "Don't you know anyone in the community who is a good Republican, a conservative . . . uh . . . businessman?"

"You've been talking to the wife of one," I replied, trying to remain cool and calm.

177

"That's not going to help one bit," he fretted. "Can't you think of anybody else?"

"Well, we know Herb and Barbara Schwab."

Just then the phone rang and it was Herbert Schwab. He was a practicing attorney at the time, active with the ACLU. Now he is the Chief Judge of the Oregon Court of Appeals.

Odell talked to him for a while and hung up, saying, "He's considered left-wing. Besides, he's Jewish."

"By the way," he added, "you know the fact that you teach at Gabel School doesn't help matters either. That's considered to be a hot-bed of Communism out there!"

Then he muttered, "Besides, I don't even know if your father is a Christian."

I was startled. What did that have to do with Lindeman's coming to Portland to do a workshop on education? One workshop had been planned as an experiment "to discover whether genuine educational problems, faced in their natural setting, and freed from the artificial incentives of assignments, examinations, and grades, will motivate serious study and effective effort." The second was to be a community study of Oregon City.

Unfortunately I could not tell Odell, because I did not know it then, that as chairman of the National Conference of Social Work that year Lindeman had chosen the parable of "The Good Samaritan" as the theme for the annual conference. What I did say was, "But his middle *name* is Christian! Eduard *Christian* Lindeman."

Odell did not think that was amusing, and he continued to ask if I knew someone who was a political conservative or business person. He had to have the name of someone to take to the board of trustees the next morning who could vouch for the fact that Lindeman was not a communist, and he needed some conservative link. He did not want to be suspected of bringing a communist to the campus.

"Well, I've never been especially proud of it," I said somewhat apologetically, "but you may be interested to know that my mother is a Taft. Her name is Hazel Taft. My grandfather is the first cousin of William Howard Taft," I blurted.

"Oh! You're related to Robert Taft?" He jolted upright in his chair and sounded much relieved. "I'm voting for Robert Taft!

That's the best news I've heard yet." He paused and then asked, "Now . . . your mother . . . She's a Republican, no!"

"No, she's not. She's a registered Democrat, but I'd call her more of an Independent. She votes for the individual rather than for the party."

"Well, uh . . . isn't she . . . doesn't she . . . have any Republican . . . tendencies you might say? With that name, Taft, doesn't she vote Republican down the line?"

"No, I'm sorry," I replied. "I can't say in all honesty she does. The fact is simply that her name is Taft, and she votes for whomever she thinks is the best man."

Odell was silent. Then he tensed up again and shook his head. "But . . . uh . . . then there's his writings? And he belongs to all those organizations. The Tenney Report has them all listed. You have them in your hand—the whole list of them."

The groups that especially worried Odell were the Friends of Soviet Russia (he apparently forgot that in 1943, Russia was an American ally), the League of Industrial Democracy, the Institute of Pacific Relations, and especially the ACLU.

"That's an obvious Communist organization," he said. "I mean, everybody knows that!"

I could only say I disagreed. He was taking his information verbatim from Gronnert and the Tenney Report, even though Lindeman had assured him it had been thoroughly discredited.

Then I reminded him that his most recent book, (co-authored with T. V. Smith), was entitled *The Democratic Way of Life.* If anything, he personified the democratic man—he *was* the democratic man. (Years later his son-in-law, Robert Gessner, wrote a biography of Lindeman called *The Democratic Man.*)

"He talked against totalitarianism whenever he saw it occurring," I argued. "Anyone who had ever taken a class from him or heard him speak, would know that he was predemocracy and antitotalitarianism. He classified communism along with fascism. He saw them as one and the same." I added, "If you had read his books, you would know."

"Well, I don't have time for that sort of reading."

"I know that Dr. Tuttle has read a lot of his books," I said "and he's a very conservative man." Tuttle, a member of the Lewis and Clark faculty, had been responsible for bringing Lindeman to Portland.

179

Odell agreed that he had always trusted Tuttle. But now Tuttle was under attack for bringing Lindeman to Portland.

The conversation with Odell was studded with telephone calls supporting Lindeman: Steiner had done his job. Someone from the League of Oregon Cities called, a cosponsor of the workshop. A man from the Anti-Defamation League, another cosponsor, also called. Of course, Odell considered them as "pink" organizations and already prejudiced.

The outcome of all this was that Odell found only one encouraging thing about Lindeman to take to his board of trustees the next day—his wife was a Taft. He would certainly use this fact to advantage.

No doubt Odell was influenced by the pending million-dollar donation when he met with the board. Even so, I resented the fact that Odell made so little attempt to stand up for Lindeman, and, even worse, he had not done his homework in finding out all he could about a man who was to teach on his campus for six weeks. He fielded attacks right and left. To one of his many attackers Odell apologized for Lindeman, saying:

> The use of Dr. Lindeman in connection with the workshops in community studies and intergroup relations does not mean that we endorse his political philosophy. His character, as far as we know, is that of a man of integrity, who has attempted to bring about the realization of the American Way of Life for all our people.

So far so good, but then he went on to say, "We all realize that our opinions vary as to the need for better conditions for some of our people, and the ways of providing corrections." Even when Odell seemed to defend my father, he always added a disclaimer.

There was an eerie quietness for several weeks after my visit to Odell's office. It was interrupted only once, when I received a telephone call from his secretary informing me that the college was going to allow Lindeman to come, and asking me not to stir up any further controversy. In other words, they wanted me *not* to discuss the matter publicly. They had been deluged with telephone calls from concerned community people wanting to make sure he was coming. But it was not until after he had arrived that I realized how they had chosen to play the game.

Lindeman and Hazel arrived on June 7, the Friday before the workshops were to begin. Odell and his wife left town the day before and stayed away the entire six weeks. No social functions were sponsored by the college. No reception of any kind was given, and there was no official recognition that Lindeman was on the campus. What I had not known was that Lewis and Clark had been totally responsible for preparing and circulating all the publicity, orginally intended to cover the entire Northwest, although the other sponsoring organizations each had a share in the planning. Apparently the board must have agreed to let Lindeman come to avoid a battle with the ACLU, but they had also made a deal—not to put out a single piece of publicity about either the workshops or Lindeman—in order to receive the million-dollar gift to the college. Louise Gronnert had, in effect, won her battle.

Consequently, nobody knew about the workshops with the exception of a handful of extraordinary individuals who found out by word of mouth. Hester Turner, who later became the national director of the Girls Clubs of America, many years later described the effect the workshop had on her:

I hadn't known what to expect. It was very intensive, many hours each day. The college hadn't advertised the workshop because of some ridiculous rumor about his being a communist. There were six, maybe eight students. Because I had no transportation I had the privilege of riding to the campus every day with Dr. Lindeman. After I met him I was enchanted. I learned more from him in that short span of time which affected my entire life—more than from any one teacher prior to or after that. I think it was his awareness of people, and acceptance. He opened my eyes to people in a way that had not occurred to me before. He also gave me a sense of courage I needed at that time. There was not only great intellectual excitement, but emotional as well. To watch this intellectual giant—as he ever so gently encouraged, probed, never insulted anyone, never made anyone feel inferior, never used sarcasm. I've never seem him since, but I've never forgotten him. The entire time was one of softness; as he ever so gently encouraged you so you never suspected how much pressure he really was putting on you—but you knew you had to do your best. You wouldn't dare come in with less than that. It was because of your father that I went on to get my doctorate in education, and then a law degree.[1]

The Portland workshops in the summer of 1952 were highly successful for the people who did attend them. When the workshops were over and Lindeman was gone, Odell returned to the campus.

Odell was invited in the fall to give a speech at Reed College in Portland on the subject of academic freedom. He did so, as far as I know, without a sense of irony.

# Chapter 17

# Harkness Pavilion: Last Days

*"This is a beautiful country.
Don't let McCarthy spoil it!
Promise me you won't!"*

Lindeman, 1953

I was shocked when I first saw my father early in June 1952. He looked so gaunt and pale. I knew that he had suffered from dysentery throughout most of the three months he was in India and that he had had a gall bladder attack just before he left. He had lost twenty pounds by the time he returned. Nevertheless, he was much worse than I had imagined. Over the past three years he had been in and out of the hospital four times.

By fall he was even worse. He could eat nothing but apples, whole-wheat bread, and yogurt. When invited to dine out he would carry along his own food, after first notifying the hostess. Several times during the six weeks he was with me in Portland the edema was so bad that I took him to my doctor for mercury treatments to dehydrate him. Privately, the doctor took me aside and asked if I realized how very ill he was. He was, in fact, in the final stages of the nephritis that had plagued him most of his life. He had pushed his body as far as it would go. Yet he put all his energy into the two workshops and never complained.

He loved to watch the birds from our back porch, nine hundred feet above sea level and overlooking a canyon of enormous Douglas fir trees. He never could understand why there were not more colorful birds around our home. But he kept watching. Our three-year-old would follow him out to the porch and he would gently lift her up, whispering, "Shh . . . Listen to the birds!"

He loved the sightseeing trips, especially one to Bonneville dam. He was intensely interested in the fish hatchery and the fish ladders at the dam. As usual he was filled with questions, eager to learn from every new experience.

But during the six weeks he was with us, I could see that he was going downhill very fast. He gave several speeches to the City Club. In fact, he was the first speaker to be invited back twice in succession to address this distinguished community group. The audience was electrified when he spoke of his recent visit to India and his meeting with Prime Minister Nehru. They were not to forget his descriptions of poverty-stricken India.

Despite his declining health and the controversy triggered by Louise Gronnert, it had been a good visit. Lindeman's students were especially sorry to see the workshops come to an end. "I felt cheated," one student said, "that I had never had, would never have again that exciting kind of person to teach me. He pinpointed the gaps in my knowledge and made me feel I had power over my own destiny."

I don't think my father was sorry to leave. In a letter to Otto he described Lewis and Clark College as "the most obnoxiously pious place I've ever been to. Full of Christian character." Obviously it had not been a pleasant experience.

By June Lindeman was too sick to attend Dewey's funeral, telling Otto that he had an "attack of nausea that morning, a severe one, and Hazel wouldn't allow me to go to the funeral. . . . I heard about your warm and human eulogy and wish I might have heard it."

In a commemorative issue of *Progressive Education* magazine he wrote about Dewey's contribution to the Doctrine of the Golden Mean. "I began," he told Otto, "by comparing Aristotle and Confucius and then indicating how Dewey transposed the doctrine into dynamics. It made sense to me, but I'm not sure how others will feel."

I was vacationing along the northern California coast in September and had just reached Big Sur when I had an uneasy feeling I should call Hazel. The only phone available was a pay phone on Highway 1, with all its traffic noise and the muffled sound of waves crashing on the rocks below. When I heard her voice I knew at once that something was wrong. Over the background noise I could barely hear her say that Lindeman had had a heart attack while resting in a dormitory of the University of Connecticut between sessions of a seminar on international affairs. They took him in an ambulance to Harkness Pavilion, a medical center on the upper east side of Manhattan.

He recovered, slowly. In February he wrote me that he was visiting their old Greensboro friends, Charles and Dorothy Shaw, in Swarthmore, Pennsylvania, and he was taking osteopathic treatments in nearby Media, Pennsylvania, which seemed to help the nausea.

These may have been the last contented days he had, where he appeared to be relatively free of pain. He wrote:

> I sleep much better than I have in a long time. What a restful time we are having with them! I sleep each a.m. until 9 or 10. After a lazy breakfast I bundle up and sit out in the sun for an hour, and we've had some lovely sunny days. Then Charles comes home for lunch, and after lunch we play Scrabble and Canasta and just talk. I feel much better than I did in Dallas. The nausea seems to have disappeared entirely and I am really enjoying food again.

February and March were filled with requests for speeches, articles, prefaces to books, plus all the duties as chairman of the National Conference of Social Work, which was being held in May. He responded to all the invitations by saying his health was too precarious to accept any engagements. Reluctantly he turned down the Minnesota Welfare Conference, the Michigan Council on Social Agencies, the Family Welfare Service of Cincinnati, a graduate course at Hunter College on "Society and the Individual," the Oregon Conference on Social Welfare, a Pacific Coast Unitarian Conference, a Child Guidance speech, and numerous other requests.

"It was a pity that your father did not live to preside as chairman of the National Conference of Social Work," Roger Baldwin told me. "This recognition from the social work profession would have been such a fitting ending for one of the pioneers in social welfare who had introduced humanistic values, rights, and responsibilities into the field of social work."

In Lindeman's acceptance speech, delivered the previous year, he had said:

> Although I have been for many years a regular and devoted participant in National Conference sessions, I have never thought of myself as an "insider" in so far as it may be said that there exists a social work "politics." I have all along thought of myself as a "plain teacher." It is true that I have taught "gladly," and the profound satisfaction

of my life has been associated with teaching experiences. . . . Social Welfare has become the target for an expanding group of disgruntled citizens. This is an age of frustration and confusion, and sadistic impulses come to the surface. It is a natural response to retaliate, condemn, and become defensive. There must be a better way of meeting current criticisms and attacks, a way which is consonant with the very principles of social work and which will bring about public enlightenment. It is my hope that the National Conference will, during the coming year, strive to find this better way, and having found it, will strive to exemplify it.

The conference was held the next year in Cleveland, Ohio. But Lindeman was not there.

He had struggled to come up with a theme for the conference. Val Keating, a good friend from the New Deal Days and former state welfare administrator for Texas, recalled in 1975 that Lindeman told her he wanted the theme to be a religious one. He finally chose "Social Welfare: Everybody's Concern," stating that it "challenges the contemptuous notion that those who genuinely care about what happens to human beings are 'dogooders.' We are saying that social welfare has become everybody's concern, that we live in an interdependent world."

In choosing this theme Lindeman reiterated that concern for human welfare is a way of expressing democratic faith and aspiration, a natural ingredient of the democratic way of life. "We must all bear responsibility for the common welfare," a belief he had expressed many times throughout his career.

In his personal message to the eightieth annual meeting in 1952, he wrote:

The Biblical account of the Good Samaritan is a disturbing, haunting story. It asks us to accept the doctrine that human welfare is an indivisible whole. It asks us to extend the concept of neighborhood until any human being in trouble becomes the object of our concern. This is a hard rule to follow, especially in a time such as the present when the world is sharply divided into two irreconcilable ideological camps.

But if we find it difficult to act as though the whole world were a welfare unit, we should at least be capable of applying this rule of conduct to our own nation and our own people. It is a bold, audacious thesis and we hope that you, America's social workers and citizen supports, will come to assist in giving it reality and purpose.

Early in April I was called to New York. Lindeman was once again in Harkness Pavilion Medical Center. He was dying, and he knew it. Only Hazel seemed not to know, or perhaps she knew but could not accept the fact.

Many people came to see him every day. The entire family was there. Hundreds of telephone calls, telegrams, flowers, cards, and letters poured in from all over the country wishing him well. To his close friends he spoke of his special concerns. He quoted Emerson. To his family he said, "This is a beautiful country. Don't let McCarthy spoil it. Promise me you won't!" He was also practical. He expressed concern about the effort to raise funds for an E. C. Lindeman chair in social philosophy.

Lindeman called for Tom Cotton, his intimate friend of thirty years and chairman of the Adult Education Council. They held hands while Cotton sang the folk songs and spirituals that they both loved so much. Cotton's voice was low and soft. "Were you there that night," he wrote my sister Ruth, "the night he said 'Tom! you're at the center of my heart.' I'm sure my face was shining extra special. I sang another of our favorite songs. I got through two verses and he was off asleep. He never spoke to me again. We were both contented. But now, Ruth, it's awful lonely, and the salt water clouds my eyes. You just can't feel close to people without feeling sad, I guess."

Lindeman's son-in-law Robert Gessner was with him when he died just as the dawn was breaking on April 13, Thomas Jefferson's birthday. Just before Lindeman died, Gessner reminded him that it was Jefferson's birthday. Lindeman shook his head and whispered, "The rock is splitting." Then he murmured softly, "What is the word!"

I had taken turns in watching over him before he died. I sat by his bedside for hours at a time. He held my hand hard. He did not want to let go unless a nurse came in and broke up our vigil.

Hazel had been incredibly stoic throughout the entire ordeal. Amazingly efficient in handling all the calls, telegrams, and visitors both at home and at the hospital, she seemed convinced right up to the end that he would somehow recover as he always had before. She insisted on feeding him the minute amount of food that he would take, and then with great excitement she would proclaim, "See how much he ate! He even finished all his spinach!" We tried to spell her off, but she insisted on riding the long distance

187

on the subway every day and staying well into the evening. The only time we could persuade her to take some time off was to insist that she get her hair done.

I had to leave on April 12, the day before he died. He begged me not to fly back. I could not understand, because he flew everywhere, and if he had had a premonition, he did not say so. The flight proved uneventful until the plane was approaching the airport, when the landing gear would not come down. We flew in circles until all the fuel had been used up, then the pilot brought the plane in for a belly landing. There were no injuries.

The memorial service for Lindeman was held on my birthday, April 17. It had been planned to a great extent by Gessner. In a letter to Otto April 20th he wrote:

> It was not so much a memorial service as it was a perpetuation service. It was simple and beautiful and positive. Lester Granger and Patrick Malin spoke briefly; there were two hymns by a black singer — favorites — "Go Down Moses" and "Swing Low Sweet Chariot." The service ended with one of those bounding Protestant hymns of assurance — and people emerged from an experience. It was Lindeman right to the end.

Gessner was haunted, he said in his book *The Democratic Man*, by Lindeman's last words:

> They had an eternal rightness of a great soul unafraid to ask, unworried by idiom — and the words asked since the dawn of man's soul. . . . In spite of the great pain and the realization of death, there was this philosophical serenity. He summoned up the oldest question — WHAT IS THE WORD? I don't feel he's gone, except on an extended lecture tour.

I wish I had been there.

# Epilogue

# By the Shores of Lake Charlevoix

*. . . but I was not there, holding her hand, not there, and then they said she was dead . . .*

Author

Hazel died July 21, 1980, in Portland, Oregon, exactly six days before her ninetieth birthday. In October I drove five days and almost 3,000 miles from the northwest coast of Washington to Lake Charlevoix, Michigan, to bury her ashes next to my father's. They had been in a plastic container in the back of my car since I picked them up in August from the Little Chapel of the Chimes in Portland. This made me uneasy and anxious to get to Michigan. Folded carefully in my purse was a letter from my sister Ruth giving me instructions as to where she thought they should be buried. I read the letter every day to be sure I would not make a mistake. "By a babbling brook, next to a bridge, on the bank, covered with a stone," she had written.

It was October 6 when I picked up Aunt Fucia, Hazel's 93-year-old sister-in-law, from her nursing home in Charlevoix.

But now Aunt Fucia and I could not find the stone. I knew I did not want to bury her ashes just anywhere. So, with the rain pouring down I carefully put the box back in the trunk of my car and covered it with a cloth, then I drove Aunt Fucia back to the nursing home.

The following morning I returned alone to the little stream with a post-hole digger I had borrowed the night before. I wandered around the shore of the lake wondering what it was like when my parents spent summers there with us children. I still could not find the stone, so I chose a spot on the bank by the stream, surrounded by small trees with silken boughs and golden leaves. I dug a hole big enough for the container and carefully laid it

189

in the ground, covering it with a layer of leaves, then some earth, then some more leaves, and finally a flat stone large enough to cover the spot.

I think they both would be pleased to know they lie buried in the state where they were born and spent the first thirty years and more of their life.

Christmas of 1981 I received a card from my cousin saying that she had taken Aunt Fucia back to the stream a year later. This time they found the stone that marked Lindeman's ashes. It was located on the opposite side of the stream and directly across from where we buried Hazel's ashes. For twenty years of their married life they had been separated by the Hudson River. Now they were only separated by a little stream.

# Notes

## Abbreviations of Archival References

ECLP: Refers to the Eduard C. Lindeman Papers, Rare Book and Manuscript Library, Butler Library, Columbia University, New York.

BLC: Refers to the Betty Leonard Collection, Social Welfare History Archives, University of Minnesota, St. Paul, Minnesota.

DHT: Dartington Hall Trust, Totnes, Devon, England.

AHC/MSU: Archives and Historical Collections, Michigan State University, East Lansing, Michigan.

CS: Refers to letters of Lindeman to Charles Shaw, librarian friend from Swarthmore, Pennsylvania. Letters are in BLC.

DWSE/ECL: Refers to correspondence between Lindeman and Dorothy Straight Elmhirst. Letters are in BLC, St. Paul, and ECLP, Butler Library, Columbia University, New York.

MO/ECL: Refers to correspondence between Max Otto, philosopher from University of Wisconsin in Madison, and Lindeman. Letters are in BLC, St. Paul.

## Prologue: On The Mountain

[1] Paul Unger, a member of Lindeman's staff in the WPA Program, "Community Organization for Leisure," directed by Lindeman, 1936-1939. Interview with author, 1974, and correspondence with author in 1986 and 1987.

[2] Sally Ringe Goldmark, Lindeman's Administrative Assistant in the WPA Program, 1936-1939. Interview with author, 1974. I am indebted to Sally Goldmark for her valuable insight into the New Deal and the special nature and contribution of Lindeman's program. (Deceased).

[3] Byron Mock, secretary to Lindeman throughout the duration of the WPA Program, 1936-1939. Interview with author in 1975. I am indebted to Byron Mock for his knowledge of New Deal history, perceptions of Lindeman's program, reasons for its demise, and his comments on Lindeman and FDR.

[4] Dorothy Cline, member of Lindeman's staff from 1936-1939. Interview with author, 1974. I am indebted to Dorothy Cline for her keen insight into the politics of the New Deal, as well as Lindeman's program. She is now Professor Emerita Political Science, University of New Mexico, Albuquerque, New Mexico.

[5] Marion Beers, intimate friend of Lindeman's during the New Deal year 1935-1940. I am especially indebted to Marion Beers for generously sharing the Lindeman letters with me, for her insight into his character, and their very special relationship. (Deceased).

[6]*The Meaning of Adult Education*. Lindeman's first and only book on adult education. New York: New Republic, Inc., 1926. (Reissued Montreal: Harvest House, Ltd., 1961: and Oklahoma Research Center for Continuing and Higher Education, University of Oklahoma, Norman, Oklahoma, 1989.)

[7]Author interview with Malcolm Knowles, 1975. Author of *The Modern Practice of Adult Education*. New York: Association Press, 1970. Protégé of Lindeman's.

[8]Author interview with Gertrude Wilson, 1975, former Professor of Group Work, Case Western Reserve University, Cleveland, Ohio.

[9]Ibid.

[10]Robert Gessner, ed. *The Democratic Man; Selected Writings*. Boston: Beacon Press, 1956.

[11]Early scrapbooks are contained in the ECLP, and later scrapbooks are in BLC.

[12]Unpublished manuscripts and other writings located in ECLP and BLC.

[13]Elmer Scott, former Director of the Dallas Civic Federation. From testimonial to Lindeman on the occasion of Lindeman's death, April, 1953. (Deceased).

[14]Patrick Malin, former Chairman American Civil Liberties Union, on the occasion of Lindeman's death, April, 1953. (Deceased).

## Chapter 1
### Early Beginnings

I am indebted to Roger Baldwin for his oral history of Lindeman. These tapes are now in the Oral History Archives, Butler Library, Columbia University. I am also indebted to Mrs. Kenneth Mayhew of St. Clair, Michigan for her recollections of the Lindeman family; and to the librarian of the St. Clair Library, St. Clair, Michigan, who steered me to Rosamund Earle's *Life and Times in Early St. Clair*. St. Clair Public Library, St. Clair, Michigan, 1973. For valuable information about Lindeman's early childhood and young adulthood I am grateful to Robert Gessner's *The Democratic Man*; Gisela Konopka's *Eduard C. Lindeman*; David Stewart's *Adult Learning in America*; and author's interview in 1976 with Flora Thurston Allen, Executive Secretary of the National Council of Parent Education and dear friend of Lindeman's. (Deceased).

[1]Gessner, *The Democratic Man*. Boston; Beacon Press, 1956. 17-18.

[2]Konopka, *Eduard C. Lindeman and Social Work Philosophy*. Minneapolis: University of Minnesota Press, 1958.

[3]Ruth O'Neil, letter from Lindeman, 1932.

[4]Charles Shaw, former colleague of Lindeman's in Greensboro, North Carolina, and librarian of Swarthmore College, Pennsylvania, and close friend until his death. BLC/ECLP.

[5]Ibid.

[6]David Stewart, *Adult Learning in America: Eduard Lindeman and his Agenda for Lifelong Education*, Malabar, FLA.: Krieger Publishing Company, 115-130.

[7]Stewart, *Adult Learning in America*. 119.

[8]Ibid. 118.

[9]Konopka, *Eduard C. Lindeman*. 11.

[10]Flora Thurston Allen, author interview in 1976. Executive Secretary of the National Council of Parent Education, and close friend of Lindeman's. BLC.

[11]Ibid.

[12]Lindeman to Straight, 1925. BLC/ECLP.

[13]Early Scrapbook, ECLP.

[14]Unpublished manuscript, *Egoism*, which he was working on in Italy in 1925. It was likely that he never published this book because his editor friend Herbert Croly did not encourage publication. BLC.

[15]Lindeman to Otto, 1949. MO/ECL. BLC.

[16]Rosamund Earle. *Life and Times in Early St. Clair*. St. Clair Public Library, St. Clair, Mich. 1973.

[17]Lindeman. *College Characters: Essays and Verse.* Port Huron, Mich.: Riverside Press, 1913.
[18]Lindeman to Straight, 1923. ECL/DWSE. BLC/ECLP.
[19]Lindeman to Straight, 1923. ECL/DWSE. BLC/ECLP.

Chapter 2
*Discovery at the St. Clair County Courthouse*

The book *Telling Lives: The Biographer's Art,* edited by Marc Pachter. University of Pennsylvania Press. 1981, provided me with invaluable insight into the art of biography, especially Justin Kaplan's chapter "The Naked Self and Other Problems" which dealt with the awesome process of changing one's name.

[1]ECL/DWSE, BLC/ECLP. Correspondence between 1923-1926.
[2]Author interview with Lucille Austin, Professor Emerita, Columbia University School of Social Work, 1976.
[3]Justin Kaplan, "The Naked Self," *Telling Lives: The Biographer's Art,* Ed. by M. Pachter, University of Pennsylvania Press, 1981, 37.
[4]Lindeman, *The Meaning of Adult Education.* New York: New Republic, Foreword xxix., 1926.
[5]DWSE/ECL, BLC/ECLP, 1925.
[6]Ibid.

Chapter 3
*College Days: From Laborer to Scholar*

I am indebted to David Stewart for his account of Lindeman at Michigan Agricultural College (MAC), and information about Cooperative Extension in Michigan. His information was obtained from the Archives and Historical Collections, Michigan State University, East Lansing, Michigan.

I am also indebted to Robert Gessner, Gisela Konopka, and J. Roby Kidd for information regarding Lindeman's early adulthood.

[1]J. Roby Kidd, adult educator, author of Editor's Preface and General Editor of 1961 edition of *The Meaning of Adult Education,* Montreal: Harvest House, 1961. xxiii, xxiv.
[2]Gessner, *The Democratic Man,* 1956. 19.
[3]Ibid.
[4]Konopka, *Eduard C. Lindeman.* 22.
[5]Ibid. 23.
[6]Gessner, *The Democratic Man.* 21.
[7]Ibid. 19.
[8]Konopka. 20.
[9]Gessner, 20.
[10]Ibid. 21.
[11]Author's interview with Sally Goldmark, Seattle, 1974.

Chapter 4
*A Career At Last*

I am indebted to David Stewart for information pertaining to Lindeman's early career, the Taft family in East Lansing (especially Hazel Taft) and details of the wedding.

[1]Konopka, *Eduard C. Lindeman.* 24.

[2]From editorial in *The Gleaner* (1913), "The Attractive Farm House," sent to me by David Stewart.

[3]Stewart, *Adult Learning*, 31.

[4]Gessner, *Democratic Man*, 22.

[5]Stewart, *Adult Learning*, 31-32.

[6]Ibid. 31-32.

[7]Letters to Harriet McGraw, 1919. ECLP.

[8]Ibid.

[9]Ibid.

[10]Ibid.

[11]Stewart, *Adult Learning*. 39.

## Chapter 5
### The Ku Klux Klan: Greensboro, N.C.

I am indebted to the University of North Carolina at Greensboro for the correspondence between Lindeman and President Foust, and between Foust and the KKK, Foust and members of his board, as well as newspaper and journal articles. Additional information regarding the Klan's activities is from Gessner's *The Democratic Man*; letters from Dorothy Shaw — wife of Lindeman's friend Charles Shaw; and from William Robbin's article "Cross of Fire," N.Y. Times, 11/5/89. The article was based on Wyn C. Wade, *Fiery Cross: The Ku Klux Klan in America*. N.Y. 1987.

[1]Lindeman, *The Community: An Introduction to Community Leadership and Organization*. New York: Association Press, 1922.

[2]William Robbin's, "Cross of Fire," N.Y. Times, November 5, 1989.

[3]Town Hall Seminars, November-December 1939, Dayton, Ohio, "The Challenge of Democracy."

[4]Gessner, *The Democratic Man*. 24-25.

[5]Konopka, *Eduard C. Lindeman*. 32.

[6]Lindeman, *Social Discovery*. New York: Republic Publishing Company, 1924. v.

## Chapter 6
### Life at Greystone

I am indebted to Dorothy Shaw, wife of Charles Shaw, who in 1975 gave me the correspondence between Eduard and Charles, and to Roger Baldwin for his memories of Eduard at Greystone and his comments on the relationship between Hazel and Eduard. I am also indebted to my sisters, Ruth O'Neil and Barbara Sanford, and to Dorothy Lemay (daughter of Charles and Dorothy Shaw) for their memories of Greystone. I am also indebted to Konopka and Stewart for their information about Lindeman at Greystone. Author's interview in 1985 with John Hader, colleague and co-author with Lindeman of *Dynamic Social Research*, 1933, provided information about the complex relationship between Mary Parker Follett and Lindeman.

[1]The Inquiry was a social reform movement founded by the Federal Council of Churches in America. Dorothy Straight was the principal financial backer, and Herbert Croly, Editor of *The New Republic*, Mary Parker Follett, Lindeman, and Dwight Sheffield played important roles. Lindeman's book *Social Education*, 1933, was an interpretation of the work of The Inquiry. I have recently learned that Senator Joseph McCarthy subpoened the reports, writings and records of the organization, and the government cannot now locate them. It appears they are lost.

[2]Lindeman to Shaw, 1922. CS. BLC.

[3]Lindeman review in *TNR*, "Joining in Public Discussion," 1922. 127-128.

[4]Lindeman to Shaw, December 29, 1922. CS. BLC.
[5]Follett to Lindeman, December 29, 1922. BLC/ECLP.
[6]Stewart, *Adult Learning*. 147.
[7]Ibid.
[8]Lindeman, *Social Discovery*. v.
[9]Lindeman to Shaw, Fall, 1922. BLC.
[10]Lindeman to Dorothy Elmhirst, 1929. ECLP.
[11]Roger Baldwin interview with author, 1975. ECLP Oral History Library, Columbia University.
[12]Tom Cotton letter to Ruth O'Neil, 1953. Cotton was a close friend of Lindeman's and of the Lindeman family when they lived in High Bridge and in New York City.
[13]Lindeman to Shaw, September 23, 1923. BLC.
[14]Lindeman to Dorothy Elmhirst, 1929. ECLP.
[15]Lindeman to Dorothy Elmhirst, 1929. ECLP.
[16]Dorothy Shaw to author, 1980. BLC.
[17]Author interview with Sally Goldmark, 1975. BLC.
[18]Author interview with Maurice Connery, former Dean of University of California School of Social Welfare, Los Angeles, 1976. BLC.
[19]Stewart, *Adult Learning*. 65.

## Chapter 7
### Dear Dorothy, Dear Eduard

I am deeply grateful to Dorothy Whitney Straight Elmhirst for sending me in 1964 and 1966 correspondence between Eduard and herself. Most of the information in this chapter is based on the early correspondence between Lindeman and Straight between 1922 to 1924, when she was still a widow and he was in her employ. I am also indebted to William A. Swanberg's book *Whitney Father, Whitney Heiress*, 1980, the first book to be written about Dorothy; and to Michael Young's book, *The Elmhirsts at Dartington*, 1982. Young was a former Dartington pupil and is a current Dartington Trustee. The book is about the Elmhirst's dream of creating a utopian community. Michael Young lives in London.

[1]Herbert Croly, *The Life of Willard Straight*, New York: MacMillan Co., 1924.
[2]Stewart, *Adult Learning*. 82.
[3]Lindeman to Harriet McGraw, 1919. BLC.

## Chapter 8
### Sunny Days by the Ligurian Sea

Much of this chapter is based on correspondence between Eduard and Charles Shaw, and Dorothy and Eduard. For details about this memorable trip, I am indebted to my mother's diary. For information about Martha Anderson (deceased), I am indebted to David Stewart. Information about the disease "glomerulonephritis" is from Dr. Raymond Herrmann, urologist, and David Stewart.

[1]Letter to author from Raymond Herrmann, M.D., urologist, Lutherville, Maryland, November 10, 1989.
[2]Letter from Lindeman to Dorothy Elmhirst, June 22, 1925, from Rapallo. As it turned out, Lindeman was awarded three Honorary Degrees: one from Springfield College in Massachusetts in 1937, one from Wagner Memorial Lutheran College in 1942, and one from Rockford College in Illinois in 1947.
[3]Max Beerbohm, English critic and caricaturist.

Chapter 9
*After Sunny Italy*

Information pertaining to the Dartington conference was obtained from Michael Young's book *The Elmhirsts at Dartington*; from Eduard's correspondence with Leonard and Dorothy Elmhirst, Charles Shaw, Wyatt Rawson; and letters to the author from Marjorie Wise and Wyatt Rawson. I am grateful to Mary Bride Nicholson, curator and archivist, Dartington Hall Trust Archives, who allowed me to use the archives during off-hours in the spring in 1985 and in the fall of 1988. I am also indebted to Michael Straight, youngest son of Dorothy Elmhirst, for his recollections of Wyatt Rawson at Dartington.

[1] *The Survey Graphic*. Special Issue on Fascism, Vol. 57:678-765. February, 1927.
[2] Stewart, *Adult Learning*. 50.
[3] Ibid.
[4] Michael Young, *The Elmhirsts at Dartington*. 142.
[5] Konopka, *Eduard C. Lindeman*. 113-114.
[6] Karen Horney, psychoanalyist, New York City.
[7] Author interview with Maurice Connery, 1976, former Dean of University of California in Los Angeles, School of Social Welfare, former student and advisee of Lindeman's.


Chapter 10
*Social Philosopher, Social Work Educator*

Material in this chapter was obtained from bulletins of the New York School of Social Work, Lindeman correspondence with Charles Shaw and Dorothy Straight Elmhirst; David Seideman's book *The New Republic*, 1986; Nathan Glazer's article "The New School for Social Research," New York Times, 1986; Bruno Lasker's *Oral Reminiscences* in the Oral History Library of Butler Library; Stewart's *Adult Learning in America*; Saul Pett's Associated Press article, 1982; Lindeman's article in the Alumna Newsletter of the New York School of Social Work, Fall, 1945; and author interview with Roger Baldwin in 1975.

[1] Porter Lee, Director of the New York School of Social Work from 1917 to 1939.
[2] Author interview with Bradley Buell, 1975, social welfare and community planning expert, author of *Community Planning for Human Services*, 1952. (Deceased).
[3] Lindeman to Shaw, Fall, 1924. CS. BLC.
[4] Konopka, *Eduard C. Lindeman*. 39.
[5] Lindeman, "What May A Professional School Reasonably Expect of Its Graduates?", Alumna Newsletter, Fall, 1945. ECLP/BLC.
[6] Elizabeth Meier, *History of the New York School of Social Work*, Columbia University Press, 1954. 91.
[7] Ibid. 108.
[8] Lester Granger's tribute to Lindeman, Memorial Service, April 17, 1953; Director, National Urban League, and former student of Lindeman's.
[9] Author interview with Roger Baldwin, 1975. BLC/ECLP.
[10] From Bruno Lasker's *Oral Reminiscences*, Oral History Library, Butler Library, Columbia University. For further information on Bruno Lasker, see Chapter 10 section on The New School for Social Research, end-note 17.
[11] Author interview with Roger Baldwin, 1975.
[12] Ibid.
[13] ECLP. Undated Lindeman Scrapbook. BLC/ECLP.
[14] David Seideman, *The New Republic*, 1980.
[15] Walter Lippmann, who with Herbert Croly founded *TNR* in 1914; Associate Editor until 1917; Editor *TNR* 1917-1922. Author *Preface to Politics*, 1913; *Preface to Morals*, 1929; *The Communist World and Ours, Coming Test With Russia*, 1961; *Essential Lippmann*, 1963.

[16]In addition to Lippmann and Croly, others who attended the Tuesday luncheons were:

Bruce Bliven, managing editor of *TNR* 1923-1930, editor 1930-1955; member of editorial board, 1923-55. He was influential in exposing the Teapot Dome oil scandals. Author of *Men Who Make the Future*, 1942; *What the Informed Citizen Needs to Know*, 1945; and *Mirror for Greatness: Six Americans*, 1976.

Francis Hackett, associate editor of *TNR* 1914-22; author of *What "Mein Kampf" Means to America*, 1941; and *On Judging Books*, 1947.

George Soule, editor, *TNR* 1924-47; professor of economics at Bennington College, Colgate and Columbia Universities; 20th Century Fund, 1948-57. Author *Introduction to Economic Science*, 1948; *Employment in the Modern U.S. Economy*, 1954; *New Science of Economics*, 1964; and *Planning USA*, 1967.

Edmund Wilson, associate editor of *TNR* 1926-31; best known books: *Travels in Two Democracies*, 1936; *Boys in the Back Room*, 1941; *Memoirs of Hecate County*, 1946; and *Window on Russia*, 1972.

Charles Merz, associate editor of *TNR* 1922-1931. In 1931 joined staff of New York Times. Author of *Centerville, USA*, 1928; *Great American Bandwagon*; and *The Dry Decade*, 1931.

H. N. Brailsford, British professor and lecturer in logic; correspondent for *TNR*. Remained convinced that the rationale of capitalism made war inevitable. Author of *Why Capitalism Means War*, 1938; *Rebel India*, 1932; *America Our Ally*, 1940.

[17]Nathan Glazer, "The New School for Social Research," N.Y. Times 1986.

In his many years of association with The New School, Lindeman had ongoing contact with the following:

Alvin Johnson, economist, editor of *TNR* 1917-23; Director New School 1923-45; author *Deliver us from Dogma*, 1934; *The Public Library: A People's University*, 1938; *Essays in Social Economics*, 1955. It was Alvin Johnson who, in 1922, welcomed Lindeman to New York City, and, in all probability, to *TNR*.

Charles A. Beard. Resigned from Columbia University in 1917 in a dispute on academic freedom. Helped found the New School for Social Research in 1919. Author, with Mary R. Beard, *The Rise of American Civilization*, 1927; *President Roosevelt and the Coming War*, 1941. Beard was critical of Roosevelt's actions and policies.

Lewis Mumford, philosopher, sociologist. Lecturer New School 1919; author of *Sticks and Stones: A Study of American Architecture and Civilization*, 1924. His magnum opus was considered to be *The City in History*, 1961.

John Dewey, philosopher known for his philosophy of instrumentalism, an innovative variant of pragmatism. Professor, Columbia University. Author of *Democracy and Education*, 1916; *Philosophy and Civilization*, 1931; and *Logic: Theory of Inquiry*, 1938.

Sidney Cohen, philosophy professor CCNY 1912-38; close friend of Felix Frankfurter. Legal philosophy became his speciality. Principal works *Reason and Nature*, 1931; *Law and the Social Order*, 1933; *Introduction to Logic and the Scientific Method*, 1934. Lectured at New School 1923-38.

Harry Elmer Barnes, historian and sociologist, affiliated with New School in 1919. Author of *Social History of Western World*, 1921; *Sociology and Political Theory*, 1924; *Story of Punishment*, 1930; and *Society in Transition*, 1939.

Horace M. Kallen, philosopher, professor at University of Wisconsin 1911-18, New School in 1952. Author *Culture and Democracy in the U.S.*, 1926, *Decline and Rise of the Consumer*, 1936; *Ideals and Experience*, 1948; *Secularism as the Will of God*, 1954; *Philosophical Issues in Adult Education*, 1962; *What I Believe and Why*, 1971.

Sidney Hook, philosopher, lecturer at New School 1931-71. Magnum opus, *Education for Modern Man*, 1946. Considered America's leading philosopher of pragmatism and democratic pluralism, heir to John Dewey's mantle in the U.S. Author of *Revolution, Reform and Social Justice*, 1975.

Bruno Lasker, associate editor of *The Survey*, 1917-23; associate secretary of The Inquiry, 1923-28; Research Associate, Institute of Pacific Relations, 1928-46; author *Unemployment—A Social Study*, 1911; *Asia On The Move*, 1945; and *Human Bondage in Southeast Asia*, 1950.

[18]Bruno Lasker's *Oral Reminiscences*. For more information on The Inquiry, see Chapter 6, end-note 1.
[19]Gessner, *Democratic Man*. 25-26.
[20]Stewart, *Adult Learning in America*. 60-61.
[21]Ibid.
[22]Lindeman, "Adult Education: A New Means for Liberals." *New Republic*, Special Issue on Adult Education, February 1928. 56.
[23]Lindeman to the Elmhirsts, January, 1932.
[24]Saul Pett, article commemorating Roosevelt's 100th birthday, Associated Press, January 30, 1982.
[25]Ibid.

## Chapter 11
### *Lindeman and the New Deal*

I am indebted to Sally Ringe Goldmark, Paul Unger, Dorothy Cline, Byron Mock, Marion Beers, Howard White, Elizabeth Wickenden, Arthur Goldschmidt, Valerie Keating, Donald Howard, Hilda Smith, and other colleagues of Lindeman's during the New Deal days, who provided me with information pertaining to the New Deal in general, and specifically, about Lindeman's WPA Program.

[1]Jacob (Jake) Baker, formerly in charge of work relief, who in 1934 became Director of Federal Relief Project No. 1, Theater, Art, Music, etc.
[2]Gilbert Wrenn and D. L. Harley, *Time on Their Hands: A Report on Leisure, Recreation and Young People*. Ayer Co., Publisher, 1941.
[3]Gertrude Wilson, Council on Social Work Education Annual Program Meeting, Washington, D.C., 1975. Professor of Group Work at Case Western Reserve University.
[4]Robert Sherwood, *Roosevelt and Hopkins: An Intimate History*, New York: Harper, 1948.
[5]Lindeman to Charles Shaw, 1935.
[6]Ibid.
[7]Ibid.
[8]Ibid.
[9]Lindeman to Dorothy Elmhirst.
[10]Author interview with Sally Goldmark, 1978.
[11]Author interview with Byron Mock, 1975.
[12]Lindeman, "Leisure—A National Issue: Planning for the Leisure of a Democratic People," Association Press, 1939. Speech given in Memphis, Tennessee, Association of Junior Leagues of America.
[13]Scrapbooks, 1938. ECLP.
[14]Aubrey Williams, Deputy WPA Administrator under Hopkins. Social Worker.
[15]Speech given in Memphis, Tennessee: Americans for Democratic Action (ADA). 1939.
[16]Ibid.
[17]Letter to Lindeman from A.S. Casgrain, National Recreation Association, 1953.

## Chapter 12
### *Marion*

[1]Lindeman, "The Common Man as Reader," *Saturday Review*, May 9, 1953.
[2]*The Yearling*, Marjorie Rawlings, 1938.

[3]*Emerson: The Basic Writings of America's Sage*, edited by Lindeman, a Mentor Book. New York: New American Library, 1947.
[4]Philip Gephardt, lawyer from Clinton, N.J., frequent tennis player at Greystone.
[5]Elliot Paul, *The Life and Death of a Spanish Town*, 1935.
[6]G. A Borgese, *Goliath, Der Marsch des Faschismus*. (1938).

## Chapter 13
### A Lifestyle Ends: A War Begins

I am indebted to Ruth O'Neill for her memories of the Lindemans' correspondence with Paul Kellogg, editor of the *Survey Graphic;* with Victor Weybright, editor of The New American Library; and to Lindeman's scrapbooks. The source of information concerning Lindeman's assignment in Germany is his report to the British Government, 1946. (ECLP) Correspondence between Lindeman and Hopkins was found in the Roosevelt Library, Hyde Park, New York.

[1]Ruth O'Neil to author, March, 1985.
[2]Ibid.
[3]Lindeman to Paul Kellogg, 1937.
[4]Stuart Chase, author of *Labor Bureau*, 1926, *Your Money's Worth*, 1927, and *Men and Machines*, 1929. Contributor to magazines and periodicals.
[5]Robert Hallowell, former business manager of *TNR*, in 1925 resigned from *TNR*, moved to Paris and became a painter. Lindeman saw a great deal of Hallowell in Paris in 1925, and again during the New Deal days when Hallowell played a role in the Federal Art Project. Hallowell also was a visitor to Greystone and Lindeman family members each own several of his water-color paintings.
[6]Lewis Mumford. See end-note No. 17 in Chapter 10.
[7]Gessner, *The Democratic Man.* 32.
[8]Author interview with Frank Karelsen, New York attorney, 1976.
[9]Hopkins to Lindeman, 1942. Roosevelt Library, Hyde Park, New York.
[10]Author interview with M. Connery, 1976.
[11]Interview in 1975 with Clara Kaizer, former professor and colleague of Lindeman's at Columbia University School of Social Work.
[12]Conversation with G. Konopka, 1986.

## Chapter 14
### Trip to India

Material for this chapter includes correspondence from Lindeman's students; the Lindemans' letters to their daughters; Lindeman's letters to Max Otto; and scrapbooks left behind in India due to their hasty departure, which were later retrieved by social worker Ruby Parnell and deposited in the Social Welfare History Archives of the University of Minnesota. Also, I quote from Lindeman's impressions of India which he presented to the Watamull Foundation upon his return in December, 1949. Other material is from Lindeman's article "The Moral Sense of India," *Survey Graphic,* September, 1950. I am indebted to anthropologist Dr. Harold A. Gould, Professor Emeritus, University of Illinois at Champaign-Urbana, whose expertise lies in the political, social and cultural history of India.

## Chapter 15
### The Sage from Wisconsin

Material for this chapter is based on correspondence between Max Otto and Lindeman between 1931 and 1952. Most of the letters were written between 1943 and 1952. I am indebted to Frederick H. Burkhardt, philosopher and 1940's colleague of Otto's, and President of Bennington College in 1948. In author's interview with Burkhardt in June, 1988, and in letters which followed concerning Logical Positivists, Realists or Critical Realists, Analytic Logic and their relationship to Pragmatism, Burkhardt warned me of the difficulties inherent in attempting to label the various schools of philosophy.

## Chapter 16
### Bigotry in the City of Roses

Material for this chapter includes correspondence between Morgan Odell, President of Lewis and Clark College, and Lindeman in the months prior to his arrival in Portland in June, 1952; letters written to the author prior to and after Lindeman's visit; and a letter from — and author interview with — Hester Turner, student in Lindeman's 1952 summer session *Like Life Itself.*

[1]Author interview with Hester Turner, 1975.

## Chapter 17
### Harkness Pavilion

Material for this chapter includes excerpts from Lindeman's letters to Otto; letters to his daughters; author's memories, and those of my sisters; interviews with Roger Baldwin, Val Keating, former State Administrator from Texas; and Lindeman's personal message to the 80th Annual Meeting of the National Conference of Social Work, May, 1953. It also includes material from a letter to Ruth O'Neil from Tom Cotton; Gessner's reference to Lindeman's death in *The Democratic Man*; and a letter to the author from Gessner describing the Memorial Service on April 17, 1953.

### Epilogue

I am indebted to Hazel's older sister, Fucia Taft, my Aunt, who in 1981 at age 90, took a shovel and tried to locate the exact spot where Lindeman's ashes were buried in order that we might bury Hazel's next to his.

# Index

Abbott, Grace, 86
Absolute (philosophical concept), The, 143
Academy of Medicine, 160
ACLU (American Civil Liberties Union)
    Lindeman as a member of, 128, 173, 179
    Roger Baldwin and, xix, 3
    support of Lindeman by, 175, 177, 178, 181
Action-Thought
    see Thought-Action
Addams, Jane, 58, 86
Adirondack Mountains, 56
Adirondacks Training School (YMCA), 29
Adler, Alfred, 80
Adult education
    Cotton and, 88
    for farmers, 25, 26
    Follett and, 44-45
    and The Inquiry, 92
    Lindeman as product of, 22
    The New Republic and, 90
    and recreation, 28
    and social work education, 86, 142
    and the WPA, 99, 100, 108
    see also Lindeman, Eduard C., and adult education
"Adult Education: A New Means for Liberals" (Lindeman), 90
Adult Education Council, New York, xvi, 187
Aiyar, C. P. Ramaswami, 145
Allegheny Mountains, 46
Allied Circle, 131
Amalfi (Italy), 63
Ambedkar, B. R., 145
American Association of Advancement of Science, Conference of, 117
American Association of Social Workers, 85
American Civil Liberties Union
    see ACLU
*American Federationist,*, 94
*American Review*, 94
*American Scholar*, xix

Americans for Democratic Action, 107, 173
American University, 112
"America Was Promises" (MacLeish), 111
Anderson, Martha, 67-68, 71
Anderson, Nels, 95
Andragogy, 68
Angell, Norman, 56
Anti-Defamation League, 180
*Antioch Review*, 157
Appennines, 66
Appadorai, A., 145
Arabian Sea, 143
Aristotle, 184
Arno River, 65
Arts, 99, 101, 103, 104-105, 108, 126-127
Asheville (North Carolina), 31, 34
Assisi (Italy), 65
Associated Press, 37, 74, 173
Association Press, xi
Atheism, 36, 150
"Attractive Farm House, The" (Lindeman), 25
Austin, Lucille, 11

Baker, Jake, 99
Baldwin, Roger, 71, 137
    interaction with Lindeman, xix, 3-4, 51, 58, 59, 87-88, 91
    on Lindeman, 46-47, 52, 86-87, 88-89, 120, 185
Bane, Frank, 101
Bangalore (India), 138, 144
Barnard College, 85
Barnes, Harry Elmer,91
*Basic Writings of America's Sage* (Emerson), 127
Bay of Naples, 63, 65, 143
Beard, Charles, 56, 91, 101
Beerbohm, Max, 68
Beers, Marion, xxii, 109-122, 123
    Lindeman's letters to, 106, 107, 115-120

Fries, Horace, 156
Frost, Robert, 51
Full Employment Bill, 134
*The Future of Experts* (Lindeman), 94


Gabel School, 178
Gandhi, Mahatma, 139, 140, 147-148
Gate City Clan #19 (North Carolina Knights
  of the Ku Klux Klan), 34
Geneva (Switzerland), 76, 77, 90, 95
Genoa (Italy), 66
George Washington University, 112
George Williams College
  *see* Lindeman, Eduard C., with the YM-
    CA College of Chicago
Germany, 76-77, 89, 128
  *see also* Lindeman, Eduard C., with the
    British Army
Gerson, Max, 75
Gessner, Doris Lindeman, 26, 47, 48, 82
  Lindeman's letters to, 52, 118
Gessner, Robert,
  on Alfred Dwight Sheffield, 44
  correspondence with Marion Beers,
    109-110
  his *Democratic Man*, ix, 1, 179
  on E. D. Carter, 92
  on Lindeman's career, 26, 32, 35, 127,
    128, 139, 170
  at Lindeman's death, 187, 188
  on Lindeman's early years, 5, 16, 19, 21
  on Lindeman's family life, 28, 125
  Lindeman's letters to, 52, 118
Girls' Clubs of America, 181
Gladstone, William Ewart, 133
Glazer, Nathan, 91
*Gleaner, The*, 6, 23, 25
God, Lindeman on, 19, 34, 146
*God-driven Man of India* (Fisher), 147
Goethe, Johann Wolfgang von, 65
Goldmark, Sally Ringe
  on Lindeman, 15, 22, 51, 128
  Lindeman's influence on, xxii
  with WPA, 99-100, 103-104
*Goliath* (Borgese), 117
Good Samaritan, The, 178, 186
Goslar (Germany), 132
*Gospel of Superman, The* (Nietzsche), 128
Gottingen (Germany), 133
Gould, Harold A., 141, 142, 145
Grace Church (New York City), 55
Gramercy Park, 125
Gramercy Park Hotel, 118, 122, 125

Granger, Lester, 86, 188
Grapevine Bar (Greenwich Village), 87
Great Depression, The, xvii, 96-98, 134
Greeks, ancient, 167-168
Greensboro (North Carolina)
  *see* Lindeman, Eduard C., with North
    Carolina College for Women
*Greensboro Daily News* (Greensboro, North
  Carolina), 33, 36
Greenwich Village
  *see* Lindeman, Eduard C., in New York
    City, Greenwich Village
Greystone, 42
  *see also* Lindeman, Eduard C., at
    Greystone; and Lindeman, Eduard
    C., move to New York City
Greystone, Lindeman's letters from, 117, 119
Gronnert, Louise, 171-173, 176, 179, 181,
  184
Group discussion, xii, xiv, xv-xvi, 44, 78, 80,
  141-142, 154
Groups
  and conflict, 92
  and democracy, xii, xix
  individuals and, 41
  and social work, ix, xiii-xiv, xviii, xxiii, 85
Grundtvig, Nikolai, 3
Gulf Terrace (Florida), 135


Hackett, Francis, 89
Hader, John, 41, 51, 92, 93, 95, 120
Hader, Mathilda, 51
Hallowell, Robert, 51, 69, 111, 126
Hamburg (Germany), 133
Hankesbuttel (Germany), 133
Hanover (Germany), 132-133
Harding, Warren G., 32
Harkness Pavilion Medical Center, 185, 187
Harriman, Edward Henry, 56
Hartz Mountains, 132
Harvard University, 24
Hayward, DuBose, 8
Hearst, William Randolph, 102
Hegel, Georg Wilhelm Friedrich, 128, 151
Hemingway, Ernest, 111
Hemingway, Pauline, 111
Hendrie, Kathleen McGraw, 88
Henry Street Settlement House, 55, 92
Hershey, Lewis B., Gen., 129
Hibbard, Sue, 88, 120
High Bridge (New Jersey), 46, 47, 95, 96, 99
High Bridge (New Jersey) PTA, 49
"History of the World," 162

Hitler, Adolf, 132-133
Hobson, J. A., xiv
*Holcad, The*, 17, 22, 24
*Homiletic Review*, 94
Honolulu, 144, 146
Hoover, Herbert Clark, 96
Hopkins, Harry Lloyd, 99-100, 101, 102, 103, 105, 106, 113, 129
  Lindeman's letters to, 106, 107, 129
Horney, Karen, 83
Hotel Bristol (Rapallo, Italy), 65-67-68
Hotel Statler (Boston), 118
Hotel Vesuve' (Naples), 63
House of Commons, 132
Housing, 88, 110, 113, 118, 159
Housing Association, National, 110
Housing Conference, National (1935), 110
Howden, Col., 109, 114, 115, 120
Howden, Marion Beers
  *see* Beers, Marion
Hudson River, 95, 123, 190
Hull House, 58
"Human Welfare in a Democratic Society" (lecture), 140
Humility, 113
Humor, 95, 96
  *see also* Lindeman, Eduard C., personal characteristics of, sense of humor
Hunter College, 185
Hyde Park Library, 129

*Ideology and Utopia* (Mannheim), 117
India
  *see* Lindeman, Eduard C., in India
Indianapolis, 117
Indian Council of World Affairs, 145
Individualism, xxiii
Individual-Groups, 41
Industrial Relations Commission (The Inquiry), 44, 92, 93
Information-Wisdom, 112
Inquiry, The, 43, 54, 74, 87, 89, 92-93
"Inside the German Mind" (Lindeman), 136
Institute of Pacific Relations, 179
Intelligence, xv, xvi, 94, 101
International Committee for Political Prisoners, 71
International House, The (Berkeley, California), 118
Interventionists, 155
*In the Hearts of the People* (Lindeman), 21
Ionia (Michigan), 24
Isolationism, 128, 134, 155, 168

Israel, 139
Issues, basic vs. derivative, 159
Italy
  *see* Lindeman, Eduard C., in Europe, Italy

James, William, 150, 151, 153, 155, 174
Japanese, 128-129
Jefferson, Thomas, 187
Jesus Christ, 59, 148
Johns Hopkins Hospital, 72, 75
Johnson, Alvin, 41, 54, 91
*Joining in Public Discussion* (Sheffield), 44
*Journal of Applied Sociology*, 94
Jung, Carl Gustav, 80
Junior Leagues of America, Association of, 55

Kaizer, Clara, 136-137
Kallen, Horace, 91
Kansas City (Kansas), 119
Kaplan, Justin, 12
Keating, Valerie, 97-98, 186
Kellogg, Paul, 72, 73, 126
Key West, 111, 119
Kidd, J. Roby, 16
Kittatinny Hills (New Jersey), 44
Kiwanis Club (Oregon City), 174
KKK
  *see* Ku Klux Klan
Kmladvi, Kamala, 145
Knowles, Malcolm, xxii
Kold, Christen, 3
Konopka, Gisela, 137
  her *Eduard C. Lindeman and Social Work Philosophy*, ix, xi, 1
  on Lindeman, 1-2, 3, 19, 23, 40-41
Korea, 148
Korean War, 163
Ku Klux Klan, 32-40

Labor unions, x, 25, 89, 104
Labour Party, 131, 132
La Follette, Robert Marion, 58
Laguna Beach (California), 157-158
Lake Charlevoix, 24, 28, 189
Lake Como (Italy), 68
Lake Conchiching (Ontario), 58
Lake Geneva (Wisconsin), 29
Lake Solitude (New Jersey), 46
Lamb, Beatrice Pitney, 145

Parent Teacher Association
see PTA
Paris (France)
see Lindeman, Eduard C., in Europe,
Paris
Parliament, 132
Peking (China), 56
Penman's Club, 20
Penguin Publishing Company
see New American Library
Perkins, Frances, 87, 101, 131
Perugia (Italy), 65
Pett, Saul, 96
Pettit, Walter, 84
Philanthropy
see Lindeman, Eduard C., and
philanthropy
Philosophy, commission on, 152, 154
*Philosophy of Right*, The (Hegel), 128
Photographs, frontispiece and ----, iv, 27, 42,
121, 124, 161
Pirandello, Luigi, 65
Pisa (Italy), 65
Pisa Brothers, 63
"Place of the Local Community in Organized
Society, The," (speech), 84
Planning Association, National, 128
*Playground*, 28
Pluralism, xvi, xix, 151, 158, 174
*Plutarch's Lives*, 127, 163
Plymouth (England), 70
Plymouth Congregational Church (Lansing,
Michigan), 25-26
Political Prisoners, International Committee
for, 71
Politics, 99, 102, 103, 104, 105-106, 122
Pompeii, 63
Ponte Vecchio, 65
Poole, Ernest, 56
Portland (Oregon), 170, 189
see also Lindeman, Eduard C., and Lewis
and Clark College
Portland City Club, 177, 184
Portofino Mare (Italy), 66
Protofino Vetta (Italy), 66
Pragmatism, xiii, xiv, 125, 134, 151, 152,
156, 158, 165
see also Lindeman, Eduard C., as a
pragmatist
"Preface to Politics" (Lippmann), 87
Presidency Women's Council (India), 140
Professionalism, x-xi, 84, 87, 157-158
"Professionals, The" (Lindeman), 157
Progressive Club (India), 140
Progressive education, 89, 151

*Progressive Education*, 184
Progressive party, 58
Progressivism, 107, 151
*Promise of American Life, The* (Croly), 90
Proust, Marcel, 65
PTA (High Bridge, New Jersey), 49
PTA (Oregon City), 174
Puerto Rico, 63
Putney (Vermont), 44

*Queen Elizabeth* (ship), 130
*Queen Mary* (ship), 133

*Races of Mankind* (Benedict and Weltfish),
173
Radcliffe College, 44
Ram, Jagjivan, 145
Rano, Rose Lindemann, 2, 5, 7, 8
Rapallo (Italy), 65, 67-68, 71, 76
Raritan River, 46
Rawson, Wyatt, 77-82, 119
*Reconstruction in Philosophy* (Dewey), 127
Recreation, xviii-xix, 97, 99, 100, 105,
126-127
Lindeman on, xv, 28, 102
see also Lindeman, Eduard C., and
recreation
"Recreation and Education" (project), 102
Recreation Association, National, 99, 108
Red Cross, xii
Reed College, 177, 182
Relief, 86, 100, 105
Reorganization Bill, 106
Richmond, Mary, xiii, 85
Richmond (Virginia), 74
Ringe, Sally
see Goldmark, Sally Ringe
Robinson, James Harvey, 56, 91
Rochester (New York), 19
Rome (Italy), 65, 71
Roosevelt, Eleanor, 56, 99, 104
Roosevelt, Franklin Delano, 96-97, 101, 105,
113, 155
and Lindeman, 102, 103, 104, 126, 127,
128-129
Roosevelt, Theodore, 90
Royal Air Force, 130
Royce, Josiah, 167
*Rural America*, 94
Russell, Bertrand Arthur William Russell, 3d
Earl, 151

211

Straight, Dorothy
    see Elmhirst, Dorothy Whitney Straight
Straight, Willard, 54, 56
Strauss, Nathan, 110
"Strengths and Weaknesses of American
    Culture" (lecture), 140
Survey, The, 87
    on Lindeman, 37-38, 39-40, 84
    see also Lindeman, Eduard C., with the
        Survey
Survey Graphic, The, 72, 73, 126, 147
Swanberg, W. A., 55, 56, 64
Swarthmore (Pennsylvania), 51, 185


Taft, Ella Maynard, 24
Taft, Fucia, 28, 189-190
Taft, Hazel
    see Lindeman, Hazel Taft
Taft, Levi Rawson, 24
Taft, Robert, 178
Taft, William Howard, 24, 178
TATA Institute of Social Sciences (India), 140
Taylor, Harold, 156
Taylor, Knox, Mrs., 49
Taylor Wharton Iron and Steel Company, 46
Teheran, 139
Tennessee Valley Authority, 97, 106
Tenney, Jack, 171
Tenney Report, 171-173, 179
Texas, 114
Theory-Application
    see Thought-Action
Third Reich, 133
"Thirty Selected Games" (Lindeman), 28, 48
Thompson, Geraldine, 88
Thoreau, Henry David, 148
Thought-Action, x, xv, 103, 145
Time (magazine), 90
Time on Their Hands (Wrenn), 100
TNR,
    see New Republic, The
Today and Tomorrow (Lindeman), 94
Tolstoy, Leo, Count, 148
"To My Father" (Leonard), xxiv
Toronto, 58
Totnes (England), 67
Trade Union College (Boston), 44
Truman, Harry S., 171
Trusts, philanthropic
    see Lindeman, Eduard C., and
        philanthropy
Turner, Hester, 181
Tuttle, Harold, Dr., 179-180

TVA
    see Tennessee Valley Authority


UCLA, 157
Un-American Activities Committee, 105
Unger, Paul, xxi, xxii, xxiv, 109, 128
Union of Soviet Socialist Republics
    see USSR
Unitarian Conference, Pacific Coast, 185
United Nations, 145
United States, Lindeman on the, 134, 140
United States Attorney General, 171
United States Department of State, 174
United States Housing Authority, 110
United States Postal Service, 25
United States Supreme Court, 105, 159
United States Treasury, 102
University of Calcutta, 145-146
University of California at Berkeley, 118, 145
University of California at Los Angeles, 157
University of Connecticut, 184
University of Delhi School of Social Work,
    138, 140, 146
University of Florida, 162
University of Kansas City, 163
University of Kansas City Review, xx
University of Minnesota, 156
University of Minnesota Social Welfare
    History Archives, ix
University of North Carolina at Chapel Hill,
    38
University of Oregon, 172
University of Pennsylvania, 111
University of Wisconsin, 152, 156-57, 159,
    163, 164
Untouchable Movement, 145
Urban League, National, 86, 127
Urban Sociology (Lindeman), 95
USSR, 51, 134, 173, 179
"Utilization of Human Resources, The"
    (Lindeman), 117


Vaile, Gertrude, 86
Values-Facts, 150
Varanasi (formerly Benares), 138, 140, 143
Veblen, Thorstein, xvii, 56, 91, 100-101
Versailles (France), 139
Virginia (state), 94